COSTUME &
fashion

Assistant editor: **Sharon Ashman**
Copy editor: **Cathy Lowne**
Creative art director: **Keith Martin**
Senior designer: **Claire Harvey**
Design: **Charlotte Barnes**
Picture research: **Wendy Gay**
Production controller: **Louise Hall**

First published in Great Britain in 2000 by Hamlyn, a division of
Octopus Publishing Group Limited
2–4 Heron Quays, London E14 4JP

ISBN 0 600 59708 3

A CIP catalogue record of this book is available from the British Library.

Produced by Toppan Printing Co. Ltd
Printed in China

COSTUME & fashion
a complete history

bronwyn **cosgrave**

hamlyn

contents

Costume & Fashion attempts to summarize the way people have dressed since Ancient Egypt, through civilizations which have contributed significantly to the development of the modern world up to the present day. Several books have been written on fashion history but many were published when research on the subject was hard to find. The information to be found in these publications, though interesting, ranged from charmingly vague to inaccurate. This does not diminish the value of past endeavours however, which, in their time, were both scholarly and authoritative.

I, however, was much more fortunate. Since the sixties, fashion information has become more accessible and information technology has progressed hugely. Fashion has been transformed from being a subject matter infrequently discussed and mused at with great suspicion by the general public (think Mick Jagger on stage in Hyde Park in an Ossie Clark white jump-suit), to a cultural force. Today, fashion is a global business with a turnover so huge that it is impossible to calculate. It is a subject studied by students at some of the world's finest institutions (from London's Royal Academy of Arts to New York's Fashion Institute of Technology). It is catalogued and displayed by museums around the globe – from the Costume Institute at New York's Metropolitan Museum of Art (whose former curator, the late Richard Martin, has written some of the best fashion books to date), to London's Victoria and Albert Museum. Fashion has also become a spectator sport or, quite simply, entertainment. It is watched on television and read about in newspapers, magazines and frothy tell-all biographies. *Costume & Fashion* focuses upon what I have concluded is fashion's true meaning – self-expression.

This book also charts fashion's progression through time. Some fashion history books target a date around which the modern meaning of fashion emerged. The Renaissance, for example, is the time some historians pinpoint. A cultural rebirth after the repressive Dark Ages, the Renaissance was a period when humans began to question their place in the world. Self-awareness increased, a development illuminated by the paintings of the artists Giotto and Michelangelo.

Fashion progressed at a steady pace from this time onward but the conclusion I drew from my research is that fashion, as a means of self-expression, has been with us since humans began to clothe themselves. The arrangement of cloth on the body – be it an animal skin or a primitive weave of natural fibres – relied on thought and consideration, just as assembling a wardrobe does today. The way a person chooses to wear garments marks them as an individual or as part of a sartorial tribe. What this book seeks to do then is trace how and why men and women have either branded themselves as individuals or assimilated into a group through their choice of clothes, accessories, hairstyles and make-up.

Through time, certain individuals stand out because of their legendary dress sense. Some – like Elizabeth I, Louis XIV and Gabrielle 'Coco' Chanel – have been singled out and their

left: Online design: *Virtual Catwalk* by Nick Knight, an image from the British fashion and art website called showstudio.com created by Nick Knight and Peter Saville.

above: Prince Mourhet clad in a *schenti* – a kilt traditionally worn in Ancient Egypt.

above: Louis Féraud's 1969 collection. His clothes were both glamorous and wearable.

right: Robert Dudley, Earl of Leicester displaying the sumptuous elegance characteristic of the Renaissance.

personal style has been elaborated upon because of its influence on the history of fashion. *Costume & Fashion* portrays the development of fashion in a digestible format, broken down into sections to make the information more accessible. It offers clues as to why people chose to dress or appear as they did to the outside world. It is not a global survey of fashion through time, nor is it entirely comprehensive in its coverage of certain cultures. A global survey of fashion would take years of research, this book was completed in approximately eight months. My assertions and conclusions are, in some areas, generalizations or approximations of what men and women looked like. Given the time period in which the project was completed it was physically impossible to travel to the countries under consideration. So my research was rendered entirely from secondary sources. My friend and colleague Isabelle Marie Creac'h conducted the research for the second half of the book. Without her help its completion would not have been possible.

Bronwyn Cosgrave

1:one

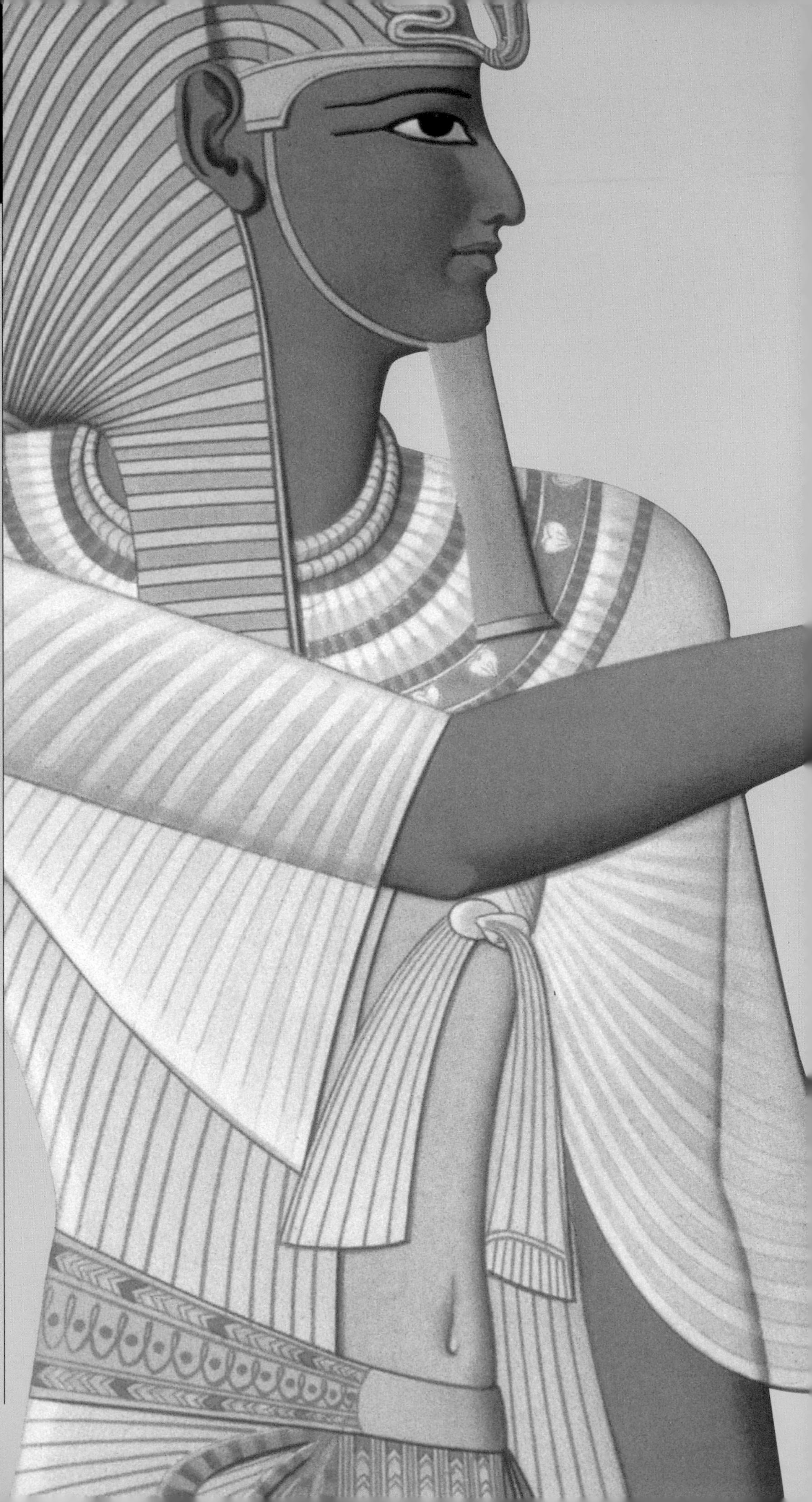

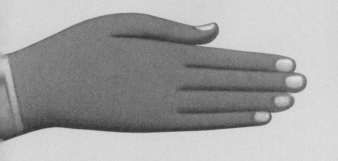

THE

ANCIENT

THE FIRST FASHION STYLE

EGYPTIANS

Background

The Egyptians originally came from the area around what we would now call Ethiopia and referred to the fertile land of the Nile valley as 'kemet', or 'the black land', so marking it as distinct from 'the red land', the 'deshert' or desert that surrounded their kingdom. They called themselves 'remet-en-kemet' or the 'people of the black land'.

Before 4000 BC their civilization had emerged on the banks of the Nile and the first king – the legendary Menes – appears to have come to power in about 3100 BC. For the next 3000 years a system of government operated which was controlled by the pharaoh. The word 'pharaoh' comes from the ancient Egyptian 'per-a', meaning 'great house' (it originally referred to the palace rather than the king, but came to be used to describe the king some time after 1000 BC). Conceived not just as king but as god, the pharaoh had absolute authority and controlled every aspect of society including art and dress. Both the government and society as a whole were strictly hierarchical and ordered: every one had their place in life. To the ancient Egyptians, tradition was everything – life and religion were seemingly unchanging, and this was reflected in such things as clothes. Eventually, after Alexander took control of Egypt in 332 BC, the Egyptians' day-to-day clothing gradually changed, but their characteristic conservative nature preserved ancient styles for both festive occasions and religious ceremonies.

Religion dominated Egyptian society. Herodotus – the Greek writer (c. 485–425 BC) who chronicled antiquity and described the places and peoples around the Mediterranean that he claimed to have seen – said that the Egyptians were the most devout people on earth. Based on the idea of eternal life beyond death, their beliefs remained fundamentally unchanged (apart from a brief period during the reign of Tutankhamun's father, Akhenaten) for some 4000 years. Egyptian religion had rituals and ceremonies to go with every act of life and death. These were reserved for the Pharaoh, priests, the nobility and warriors; ordinary people were not involved. Because they believed in life after death, they regarded the latter as a painful event, but one that could lead to a life beyond the present. Homes were seen as merely temporary dwellings and anyone who could afford to had a tomb built. The most magnificent were, naturally, the funerary temples and tombs of the pharaohs, especially the pyramids. The earliest pyramid structures, built in about 2700 BC, were the step pyramids, from which the great, towering true pyramids developed – the most astounding of which was the Great Pyramid at Giza, erected in about 2500 BC.

Pyramids had immense symbolic significance: their shape symbolized the sun's rays slanting to earth and they could be seen to function as a 'stairway to heaven' for the pharaoh's soul. Their internal structure was symbolic as well, as were some of the paintings on the walls which showed aspects of the occupants' daily lives and symbolized how they would spend their time in the next life. Everyday scenes were also painted on the walls of other tombs, temples and palaces, and it is from these that archaeologists have gleaned much of their knowledge about Egyptian clothes. In fact, so complete was their depiction of the lifestyle led by the upper classes that the evidence they provide has been likened to the pages of an encyclopedia.

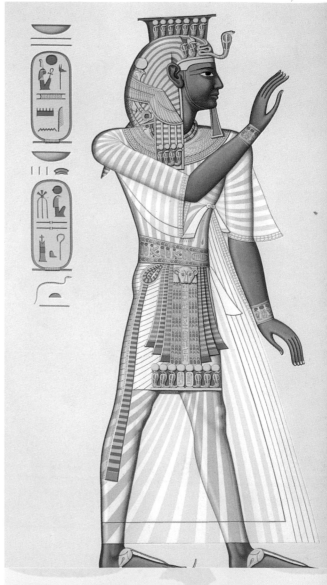

left: The Egyptians, originally from what we now know as Ethiopia, called themselves 'remet-en-kemet' – 'people of the black land'. This Egyptian painting (Middle Kingdom, 19th century BC) shows a travelling Semitic tribe (above) with Egyptians (below).

above: The pharaoh was conceived not just as king but as god. He had absolute authority and controlled every aspect of society, including art and dress. This portrait is of Ramesses III who reigned as pharaoh in the 20th Dynasty.

THE ANCIENT EGYPTIANS

above: Boys were educated, girls were not. Women, though honoured and respected by men in Ancient Egypt, did not share an equal place in society. This mural painting shows Nefertari's daughters, depicted as erotic icons, with slender waists and rounded buttocks and thighs.

Women

Women – in particular, mothers – were honoured and treated with respect in ancient Egypt. A papyrus of the time provides the evidence:

'Never forget your mother ... Remember you burdened her womb for a long time and when her time had passed she gave birth to you. For three long years she carried you on her shoulders and offered her breast to your mouth. She reared you and was not offended by your dirty ways. When you went to school and received instruction there in writing and counting, she came daily to your teacher with bread and beer brought from home.'

But women did not have an equal place in society with men. Boys went to school – girls did not. For a girl expectations did not exceed marriage and motherhood, but within this entrenched role, women played an important part in family life, running the household and managing its finance, providing food and weaving the textiles to make clothes.

Costume

Egyptian culture has been a source of inspiration for art and architecture for centuries, but the clothing has largely been forgotten. Perhaps this is because the image that Egyptian costume conjures up is somewhat kitsch. Today, when most people think of ancient Egyptian clothing, what come to mind are the stunning, elaborate costumes from some of the great Egyptian-inspired Hollywood movies such as those worn by Elizabeth Taylor in Joseph L. Mankiewicz's 1963 epic *Cleopatra*. Some of the world's best fashion designers cite these Hollywood films as sources of inspiration. In 1997, John Galliano produced 'Suzie Sphinx' – a collection inspired by Cecil B. De Mille's 1934 production of *Cleopatra*. Salvatore Ferragamo had collaborated with De Mille designing 75 pairs of sandals for his 1956 production of *The Ten Commandments*. The lavish costumes in these lush epics have overshadowed the actual simplicity involved in Ancient Egyptian dress. The white linen *schenti* – a man's loincloth, or kilt – and the *kalasiris* – the long, close-fitting sheath dress worn mainly by women – and other simple items like them are the basics from which clothing has evolved.

Because of the environmental conditions at many burial sites – the dryness of the soil and hot climate – costume, jewellery, artefacts and tools that would rot in damper conditions have been well preserved, and this is why historians know so much about Egyptian daily life and costume. More artefacts and relics survived from ancient Egyptian times than of any other western culture between the Roman and Gothic periods. Tutankhamun's tomb, excavated by the British archaeologist Howard Carter between 1922 and 1932, was a particularly rewarding source of well-preserved clothing. Among the items found was a linen shirt, dating from about 1360 BC, which is now in the Victoria and Albert Museum in London. Even in Egypt, such findings are relatively rare and they are virtually unknown from other civilizations.

Clothing styles changed little throughout the history of ancient Egypt, and when new garments or styles were introduced, they were worn alongside the old. Initially, most garments were simple in shape, and roughly triangular. Because of the extreme heat, clothing was characterized by three constant qualities: it was roomy, light and spare. Complete nakedness, however, was not condoned as it was considered lowly and immoral for anyone other than children, slaves or commoners to appear naked.

Both men and women could keep their upper body bare, although women did cover themselves up much more than men. The proportions of clothing lines were similar, too, although the emphasis was slightly different. Female dress was characterized by a high waistline, while men's clothing emphasized the hips. Women's clothing, too, was far more restrictive than that worn by men: the *kalasiris* was tight-fitting whereas the male kilt allowed the wearer to move more freely, perhaps an indication of men having a more active lifestyle.

Clothes reflected the strictly hierarchical nature of Egyptian society and distinguished social rank. But it was not the clothing styles that were determined by a person's position, it was the cloth used to make them. So, the higher a person's rank, the better the cloth he

above: A portrait of Queen Nebto, 19th Dynasty. She is wearing a white, tight-fitting *kalasiris* and on her head is the so-called Vulture cap, the symbol of royal power.

could wear: the Pharaoh's kilt would be made of fine linen, possibly enriched with gold thread, whereas, at the other end of the scale, the standard loincloth worn by a commoner was made of vegetable fibres or leather. Its weave varied according to social rank.

Women's clothing

Until the mid-18th Dynasty the average woman wore the *kalasiris*, or sheath dress. It was simple in shape, falling from below the breasts to above the ankles and held up by two shoulder straps. Those found by archaeologists were made from a tube of material sewn along one side. It was probably not as form-fitting as paintings and statues suggest and certainly could vary a little in shape: paintings show that it could extend over the breast or even up to the neck; some examples that have survived are supported by sleeves, not straps, and others have only one strap. Women would wear a light shawl over the *kalasiris*, to protect their skin from the sun during the day and to keep themselves warm in the evening.

Another ensemble consisted of two separate pieces. A short, tight bodice that opened back and front was worn on the upper body. It had slim-fitting sleeves and was secured on to the body with thin cords. It was accompanied by a wide skirt with horizontal folds.

The wives of pharaohs and nobility are also shown in draped garments made from bleached linen that was pleated by hand and starched. The upkeep of these garments would have required great care, and servants would have spent hours starching them.

In the 18th Dynasty new dress styles came in, perhaps reflecting the immense changes in religion occurring at the time. Depictions of Akhenaten's wife, Nefertari, and her six daughters show them in long, flowing, pleated linen drapery. They are portrayed as what we would think of as erotic icons, with slender waists and rounded buttocks and thighs. In some tomb paintings and statues Nefertari is shown wearing a long, tight dress under a pleated tunic with wide sleeves that came down to the elbow. A belt fastened below her breasts to form an Empire line, while a beaded collar hung at her neckline.

There was remarkably little change in women's clothing after the 18th Dynasty, even when the Greek Ptolemaic Dynasty were in power from 304–30 BC. The last ruler of Egypt was Cleopatra VII. Her wardrobe of clothes and jewellery is legendary, and included dresses of linen woven with gold, but she is always depicted in traditional wear.

Men's clothing

The traditional male garment was the *schenti*. A simple kilt, it was wrapped around the hips with the ends hanging down in folds at the front of the body. Initially made of leather or hide, it was later constructed of a light cloth, usually linen. Pharaohs are sometimes shown with a lion's tail hanging down at the back of their kilt, while soldiers sometimes wore a kilt that was striped or cut from coloured cloth.

As time moved on, the kilt was cut in a more angular fashion and starched so that the cloth was stiff enough to stick out and create a triangle at the front of the body. For men, costume that emphasized the front of the body was universally worn. This emphasis on the genital area was due to the fact that it was regarded as sacred because of its involvement

left: A wall painting, dating from the New Kingdom (1555–1080 BC), depicting a procession of women.

above: A quartzite statue of a female torso – probably that of Nefertari – dating from the Armana period (1365–1349 BC).

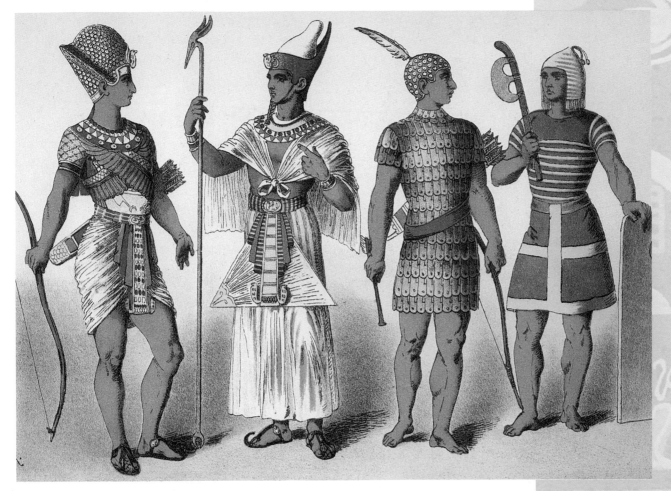

left: The *schenti* was a garment worn by most men except slaves, who wore a loincloth. This ivory carving, a figure of a man (2000 BC), displays the *schenti*, possibly made of a light linen cloth.

above: Kings in war and ceremonial costume. The figure on the left shows the kilt cut and starched in such a way as to create a triangle at the front of the body.

in procreation. Attention to this body zone was also achieved by draping cloth from the waist down over the pubic area.

Men's costume evolved gradually. One of the first innovations to follow the schenti was the loin skirt. King Menes is depicted wearing one in the palette of Narmer, a piece of art dating to about 2900 BC and now in the Egyptian Museum in Cairo. Its top edge was extended to run up over the left shoulder.

In the Middle Kingdom (2040–1640 BC), men wore long skirts over the kilt. Made from a single rectangle of linen, these varied in length from mid-thigh to calf and were sometimes held in place by a decorative belt.

The introduction of two garments – the tunic and the robe – is thought to be a consequence of Egypt's conquest of Syria in the 15th century BC. At that time, foreign weavers came and settled in Egypt (to such an extent that the term Syrian became synonymous with weaver). As a result, sophisticated weaving techniques were introduced to the country thus allowing for better textile production. The tunic – resembling a short sleeved nightshirt – could be worn over the *schenti*. The long robe was complicated in form and made from a piece of cloth approximately twice as long as the intended wearer's height. It had a wide neckline and, because it was so full, had wide sleeves while the skirt was gathered at the waist. The robe has been considered the most unusual style worn by the Egyptians. There was also a garment consisting of a piece of cloth draped over the shoulder and kept in place by a *fibula* – a brooch-style fastener.

Textiles and colours

Linen was the fabric most commonly used for clothes in Ancient Egypt. It offered several advantages over other materials: its fibre could be woven into a fine, light weave so that it was neither heavy, nor hot, and it could also be draped over the body simply. It was also easy to launder. Initially, linen was woven from vegetable fibres – a technique invented in Egypt – but, as irrigation techniques improved throughout the country, flax became the common raw material used in the production of linen. After the Syrian weavers came to Egypt, their sophisticated weaving techniques allowed better textile production and the quality of the cloth improved. Household goods such as baskets and sieves were also made from matted plant fibres.

Although linen was the cloth mostly used, it was not the only one: reeds were matted and fashioned into the simple garments worn by slaves; byblus and papyrus plants were worked into short, tight-fitting costumes like aprons. In addition to linen, cotton was fashioned into ample garments such as tunics and robes and could be embroidered with gold. Wool was used for shawls and for making overgarments. Leather was used to make battle dress, such as soldiers' aprons. Silk was not known in Egypt until it was introduced by the Greeks and the Romans around 323 BC. Neither woollen nor leather garments were worn in the temples because it was considered profane to worship the gods in any garment made from animal fibres.

Colours were symbolic, for example, green symbolized life and youth and yellow was the symbol of gold, the flesh of the immortal gods. The colour that rarely appeared in Egyptian costume was black – it was used exclusively for wigs. White, the symbol of happiness, was the colour commonly found in the Egyptian wardrobe, although this was partly for practical reasons. Linen did not accept dye easily using techniques available then, so clothes were normally made from natural, bleached linen. The dyeing of cloth using natural, indigenous ingredients had been developed in Egypt. Though this was a tricky technique, the Egyptians did dye some cloth, slaves were often dressed in blue linen, for instance. Red dye was extracted from plants including *Alkanna tinctoria*, *Rubia tinctorum* and flowers such as *Cathamus tinctorius* (safflower). Thread was dyed gold and used as weave for royal tunics and gloves. Leather was also dyed red, yellow and green.

Jewellery and ornaments

Despite the riches gained through foreign conquests, such as those into the near east during the 18th Dynasty, and the tribute exacted from defeated countries, Egyptian clothing was virtually unadorned and almost austere (except royal garments). Wealth was displayed in jewellery – and this also served to inject colour into the Ancient Egyptian wardrobe. Sculpture, carvings and wall paintings portray both men and women wearing jewellery.

above: The goddess Isis leads Queen Nefertari into the next world. Nefertari is in a white *kalasiris* with a gold collar; the goddess is wearing a far more colourful, patterned garment.

right: Environmental conditions – dry soil and hot climate – meant that Ancient Egyptian objects and artefacts were well preserved. This pleated dress is thought to be the earliest extant garment in the world, dating from the 1st Dynasty, 3100–2890 BC.

Pieces such as collars had been worn since pre-Dynastic times. Necklaces, armlets, bracelets and anklets were made of gold, coral, pearl, agate, onyx and chalcedony. Silver was used more rarely for jewellery. It was called the 'white metal' and considered the substance of which the gods' bones were made, and was generally used for ornamentation – hammered into thin plates and encrustations which were then applied to statues, furniture and trinkets.

Collars were made of shells, beads, flowers and precious stones set into gold. They could be worn either as a necklace or attached to a neckline made of leather or cloth – a style that originated during the Old Kingdom. A new design introduced during the 18th Dynasty was a necklace that consisted of between two and four rows of metal discs, which might reflect the greater abundance of metal available. Beaded bracelets seen in wall paintings of the time are thought to have originated – or been inspired – by near-eastern examples. Pendants and earrings were often enormous and must have been heavy to wear.

Royalty had an appetite for gold jewellery and it was the large amounts of it buried with them that has tempted tomb-robbers ever since, so complete finds are rare. One collection was discovered in 1834 by the Italian explorer Giuseppe Ferlini, who came across a pyramid at Meroë in the Sudan that belonged to Queen Amanishakheto. Scientific examination of the items discovered revealed how they were worn because they showed traces of wear and tear. For example, she wore her set of ten bracelets in a stack of five on either arm. Nine shield rings were also discovered in her tomb. These were everyday rings, but rather than wearing them on her fingers, she attached them to her hair and hung them over her forehead.

Other ornaments were ingrained with religious or political significance. Priests wore feathers, lotus leaves and birds to symbolize their rank. The pharoahs' regalia was deeply symbolic. The crook and flail that they held represented authority over their territory, shepherds and grain farmers. The ankh was a sacred sign of life normally reserved for kings, queens and gods. Its origin is uncertain but it is said to represent the tie straps of sandals. The cobra was a symbol exclusive to kings in Egypt: it was worn on both the crown and the hood-like head-dress made familiar by the well-known funerary mask of Tutankhamun and statues of Ramesses II. Cleopatra, like other rulers before her, wore a complicated head-dress bearing two feathers, which signified her exalted rank, while other common symbols like the sun, a globe and ram's horns were symbols of fertility. Throughout life, amulets, such as scarab beetles, were kept close to the body for protection and then placed with the dead for ultimate preservation. The wedjat eye – which was also known as the Eye of Horus – was a popular good luck charm and gold necklaces have been found with a string of wedjat eyes on them.

Flowers were also worn as ornaments: collars of freshly cut flowers were made for religious ceremonies, including funerals, and festivals. The Egyptians admired flowers not just for their beauty but also for their sacred and symbolic qualities. The lotus flower – or *nenuphar* – has become known as the symbol of Egypt. According to tradition, a great lotus grew from the primeval waters, and was the cradle of the sun on the First Morning.

left: Since pre-Dynastic times the Egyptians wore jewellery such as anklets, bracelets and necklaces like those made of semi-precious stones seen here .

above: Ornaments and objects were engrained with symbolic significance. This pendant, found in the tomb of Tutankhamun, is in the form of a wedjat eye, the symbol of protection. The counterpoise is in the form of two djed pillars, a symbol of stability and power.

above: This golden collar (c 1316–1352 BC), thought to have come from the tomb of Tutankhamun, shows Horus, the ancient falcon-god. The pharoah was counted among the gods and was said to be an embodiment of Horus.

Mummies have been found in tombs wearing collars of fresh-cut flowers. Tutankhamun's coffins were laden with numerous floral ornaments made from petals of the blue lotus, thin strands of papyrus (symbolizing rebirth) and olive leaves. Fifteen years before his tomb was discovered, explorers came upon the remains of a funerary banquet held in honour of Tutankhamun in the Valley of the Kings including collars of cornflowers, olive leaves and woody nightshade. Some mourners, however, may have worn collars made from faience (tin-glazed earthenware) beads shaped like fruits, leaves, petals and pods.

Footwear

Sandals are the oldest known form of footwear, and were considered an ideal way of protecting the feet from the hot desert sand, while allowing air to circulate round them and keep them cool. The basic Egyptian sandal was thong shaped and consisted of two straps

above: Shoes were
regarded as the most
precious item in the
Egyptian wardrobe. These
gold shoes were found on
the mummified body of
King Shoshenq II, thus
ensuring that the king
would be shod like the
gods in the afterlife.

and a sole. One strap passed between the first and second toes to join the other, which ran over the arch of the foot. Both men and women wore sandals made of wood, papyrus, goat skin and palm fibre. A servant is shown carrying Pharaoh's sandals on the palette of Narmer, and the Bata Shoe Museum in Toronto has the wooden soles from a pair of 4500-year-old Egyptian sandals, although the straps (probably made of woven papyrus) have not survived. A number of pairs of sandals were found in Tutankhamun's tomb, including a beautiful jewelled pair that he would have worn for ceremonial purposes and a pair with pictures of his enemies on the soles so that he trampled them, symbolically, as he walked.

Shoes were for indoor wear and were regarded as the most precious item in the Egyptian wardrobe. They would be carried during a journey, and only put on when a party arrived at their destination. Examples woven from palm fibre and grass, with curled-up toes and found at Thebes, are thought to have been funerary shoes.

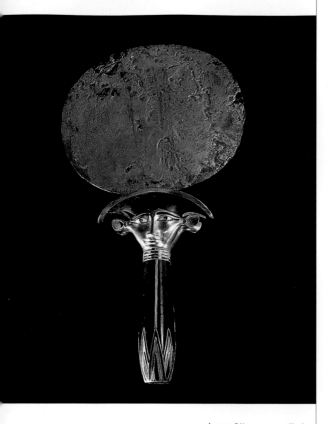

above: Silver was called the 'white metal' and was generally used to make trinkets, such as this silver mirror used by Princess Sathathoryunet. Its handle is in the form of a papyrus stem with the double-sided face of the cow goddess, Hathor, at the top. It dates from the New Kingdom, 12th Dynasty (c 1842–1798 BC).

Beauty and grooming

Herodotus wrote that the Egyptians were preoccupied with cleanliness, but this would have been a necessity in any warm country. Insects and rodents, like mice, were common pests in households: at the ancient site of Illahun, in Middle Egypt, houses were discovered during excavations to have been tunnelled through by rodents. Fleas, parasites and lice – the last two of which have been found in the hair of mummies – were among other pests.

Priests adhered to strict rituals of cleanliness, washing several times a day and shaving their bodies to keep them smooth and free of hair. Like clothing and dress, the grooming regime was passed on through generations and dictated by religious and royal decree. The Egyptians followed a beauty regime from which numerous modern grooming rituals have evolved. For example, a relief in the tomb of the nobleman Ptahhotep (who lived in about 2400 BC) shows him receiving a pedicure. Queen Nitocris claimed that women should bathe every morning and have a daily massage to keep slim. Skin on the knees and elbows was exfoliated with a pumice stone and a body rub with scented oil was prescribed to ease sunburn and insect bites. Body scrubs – some composed of a paste of honey, calcite and salt – were commonly used and women oiled themselves to keep their skin soft and supple. Evidence suggests that pellets of ground carob were rubbed into the skin and balls of incense and porridge were placed on sweat-prone body parts as deodorants. Egyptians cleaned their teeth by chewing the root of *Salvadora persica* – a tree found in southern Egypt and the Sudan, and used over the centuries in Arabic countries for the same purpose – and kept their breath fresh by gargling with milk, chewing herbs and frankincense.

Excavations in the 19th century revealed the high degree of care that went into the ancient Egyptian grooming ritual. They had devised in primitive form most make-up tools that exist today. Glazed urns, pots, boxes, razors, palm fans, ivory combs, an array of brushes, mirrors and jars – all used for cosmetic purposes – have been discovered in tombs. Mirrors were composed of polished metal and set into handles of wood, bronze, ivory or Egyptian faience. These items were stored in boxes for safety.

Both men and women used cosmetics in ancient Egypt. Women lightened their skin with a yellow ochre colour, whereas men applied an orange-tinted paint to their face to darken its skin tone. They used black kohl or green malachite powder – brought to the Nile from the mountain regions of the Sinai – to underline and, so they believed, widen the eyes. This expensive material was kept in lumps and stored in tiny bags made from linen or leather, which was ground into a powder and then applied to the lids with moistened sticks. They enhanced their eyebrows and lengthened them with a grey powder, sometimes tracing lines from the brows that arched down on to the cheek in the form of an arabesque, the symbol of clairvoyance. Eye paint was used for both therapeutic and beautifying purposes: often it was mixed from kohl and goose fat, and they believed that this could prevent eye disease, like an eye wash made from ground celery and hemp.

Red lip gloss – mixed from fat and ochre and applied with a brush – and rouge, to flush the cheeks or to camouflage problem skin, were both popular, as were white foundation and orange lipstick. Women sometimes traced the veins on the forehead with blue face paint

above: Servants attended to royal costume. Here a painting found in Thebes inside the tomb of Nakht, a scribe and priest under Thutmose IV, depicts a typical scene: a slave girl helps three ladies dress for a festive occasion.

and wrinkle treatments, composed of plant extract oils, gum of frankincense, wax and grass, were also applied to the face.

A red tint (probably henna) was used to stain the fingernails. Men and women wore make-up, employing a technique that was vivid and intricate but probably not as obvious as it might seem from paintings and sculptures. Both sexes painted and tattooed their bodies and the pigment used for tattoos may have been injected under the surface of the skin.

In early times, priests concocted make-up and perfumes, keeping their formulas secret and selling them to those who could afford to buy them.

A variety of perfumes were popular, but the formulas were fairly primitive as they did not know how to distil alcohol. Scent was extracted from plants and flowers by steeping them in oil to create an essential oil. Other fats and oils were added to this and these ingredients were then stored in cloth which was later tightly wrung and the fragrant drops collected. They may also have burned scented oils in the home, as a lamp found in the tomb of Kha at Deir el-Medina held the remains of fat.

Egyptian men were clean-shaven; a smooth chin was a mark of distinction for men of high birth and rank. A beard was only really permissible during mourning periods. Oddly, a pharaoh would wear a stylized false beard on the end of his chin during ceremonies, but this had a particular symbolism. Copper razors have been found in many tombs.

Hair and head-dresses

Hair care was an intricate part of grooming. Hair-conditioning formulas were found in tombs and descriptions exist of remedies for a variety of problems. Setting lotions were often composed of a mixture of bee's wax and resin. Egyptians also concocted remedies for baldness and greying hair, for instance, chopped lettuce could be placed on a bald patch to encourage hair growth and the blood of a black ox was heated with oil, cooled and applied to the hair to cure greyness. The blackness of the animal, they believed, would transform the hair's grey colour.

Time was also devoted to styling the hair. Women sometimes plaited their hair or wore it in ringlets. Extensions of artificial hair were sometimes added to the natural hair. If hair was worn short it was cut in a severe crop, such as that of Nefertari.

Hair styles, just like costume, could indicate a person's position. Children, for example, wore their hair cut short often with a long strand — or side-lock — falling from the right hand side of the head. By the 19th Dynasty, royal adolescents wore a loose side-lock over a wig. The side-lock, it was believed, was meant to indicate their link to the king. Married women wore what has become known as a *triparti* hairstyle. Shoulder-length locks framed the face at each side while the rest of the hair fell behind, down the back of the head. Premarital women and young servant girls sometimes adopted a hairstyle that fell just below the shoulders, with ringlets to either side of the face. Another possibility for married women was the enveloping wig — where the hair fell evenly at the shoulders all around the head. Pictures of Cleopatra often show her with her hair in plaits, with a ribbon bearing the royal cobra around her temples.

The Egyptians were expert wig-makers. Wigs were worn by both men and women. Because of the heat and the habitual preoccupation with cleanliness, royalty and the nobility shaved their heads and wore wigs made of real hair, which were groomed and dressed carefully by slaves. Cleopatra is known to have possessed wigs in several hair shades. Men wore wigs mainly for religious feasts and ceremonies. Women's wigs reached their greatest proportions in the New Kingdom, falling below the shoulder and featuring ornate accessories such as gold bands and rings, coloured glass and jewels. The poor, on the other hand, wore wigs made of wool.

Hair could be either concealed or revealed by a head-dress. The pharaoh's *pschent* was a tall head-dress composed of the two crowns symbolizing the old kingdoms of Upper and Lower Egypt, and this concealed the wearer's hair completely. Many pharaohs, including Ramesses II, are seen wearing a version of this in paintings, reliefs and statues. Ramesses II is also sometimes shown wearing something like a skull-cap, to which hair extensions could be added.

Like other aspects of Egyptian costume, head-dresses incorporated symbolic elements. One ceremonial form of head-dress worn by pharaohs included two upright feathers (symbolizing Amon, regarded during the New Kingdom as the 'king of the gods'), ostrich feathers (for Osiris, the god of the underworld), rams' horns (an attribute of Khnum, the god who created life and all living things) and the sun disc of Re. As time progressed styles

above: Hairstyles indicated a person's position. This wall painting, found in the tomb of Amen-hor-khepeshef, displays the son of Ramesses III wearing a side-lock. The side-lock indicated a link to the king, behind whom he is standing.

above: Hair could be
concealed or revealed by
a head-dress. Here a
relief of General
Amenemonet (New
Kingdom, 18th Dynasty,
1555–1337 BC), shows a
head-dress concealing the
hair.

reached extravagant proportions. During the New Kingdom, a preoccupation with fantasy
reached a peak and the symbolic motifs incorporated into the tall ceremonial head-dress
could include the sun disc, and protective wings of the sacred hawk or vulture, the royal
plumes and the royal cobra.

The ubiquitous fabric head-dress, the bulky *klaft*, primarily served an absolutely
functional purpose – to protect the wearer from the heat of the sun. Made from thick, stripy
material, it was fixed at the temples and fell in folds over the shoulders, and could either
cover or reveal the ears.

Again, it is Nefertari, the epitome of Egyptian beauty, who provides the most enduring
image of an Egyptian head-dress in the limestone head in the Staatliches Museen in Berlin:
concealing her hair and angular in shape, it was fashioned by a stiff blue mitre that was
banded with a polychrome ribbon, highlighted in gold.

MINOAN SPLENDOUR

CRETE

Background

Minoan – or Bronze-Age – Crete is regarded as the first European civilization. The earliest known inhabitants are thought to have been animal-skin-clad cave dwellers, but they disappeared as settlers arrived on Crete from Asia Minor before 6000 BC. For the next 3000 years or so, a Neolithic settlement, which would eventually become known as Knossos, prospered a few miles inland from the island's north coast.

Crete became a centre for bronze production and export due to two main factors. By roughly 3000 BC, techniques for manufacturing and casting bronze had developed. Simultaneously an influx of immigrants from the Cyclades brought new navigational skills to Crete. Cretan civilization initially was heavily influenced by its most important trading partners, Egypt and Babylon.

Archaeologists divide the Minoan Bronze Age – with its distinctive style – into three periods: Early (3000–2000 BC), Middle (2000–1700 BC), and Late Minoan (1700–1450 BC). In the Middle Minoan period, metalworking techniques became more sophisticated, featuring filigree patterns and granulation. The first palace at Knossos was built at this time, but it was destroyed in about 1700 BC, and rebuilt during the next 100 years or so. Sadly, the destruction of the original palace means that no frescoes survive from before the 17th century BC.

Knossos stands out as the most significant site on Crete. The area was excavated by Sir Arthur Evans between 1900 and 1935, and he uncovered frescoes, delicate and beautiful painted pots and ivory and faience statuettes, all of which provide significant information about Minoan costume. Some fantastic gold jewellery was also found.

In about 1450 BC Crete was invaded by Mycenaeans from the Greek mainland. The art and pottery found from this time on is Mycenaean in character. The palace was destroyed, probably by a natural disaster, in the 14th or early 13th century BC and was never rebuilt, although the city continued to be inhabited until the 4th century AD. The Mycenaeans' culture was in decline by the time of the Dorian invasion in c. 1100 BC, and although Knossos remained an important state until the Roman invasion of 67 BC, it never regained its Bronze Age pre-eminence.

Women

Women seem to have enjoyed a prominent place in society and to have been relatively free. They played an important role in society, particularly religious life. Clay and stone figurines from the early period indicate that there was a cult dedicated to a great mother goddess.

Costume

Crete's temperate, damper climate means that, unlike in Egypt, no clothing specimens survive, as they have all rotted away. What we know of Minoan costume has come from statuettes, vase paintings and frescoes which provide clues but can never reveal exactly what was worn. Images of the snake goddess provide an idea of female dress, and a Late Minoan picture of a priest king at Knossos wearing an iris crown with three feathers (rose,

left: Information about Minoan costume has been rendered from frescoes – like the one seen here, depicting a procession of gift-bearers from the Minoan Palace of Knossos, Crete (16th century BC).

above: The terracotta Petsofa statuette – the 'snake priestess' or 'snake goddess' (17th century BC) – shows an early example of typical Minoan dress, including the tiered flounced skirt.

above: The cinched-in waist – a feature of female Cretan costume seen here on ladies of the Minoan Court (1100 BC) – has been compared to the silhouette of 19th century women's fashion.

purple and blue), a red-and-white rolled girdle gathered tightly at the waist and a short, leather loin skirt may provide evidence of male costume of that era. The Minoans appear to have been, on the whole, a tall, slender race and their clothing styles seem to suit these proportions.

Signs indicate that the concept of 'cut' could have emerged in ancient Crete. While other early civilizations wore draped cloth and folds of fabric, the Minoans wore fitted clothes. The hat, too, is believed to have originated in Crete.

Minoan costume was one of the four discernible styles that led to the eventual development of Greek clothing. It was also influential in the coastal regions of the Black Sea, the eastern Mediterranean and even in some areas of inland Asia.

Women's clothing

In the early stages of civilization in Crete, women wore loincloths that probably fell longer at the thighs, almost like a skirt. With time, this loincloth evolved into a rounded apron that was worn over a skirt.

A statuette from 2000 BC found at Petsofa, in the east of the island, shows an early example of the typical Minoan dress. The lower portion of this primitive garment fell in a flounced or tiered skirt, and it may have been stretched over hoops of rushes, wood or metal, possibly the first type of crinoline. The form of the bodice might have evolved from a way of wrapping a stiff shawl around the body and then girdling it at the waist, producing a collar that framed the head and a pronounced shape that left the breasts exposed, even pushed up. This dress was often worn with a peaked head-dress. By the 18th century BC, a bell-shaped skirt had developed, and this can be seen in images of the snake goddess. She appears with exposed breasts and a long, tiered, circular skirt. She may be wearing a corset made of a frame of metal plates and allowing the skirt to lie flat on the hips, thus accentuating her slim waist. A long cloak or a short, sleeveless cape could be worn over the dress in colder weather.

As the skirt evolved, it became more elaborate and often featured embroidery and colourful decoration as well as pleats and flounces. Flounces, narrow strips of patterned material, fell over each other to form a checkerboard pattern of light blue, brown and beige cloth. A fresco at Hagia Triada even depicts a woman wearing a skirt in which two tiers of flounced fabric with white, red and brown rectangles and a red-and-white binding were sewn on to a skirt with a white-and-red cross pattern.

The late Middle Minoan version of the dress is again known from snake goddess figures and frescoes of women. The tightly fitting bodice was laced below bare breasts (and some images show a transparent bolero top over the bodice). Sleeves fell to the elbow and could be tight-fitting, puffed or 'leg-of-mutton' in style. They were held in place by ribbons fastened at the back of the neck or by shoulder straps crossed over the back. A girdle cinched in the waist, with a rolled, twisted effect at the top and bottom. The conical skirt was stiff, and sometimes layered in a series of tiers. Another skirt worn at the time was tight, patterned and colourful, with a stiff apron circling the lower body.

The cinched-in waist produced a silhouette that has been compared to female fashions of late 19th-century Europe, with the accentuated chest, nipped-in waist and sweeping skirt. The resemblance is so strong that one image, a fragment of a fresco from Knossos (c. 1500–1450 BC) is known as La Parisienne.

Minoan costume reached its most elaborate between 1700 and 1500 BC. Wardrobe staples included the gown, the apron, bodices, culottes-type skirts and numerous styles of hats. Rich textiles appeared and luxury and elegance are the two words which best sum up the Minoan attitude towards dress at this time. Vivid colour, including red, yellow, blue and purple, was a marked characteristic of female Minoan dress, throughout the Middle and Late periods. After the Mycenaean invasion in 1450, Mycenaean women took Minoan colours and costume shape, and these eventually made their way into Greek styles.

Men's clothing

The Minoans displayed a permissive attitude towards male nudity. Men of any rank or status roamed freely in the nude. They also wore short skirts similar to those worn in pre-dynastic Egypt and belts to which small aprons were attached.

Another wardrobe staple was the loincloth. It could be made from soft fibres like linen or from stiffer fabrics such as wool or leather, and its shape depended on the fabric. One form was gathered at the back in a long, oblique point, an upturned shape which resembled an animal's tail. In a variation on this style, another loincloth could be worn over the first, but back to front, forming a flounce that extended to mid-thigh with two points, one each at the back and front. The torso was not covered.

Tight, cloth belts decorated with spirals and rosettes emphasized the typical male wasp waist. Men also wore a loin skirt that by the Late Minoan period had evolved to reach mid-thigh. It featured a heavy beaded tassel. Like women's skirts, men's could be made from bright cloth decorated with geometric patterns.

At ceremonies, princes, the nobility, priests and priestesses (and sometimes high-ranking women) wore a long gown, or *chiton*, made of bright-coloured fabric. Tunic-shaped, it fell from the neck to the calf or ankle. Priests and priestesses wore stiff, sometimes full, gowns that might be made of spotted cloth to resemble animal skins. A short cape or a cloak made from animal skin or wool was worn over the loincloth or gown for warmth.

After the Mycenaean invasion, men wore tight-fitting shorts with decorative tassels. This style prevailed until the Dorians invaded Crete in about 1100 BC.

Footwear

Nobility wore shoes or sandals out of doors, but some archaeologists believe that they went barefoot indoors – on the staircases at Knossos the treads are worn as far as the threshold but unworn beyond it, suggesting that people took their shoes off there. Minoans' shoe-types include slipper shoes, moccasin-style socks, sandals fastened just above the ankle (some with beaded straps) and high, closed boots for journeys. Men wore half-boots of white or red leather or chamois skin. Women also wore high boots and a shoe with a raised heel.

above: Minoan traders, like those depicted here, centred their livelihood around Knossos.

above: Cretan costume was sophisticated as the female head of the so-called 'La Parisienne' shown here suggests. This fragment of a fresco is from the columned state hall in the west wing of the Palace of Knossos (c 1500–1450 BC).

Textiles

Early Minoans wore animal skins, but by 3000 BC they had mastered the art of weaving flax and, later, wool. Spinning was done both in centralized workshops at Knossos and by women at home, but skilled professionals dyed the cloth. Embroidery, too, was an integral part of Minoan costume and simple line patterns, flowers, rows of crocuses, birds and fish were popular motifs, especially in the Late period.

Jewellery

Arthur Evans' excavations of Knossos produced relatively few jewellery pieces: most examples have tended to be found in tombs, where they were buried with their owners. Many of the jewellery items that survived from the Early Minoan period were found near Mochlos and display a distinct Babylonian influence. Jewellery produced in the Middle Minoan period featured a filigree pattern and examples of typical granulated gold jewellery have also been found.

Minoan women have been depicted wearing thin necklaces with long strands that could be wrapped up to three times around the neck. They also wore rings, dangling gold earrings and pendants and in the Late Minoan period jewellery could feature animal motifs, such as the pendant of two wasps sharing a drop of honey, or scenes with people. Minoan men also had a taste for rich adornment. Some loincloths featured nets of pearls hanging in the front. Bracelets might be carved and were worn stacked on the arms.

The average Minoan wore necklaces of stones, while the wealthy proudly displayed semi-precious jewellery accentuated with beads of amethyst, rock crystal and agate. Pins were made of gold (some featured hunting motifs). These were worn by women. Copper and gold were used for hair pins. Gold buttons – shaped like leaves and animal figures – also appeared on women's garments. Excavations have also produced gemstones which were engraved and carved as seals.

Beauty and grooming

The Minoans adhered to a strict grooming ritual. Both men and women bathed daily and oiled their bodies to keep the skin supple. Men were clean-shaven. The Minoans' trading links with the Egyptians led to them using similar beautifying tools.

Hair was often styled intricately. Women wore their hair in a variety of ways: in a ponytail hanging at the back of the neck, in long waves and plaits or with a single or double lock curling above the ear and hanging down by the neck. The hair could be pulled back from the face with a ribbon; by the 17th century BC a band across the forehead was used for this purpose: there are images of them decorated with flowers. Women of high rank wore ornamental gold pins in their hair and gold or copper hairpins were also used to hold the hair in place. Hairstyles could also feature lavish ornamentation such as pearls and gems held together by gold filigree fillets – narrow hair bands – or a small gold crown. Alternatively, the hair could be braided with strings of pearls. Late Minoan men wore their hair in a long wavy style.

Hats and head-dresses

Hats are believed to have originated in Minoan Crete. Terracotta figurines display two popular styles: one, which seems to be part of the tiered-skirt ensemble, looks like an inverted plant pot, while another resembles a beret. A range of styles developed, including high caps, pointed hats, turbans and bonnets. Some hats featured white trimming, while others featured black. Ceremonies required special headgear such as the tiara, a toque or a flat, round hat. In the Late Minoan period men sometimes wore a beret-style cap.

above: Women enjoyed a prominent place in Cretan society. They can be seen here socializing in the Palace of Minos in Knossos.

3:three

ANCIENT

CLASSICAL ELEGANCE

GREECE

Background

The Greeks were innovators. In just 400 years, the Greeks invented politics and philosophy, as well as much of mathematics and geometry. Hippocrates provided the foundation of modern medicine and Herodotus first pondered history. The arts – the western concept of theatre and acting – can be seen as Greek innovations.

The ancient Greeks were not one people, but descended from successive waves of Indo-European invaders who arrived in the Aegean and eastern Mediterranean over a period of hundreds of years. They first occupied the territory between 2000 and 1600 BC. The Mycenaeans arrived from the north in the early 16th century BC, but were in turn invaded by the Dorians from Macedonia and the Balkans in about 1100 BC, and the Aeolians arrived in the coastal region of northwestern Asia Minor about 100 years later. All three groups spoke Greek, though with their own dialects. Forward thinking, if heavily influenced by the Egyptians, the Dorians built up a civilization that was unchallenged in terms of its sophistication.

The regions were divided into squabbling city-states, each usually ruled by a king, and would band together only to fight a common enemy. Eventually, different forms of government evolved: some cities were ruled by a wealthy group while others had a democratic system where all citizens (men who met stringent financial and social qualifications) had a direct input into the way the city was run.

The Greek diet was healthy yet spare, consisting of stone-ground bread, goat's cheese, olives, figs, eggs, dried fish and diluted wine. The ground was poor, making grazing difficult, so meat was eaten only on feast days. Although their society was sophisticated, there were few skilled professionals except smiths, stone cutters, armourers and jewellers. Most people lived off the land. Although public buildings such as the temples and the Parthenon at Athens were exquisitely grand, the average Greek lived a simple life in a small house and few had slaves or servants.

Women

Homer's *Iliad* sheds light on women of the Archaic Age. For example, the hero Hector tells his wife, Andromache to go back to her weaving rather than watch the battle, and describes how King Priam built a separate area of the palace for the women. Customs differed between cities and varied with time, but a general picture emerges in Greek writings of women living in complete anonymity, in some cases segregated in a separate part of the house: 'The slave has no will of his own; the child has a will, but an incomplete one; woman too has a will but it is impotent...'

Marriage was not a matter of choice for women. It was a financial arrangement set up between the parents of the bride and bridegroom. Running the household was the job of all Greek women, regardless of their social rank. A wife's main responsibilities lay in raising children and providing food and clothing. Weaving, particularly, was an important job for a woman. As Homer's poems testify, even queens spun and wove. This was back-breaking and laborious work, as Greek garments used large amounts of material. Fortunately, they

left: These exquisitely decorated Greek vases show women dressed in richly draped *chitons*. The fact that these garments are ankle-length suggests that the women depicted are from the upper echelons of society.

above: Although Greek clothing was simple, the Greeks were fond of patterns as their textiles and mosaics (such as this mosaic from the Palace of Attalos II, Pergamon, 159–138 BC) suggest.

ANCIENT GREECE

41

WOMEN

above: Elegant and feminine, ancient Greek female fashions ranged from draped to layered and fitted.

involved only minimal amounts of sewing. Women also made items for the home such as wall hangings, bed covers and cushions. An upper-class woman also had slaves or servants to manage, but even where slaves or servants prepared a meal, the woman of the house served food to both the family and guests. Women were also responsible for bathing their husbands. A girl from a wealthy family would be educated in home management by her mother or nurse. She could learn to read, write, spin, weave and embroider. Women also learned how to sing, play an instrument and dance – an activity that they engaged in both to exercise and to entertain their husbands.

Although society placed women in the home, they were not always completely secluded – upper-class women in the Archaic Age could mix uninhibitedly with men. Although they were not allowed to attend the gymnasium or the theatre, outside the home many women enjoyed some degree of freedom, although they would wear a veil to shield the face, and would always be accompanied by a slave or servant. Housewives would stand at their doors to watch passing events such as wedding processions.

Costume

Historians claim that Greece was to Rome what Paris was to the 18th and 19th centuries in Europe – the source of art and style. But when it came to costume, Greece can be considered the Gap of the ancient world. The Greeks wore clothes that were basic and simple; most garments originated from a rectangular piece of cloth. The amount of sewing involved was minimal, as the clothes were wrapped or draped. Tradition determined the ways in which men and women arranged their drapery, although there was a little leeway for personal style or individuality.

Ancient Greece can claim four main costume silhouettes as their own: Cretan Minoan, Mycenaean, Archaic and Classical. Each was named after the era during which it appeared, and styles reflected the values that governed each society. The Minoan style is discussed in the previous chapter, and although Mycenaean costume was influenced by Minoan fashion, it was also quite crude, incorporating items made of leather – like thongs and fringes – and even some made of metal. Archaic Greek clothing was based around the basics of a tunic and shawl and was meant to frame and shape the human body in a specific way. In the Classical era fabric was softer and draping became more sophisticated so that clothes fell naturally over the body. Minimal cutting and sewing was involved – or abandoned completely, and attention was devoted to draping. In its ideal form, clothing was meant to be so subtle that it was difficult to differentiate between the body and the cloth. This corresponds to the Classical Greek ideal in art where statues, once stiff and ritualistic, became more natural and easy.

The indispensable wardrobe item of Greece was the *chiton*, or tunic. Worn by both men and women, a *chiton* was no more than a large, rectangular piece of woollen cloth, draped over the body, covering the left arm while the right arm was uncovered. Pins or brooches (*fibulae*) fastened it on the left shoulder or on both shoulders. The *chiton* could be knee- or ankle-length, but its length as well as the amount of leg-room varied depending on the social position of the person who wore it. For ease of movement a labourer, for example, would wear a *chiton* that was shorter than that worn by an aristocrat. More luxurious examples could also be dyed, embroidered or edged with geometric designs or other decorative elements.

Women's clothing

A woman's wardrobe staple was the Doric *peplos*. Worn until the beginning of the 6th century BC, the *peplos* originated from a simple rectangle of woven woollen cloth. It was 6 feet (180cm) wide and its length has been estimated as approximately half as tall as the person wearing it. It was wrapped around the body and fastened by pins or *fibulae* at the shoulders, with any excess material being folded at the top, forming a flap at the back that

above: The Greeks wore clothes that were uncomplicated and simple. This Nereid sculpture from the west pediment of the Parthenon depicts Iris, the messenger of the gods.

WOMEN'S CLOTHING

above: The *chiton*, or tunic, was the indispensable wardrobe item of the Greeks. Worn by men and women alike, its hem reached either knee or ankle.

right: Women's *chitons* — such as the one worn here by a teenage girl — were draped differently from those worn by men. Women adapted the fabric to suit the shape of their bodies and sometimes put oval weights into the hem so that the *chiton* would drape better and cling to the body.

resembled an abbreviated cape. There were elegant variations on the basic *peplos*. For example, it could be worn without a belt, leaving it open at the side, or a skirt-and-blouse effect could be achieved by sewing the side slit from the waist to the hem, and tucking the excess material through a girdle or belt underneath the breasts with another belt fastened over a fold above the waist.

Women's *chitons* were made of narrower material than those of men and were draped differently. They adapted it to suit their body shape and could put oval weights into the hem so that it would drape better and cling to the body. If they wanted to flatten their chests, women would wrap themselves round with tight bands of cloth. A Greek woman's wardrobe featured a number of garments that were distinctly female and there was a ritual involved in the way a Greek woman dressed. First she wrapped a band of material beneath her breasts, then slipped a tunic of transparent material over that and finally added a short, sleeveless overtunic.

The Doric *podere* tunic was another elegant feminine garment, which could be embroidered and paired with jewellery and a light linen shawl, or *pharos*. Made of fine material, the *pharos* could be fastened together with a pin and could also take the shape of a scarf, worn diagonally across the body. It served both decorative and functional purposes as it could be wrapped around the body or the head for warmth in winter. The *palla* was an overgarment that resembled the *chiton*. It was sleeveless and fixed at the shoulders and gathered in at the waist by a belt fastened at the hips. Women also wore the men's *himation* (see page 47) over their tunics.

Men's clothing

Men's *chitons* were much wider than those worn by women, and sometimes sleeves were fashioned out of the extra width of cloth. Another form had a blouse-and-skirt type effect created by fastening two belts at the waist and on the hips, allowing material to flop over the belts. Extra material could also be doubled at the shoulders. The basic form of the *chiton* changed with time: during the 7th century BC it had no overfold of cloth (this version is called an Ionic *chiton*) and was ankle-length, but by the 5th century, it had been replaced by a short, knee-length version. This was fuller and softer, often made of linen rather than wool, and could be pleated and cinched at the waist with the help of a girdle. Small *fibulae* fastened the material across the shoulders to form sleeves, which were seamed rather than pinned.

The *himation* was another indispensable element of the male Greek wardrobe. During the Archaic period it was a short cloak-like garment made from a rectangle of wool and worn over the shoulders. It was wrapped around the torso, passed under the left arm and was pinned at the right shoulder so the extra material fell along the right arm and could be fastened with a number of small pins. An even simpler method of draping arranged the cloth around the back, so the loose ends fell over the forearms. In time, when the *himation* was made of lighter wool, it became more versatile and it reached 12 by 5ft (360 by 150cm) and was draped to give it a more elegant look.

The *chlamys* – a short, oblong garment which was fastened at the right shoulder – was sometimes worn over the knee-length *chiton*.

The Hellenistic age, following the death of Alexander the Great, heralded the most decorative era in Greek costume, partly because of the introduction of cotton, silk and gold and silver threads from India. Dress varied in cut, and oriental embroidery and metallic additions were used for decoration. Costume in the Hellenistic age emphasized a person's individuality. It was a time of prosperity for the Greeks, due to a thriving mercantile economy, and the luxurious materials used for clothing reflected the richness of the time.

Textiles

Some specimens of ancient Greek textiles have survived through until today. These were found at Kertch in the Crimea and date back to the 5th or 4th century BC. One fragment is of silk, but this material would have been very rare at the time: according to Herodotus, wool and linen were the two most commonly used fabrics in ancient Greece. Both were woven into a variety of textures ranging from thin and loose to a heavier weave, similar to a thick blanket.

Wool felt was used for caps and hats and woollen cloth was used to make both the *himation* and the *chlamys*. The use of wool for clothing has been traced back to the mountain-dwelling Dorians, who kept sheep. By 1000 BC, clothmaking had developed into an industry, and the different stages of production – shearing, washing, carding, spinning, weaving and dyeing – were divided between specialized workers. The use of linen, it is believed, originated from Egypt via the Ionians, although Plato claimed that linen had first

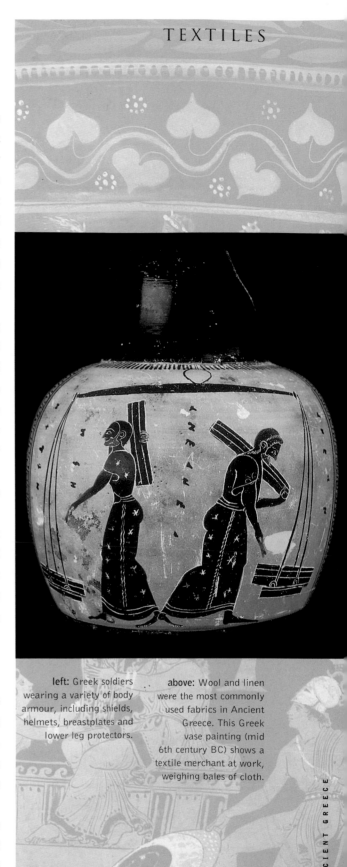

left: Greek soldiers wearing a variety of body armour, including shields, helmets, breastplates and lower leg protectors.

above: Wool and linen were the most commonly used fabrics in Ancient Greece. This Greek vase painting (mid 6th century BC) shows a textile merchant at work, weighing bales of cloth.

TEXTILES

above: This gold crown of ivy leaves (4th century BC) would have been worn as evidence of the owner's wealth. Gold jewellery became more prevalent as the value of this precious metal was appreciated.

been brought to Greece from Sicily. It could be woven so finely that it became almost transparent and could be pleated by hand.

Silk – imported from China, probably via India – was added to the Greek wardrobe in Hellenistic times. The texture would have been rough and uneven, comparable to raw silk or *shantung*.

The prevalence of woollen clothing in the ancient Greek wardrobe meant that most garments were off-white, at least until other textiles were introduced during the Archaic period. Cloaks were often dyed in dark colours such as rusty reds and earthy shades of brown and, by the 5th century other garments began to appear in a range of shades. According to Pliny, women had a liking for clothes made in floral shades and this is borne out by traces of paint on a number of female statues, including one whose cloak was originally green.

Warriors' garments were also coloured: a soldier's *chlamys* was decorated with bands of colour along the upper edges on the neck and shoulders or down the side seams. Homer relates that gold and silver thread could also be woven into the cloth to provide a decorative element and Herodotus described the use of yellow, indigo, violet, red and purple thread sewn into one garment. The textile fragments found at Kertch reveal that the Greeks employed numerous types of decoration on clothing, including a honeysuckle and palmette pattern. Garment borders were also dye-painted. Motifs from architecture and vase painting – such as wavy lines, egg and tongue moulding, animals and foliage patterns – were also dye-painted onto cloth.

Footwear

Although the Greeks went barefoot indoors only the lower classes did so outdoors. Both men and women wore sandals, which could be fastened in a variety of ways. The basic sandal featured a fan-shaped splay of straps passing from between the toes up to the top of the ankle. The straps were minimal and light so the foot was left almost bare. Sandals could be made of tooled leather or of purple leather with piped edges that were attached to the sandal by a clasp hanging on a strand of plaited leather. Boots were common footwear for soldiers, hunters and active men. Most of them were calf-length and while some laced up, others stayed on the foot with the help of a criss-cross thong at the toe. To make themselves look taller, women attached cork soles to their shoes.

Jewellery

Greeks, like many other peoples, wore jewellery in order to display their wealth. Earrings, bracelets, necklaces, brooches and rings – made of metal and semi-precious stones, including chalcedony, carnelian, amethyst, quartz (pink, green and grey), rock crystal, lapis lazuli, turquoise, garnet and crystalline calcite have been found. Precious metals were also used for both jewellery and decorative pieces such as tableware. But gold was in short supply: it was mined in the outer reaches of Thrace and Macedonia and on a few of the Aegean islands, but only in very small quantities. Oriental jewellery was imported and later,

left: Perfume was used profusely in Greece. It was stored in bottles, such as this one made of ceramic which is in the shape of a sandled foot (from Taranto, 7th century BC).

during what has become known as the Greek Orientalizing period, the eastern style of jewellery-making was copied. By the 6th century BC when gold's value became appreciated, an economy had developed which was fuelled by gold coins, leading to an increase in the prevalence of gold jewellery.

During the Archaic period Greek men wore only a few simple, functional items of jewellery, such as a pin or brooch to fasten a *himation* or *chiton* and a functional seal ring that could be used to seal letters and important documents. Men also carried walking sticks with metal heads: originally these were of iron but eventually, in later periods, silver and gold were used. With time, women's jewellery also evolved from mainly functional pieces into more lavish objects. The *fibula*, for example, had evolved by Hellenistic times into a decorative stickpin and keepsake. The most treasured items of jewellery could feature precious stones or be carved like a cameo. Hellenistic goldsmiths are said to have created the best Greek jewellery, which was well known for being rich in design and outstanding in its weight and composition.

above: Women in Ancient Greece wore make-up and took care of their skin. This woman, depicted on a vase painted c 480 BC, is shown standing in front of a wash basin and holding a mirror.

Beauty and grooming

Archaic Greeks wore little make-up, but later, by the 4th century BC, it was in use by all except lower-class women. Those women who did wear make-up applied paints and colour washes to the skin to accentuate their natural features. But the white base colour women applied to their faces was often made from white lead which could destroy the complexion and cause fatal lead poisoning. Rouge was a gentler beautifier. An earthy shade of red, it could be blended from vermilion or vegetables such as mulberry or seaweed. Greek women often blended it into their cheekbones in a round shape, although this could vary. Flushed cheeks were often accompanied by red lips, although sometimes women wore colour on their lips alone.

Eye make-up was also a part of Greek women's beauty regime. They probably applied shadow and Egyptian kohl to the eyes, but sometimes even soot and lampblack were used. More than one colour of eye shadow could be used at once. Richard Corson describes one popular way of wearing eye make-up where the upper lid was shaded a reddish brown while the lower edge of the bone and above was shaded with a jade green. The upper lid was then lined with the same green and this extended beyond the lid out to the corners. Meanwhile, eyebrows were groomed and, whatever the woman's hair colour, painted black. Greek women also appear to have favoured a 'uni-brow' – thick eyebrows which met just above the nose, and some even wore false eyebrows. Petronius describes a woman taking her eyebrows out of a small box.

Perfumes were used profusely. Violet was a popular scent. Women also sprayed their skins with essences of mint, myrrh, marjoram and thyme. The Greeks often applied different scents to different body zones. Antiphanes described the perfuming ritual:

> In gilded tub, and steeps his feet
> And legs in rich Egyptian unguents;
> His neck and chest he rubs with oil of palm
> And both his arms with sweet extract of mint,
> His eyebrows and his hair with marjoram,
> His knees and face with essence of wild thyme.

The use of scent and make-up went in and out of fashion, sometimes because of laws. Some young Athenian men – the equivalent to English dandies – used so much scent that Solon (c. 640– c. 559 BC) established a law banning the sale of scented oil to Athenian men. Meanwhile, Plutarch reveals that Lycurgus banished cosmetics from Sparta as he claimed that painting the body corrupted men's manners.

Greek women took care to condition their skin on a daily basis. They used depilatories to remove hair and smooth the skin, applied meal face packs at night and removed them the next morning with milk, and rubbed ointments, pomades and oils all over the body. Oils were used for therapeutic reasons (both during massage and as medicine) as well as animal fats, goose fat and butter were used in cosmetics. Both men and women cleaned their teeth and, after bathing, scrubbed their body with a *strigil*, an implement that worked like a modern body brush. The Scythians were reputed never to wash because they believed it would disrupt the natural beauty of the skin. Instead, to clean the face they used *succedaneium*: a paste mixture made by pounding cypress and cedar incense, then infusing the powder with water. Once removed, they believed that it left the skin smooth and glowing.

Men also maintained their physique. Gymnastics – physical exercise often performed in the nude – was a way of life for the Greek male. Physical education was taught to the young and every city had a *gymnasium* – a network of buildings similar to a college campus, including a *palestra*, a complex devoted to exercise, complete with changing rooms and fountains. Although women were prohibited from the *palestra*, they were encouraged to maintain their figures. Socrates, for example, advised women to sing to develop a shapelier chest.

The Greeks believed that hair was imbued with a religious and a symbolic significance. Mourners would tear, cut off or shave some of their own hair and lay it upon the corpse or throw it in a pile to be burned with the dead person. A bride's hair was cut on her wedding day to symbolize her humility and renunciation of her vanity, and during the ceremony virgins offered a lock of hair to the goddesses. An unfaithful wife could have her head shaved by her husband. Young boys did not cut their hair until the first signs of facial hair appeared, when they would sacrifice it to Apollo. In Athens, young men cut their hair and ceremoniously offered it to Hercules.

Hair styles for men and women were, like clothing, initially similar. The Greeks had hair of all shades – from blond to black. But both sexes admired blond hair and some went to great lengths to lighten theirs, washing it in yellow flowers or using a special ointment formulated in Athens. This was massaged into damp hair and left there until it dried in the sun. Potash water was also used to bleach the hair.

With time – probably by the 6th century BC – men wore their hair cut short. At first, men's hairstyles had been fussy with curls forming a crown around the forehead or braids wound around the head. But styles eventually were simplified and from then on, long hair was considered effeminate, acceptable as a style for the elderly male, young men or boys. Sometimes men wore trinkets in their hair. Hair styles were also known by names: the *kepos* was unkempt, the Hectorean style involved cutting and combing the hair backward into curls and the Theseid cut featured strands of hair worn short at the forehead while the rest hung down longer at the back of the neck.

Young girls let their hair fall freely and older women wore their hair long and let it fall loose over the shoulders. The Greeks considered a low forehead a mark of beauty, so hair was often styled in such a way as to diminish its size. Women also wore their hair parted in the middle, waved (by using hot irons) and scraped back so as to expose the ears. Sometimes, three or four strands, or spiral curls, were sectioned from the rest of the hair and styled so they hung down over the forehead while the rest of the hair hung down loosely at the back.

above: It was not only women in Ancient Greece who cared about their appearance. Men devoted a lot of time to improving their physique and they also wore make-up and sprayed their skin with scent.

BEAUTY AND GROOMING

By the 7th and 6th centuries BC the hair was bound by a band, ribbon, diadem or string of pearls. Women of high rank wore precious hair accessories including gold spirals, and silver or bronze bands. By the 5th century BC, another style had become popular – women pulled up the back hair and looped it over a fillet. Triangles of fabric and folded handkerchiefs were both used to pull back the hair and, until Alexander's time, women often bound ribbons into their hair. After Alexander, hairstyles seemed to become more sophisticated – knots and chignons were held in place with ornate hairpins and, through the Hellenistic period, ringlets and corkscrew curls were used to accentuate chignons.

Wigs were not as popular as in Ancient Egypt but they were worn. It was suggested that Thespis invented acting after observing the change in his appearance a wig had made. And it is presumed that Pythagoras wore an Egyptian wig while travelling there (he had been so attacked by insects that he had his hair shorn).

Greek women washed their hair with scented water. Hair grooming products for the Greeks included oils and perfumes. Hair oils were scented with floral notes including rose oil amaricium which originated from the island of Cos. Other blends included extracts of marjoram and elder. The Greeks became known for these hair oils and they were exported to nearby countries. There was special mud as well as pomades to add shine to the hair. Unguents were used as setting lotions.

Though blonde was the preferred hair shade, from 444 BC both sexes dyed their hair other colours by using gold, white, ebony, sky blue, honey and red coloured powders which could be easily washed out. Dyes and false hairpieces were also utilized, but, like the use of cosmetics, altering the natural colour of hair became frowned upon.

Like the hair, beards also had symbolic significance. Beards (real, false and often cut into a rounded or pointed shape) were worn throughout Mycenaean Greece and the Archaic Age. But by the Classical Age, only philosophers and older men wore beards. According to Herodotus, a beard gave a man an air of seriousness. The Epicureans wore long beards and the Stoics went unshaven, whereas slaves wore beards but shaved their heads. In the 5th century BC there was a trend of letting only a moustache grow. With time it became increasingly unfashionable for men to show body hair. The ideal man, as sculpture rendered, was smooth-skinned and youthful.

Men devoted time to grooming. The Greek barber shop – complete with specially designed chairs – was a meeting point where men gathered to gossip and served as a place where intellectuals could meet and exchange ideas.

Hats and head-dresses

Greek headgear, for men, took many shapes. There were several variations on a cone-shaped hat: a truncated cone, a cone with a small brim and an extended truncated cone. The Phrygian cap appeared, too, in Classical Greece. It proved to be the model for the medieval caps worn by the *doges* of Venice and the liberty cap of the French Revolution. The bonnet was another known style, as was a hat shaped like a pagoda. The latter may have been introduced after Alexander the Great's campaign in the Far East. The *pilos* was

above: Greek women often washed their hair with scented water. The bust depicting the back of Queen Arsinoe III's head (235–204 BC) reflects the hair styles of the period.

a brimless skull cap made from felt or wool which was sometimes worn underneath a helmet.

Women in Classical Greece wore scarves, which were wrapped around the head twice. The *saccus* was a Classical style of hat featuring a tassel at the back as well as nets or snoods to hold the hair back. The tiara-like *stephanie* was a very popular form of headgear. The *petasos* was worn by women, as well as men on journeys. This was a sun hat made of woven straw. It featured a brim which could be turned up or down as well as a flap which fell on one ear. The *petasos* could be fastened at the neck by a ribbon that hung down when the hat was worn on the head. On festive occasions a *petasos* featuring brightly coloured streamers could be worn.

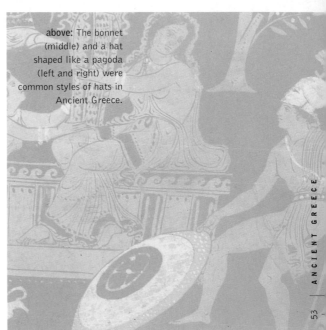

above: The bonnet (middle) and a hat shaped like a pagoda (left and right) were common styles of hats in Ancient Greece.

ANCIENT GREECE

53

THE

ATHLETIC AND COLOURFUL CLOTHES

ETRUSCANS

Background

As the Mycenean palaces began to crumble, the hill towns in Etruria – present day Tuscany – began to develop. Though Etruscan culture was to have a profound influence on the religious and political life of Rome, archaeologists are still uncertain about the origins of the Etruscans. It is known that they were not natives of Italy. There was probably one influx of settlers from the Balkans (or Asia Minor) before 1000 BC and another from Asia Minor during the 8th century BC, and it is from this time that Etruscan civilization begins to flourish. Etruscan society has unique elements unlike anything found in Asia Minor or Greece, possibly indicating that the invaders adopted parts of the native culture. This is particularly evident in the few early Etruscan inscriptions that were found on a group of objects preserved in tombs discovered in a village near Bologna. Although written in an early Greek alphabet, the language used is not Greek and unrelated to any other known language. During the Archaic Period (700–650 BC), the main cultural influence came from Asia Minor, but from 650 BC Greek culture was dominant.

The Etruscans dominated much of the western Mediterranean, competing with the Phoenicians and Greeks for maritime supremacy. At their height they had territories that spread from Venice in the northeast to the Po Valley in the northwest and down the western side of Italy as far as Naples in the south. Their empire was a loose federation of independent city-states, each governed by its own kings, much like the Greeks. Until the late 6th century BC there was no major threat to Etruscan expansion and rule, but battles with Greek cities in Italy led to loss of trade and power, and during the 5th and 4th centuries BC their territories were gradually overrun by Gauls from the north and alliances of states and tribes (including their own former city-state of Rome) in the south. They were under Roman rule by 250 BC and their cities and culture were more or less destroyed in 80 BC by the Roman general Sulla.

But the Etruscans were not always at war. Their community prospered due to the work of skilled craftsmen like metal workers who used Italy's wealth of minerals, such as copper, lead and iron, to make a wide variety of items, from bronze household and religious objects to iron weapons. The Etruscans were also able goldsmiths, importing the precious metal from Africa and Asia. Stylistically, Etruscan art follows the phases of Greek art although it has a vigour and a vividness that is all its own.

Social divisions appear to have been prominent. The upper echelons of society were, typically, architects, warriors and merchants. Below them, archaeologists believe, there was a middle class – the *etera* – who worked for the elite as farm managers or servants. In return, they would be given protection and even a burial plot in the family tomb of those they served. As for the lower classes, the masses were labourers – farmers and food producers, sailors, soldier and miners. Below them were the slaves.

Few historians claim to have detailed knowledge about the Etruscans' daily lives. Because they left few written records of their culture, clues about how they lived have been pieced together from paintings, sculpture, pottery and from references in Roman writings. The vivid tomb-paintings showing their lives, banqueting, hunting and fishing, dancers and

left: Because the Etruscans left so few written records of their culture, clues have been pieced together from artefacts such as this wall painting (c 470 BC) which shows dancers from the time.

right: This bronze statue shows the hair style typical of Etruscan women – the long hair is braided and the fringe is frizzed.

BACKGROUND

above: A bronze statue (early 4th century) shows a young Etruscan clad in a *tebenna*.

animals, give us a small insight into their culture. These paintings, along with the items buried with the dead, also indicate that they believed in a life after death.

Some of what archaeologists know about Etruscan houses comes from their tombs, which were, in fact, copies of their timber, mud-brick and terracotta homes, hewn out of rock. Aristocrats lived in single-storey homes with gabled roofs covered in terracotta tiles. Within the house was a vestibule – a multi-purpose hallway: during the day it could function as an office, by night it would become a hall for dining and entertainment and servants might sleep there. The vestibule form would later be adopted by the Romans and become the central, open atrium of a house. The Romans would also use many other Etruscan innovations in building, including the town plan of a grid centred on a crossroads, aqueducts and sophisticated domestic plumbing, drains, fortifications and semi-circular arches used as architectural features in combination with classic Greek forms.

Women

Theopompus, a Greek historian who wrote in the 4th century BC, described Etruscan women as vain, promiscuous exhibitionists who thought nothing of appearing naked in public. But his description can now be considered sensationalist and his disparaging remarks probably stem from chauvinism, jealousy or resentment of the Etruscans' military might. Women living in Etruria enjoyed a freedom unrivalled in the ancient world, some say near equality with men, and this would, no doubt, have shocked Greek and Roman writers. Wives still performed the usual household chores, including spinning and weaving cloth, making clothes and rearing children, but, unlike their counterparts in Greece and Rome, they were not segregated into separate quarters. They freely attended public entertainment – dances, boxing matches, acrobatic displays and chariot races. Etruscan women drank wine while Roman women were forbidden to do so. It is also likely that aristocratic ladies were able to read and write. Clues confirming this were found on hand mirrors, many of which were engraved with mythological figures and written inscriptions providing the identity of each character as well as the details of the scenes depicted. Such inscriptions would have been pointless if their owner was illiterate.

Costume

Etruscan men and women followed Greek fashions and, as in Greece, fashions changed through time. From 700 to 575 BC, both sexes were depicted in tunic gowns of varying lengths. The tunic was cinched in at the waist by a wide belt. It featured half-sleeves fastened at the shoulder by *fibulae*. Over the tunic women wore a semi-circular cape with two panels thrown back over the shoulders which hung down to the waist. Men wore a long cloak as an outer garment.

Women's clothing

Aristocratic women readily adopted changing fashions, adding new ideas. For example, some wore a scarlet cloak with a Greek *chiton* (see page 43). One tomb-painting depicts a woman wearing a long, sheer tunic under another heavier one with decorative borders at the neckline, hem and at the elbow-length sleeves. Women wore shawls, draped either like the *himation* (see page 47), or over the head with the ends flung over the shoulders.

Men's clothing

Loin skirts (see page 35) and T-shaped tunics were typical garments worn by 7th-century BC Etruscan men. By the 6th century BC the Greek-style tunic had dropped to ankle-length and featured a geometric pattern. The universally-worn *lacerna* was a short, narrow woollen cloak. Men of high rank could also wear a rectangular shawl or mantle often featuring a plaid pattern. Etruscan men sometimes wore brightly coloured scarves instead of cloaks.

By the mid-6th century BC, the men's long cloak was giving way to the *tebenna* – a semi-circular cape draped over the left shoulder and under the right arm. It may have derived from the Greek *chlamys* (which men also wore) and inspired the Roman toga. Preferred by

above: An Etruscan female figure from the tomb of Larthia Seianti from Chiusi. A long, sheer tunic was worn under a heavier tunic, featuring a decorative border at the neckline, hem and at the elbow-length sleeves.

kings and aristocrats, the *tebenna* could be worn over a white embroidered tunic. Originally short, it progressed to knee-length and then ankle-length. A terracotta sculpture of Apollo from Veii – representing the high point of Etruscan art, from about 510 BC – wears a knee-length tunic and *tebenna*. The middle and lower classes wore plainer versions of the same items, and peasants dressed simply in a tunic and a cloak, sometimes with leather leggings.

Footwear

In the early period no one wore shoes, but eventually, shoes became a status symbol among the rich. By the 6th century BC specialist cobblers were creating a variety of custom shoes for aristocrats: sandals, laced boots, soft, comfortable shoes, shoes with ankle straps and some with upturned toes in blue, black or red leather. The Bally Museum at Schönenwerd, Switzerland, has a 6th-century BC Etruscan wooden-soled sandal in its collection. It is split, hinged with leather and tied with a lace, and suggests comfort and flexibility. Shoes with upturned toes or points could be cut low or laced up high. Etruscan women wore soft moccasin-style shoes. By the 5th century BC a Greek influence was noticeable; pointed shoes were replaced with more comfortable sandals. Shoes were valued items: when they were taken off at mealtimes, they were placed on low benches rather than left on the floor.

Jewellery

Etruscan jewellery is of very high quality and is very recognizable because of a unique decorative technique they developed called granulation. This involved soldering tiny gold particles on to a smooth, gold background to create a sparkling effect. This was used on a whole range of jewellery – clasps, wreaths, pendants, breastplates, *fibulae* and bracelets. The quality of 7th-century BC workmanship makes it evident that Etruscan civilization was thriving. The Etruscan upper classes took great pride in their jewellery, wearing lots of it (one fashion, shared with the Cypriots and the Spanish, was to wear several rings at once on the left hand). They stored it carefully in wooden and bronze boxes. Jewellery could be enriched with engravings of animals or arabesques and floral motifs. Necklaces featured lockets and dangling jewels, and pendants were also worn. Earrings could be disc-shaped and very long (sometimes 7.5cm (3in)), spiral or sculpted like snakes with human heads.

Textiles

The Etruscans used a variety of materials to make their clothes, chiefly cotton and wool, in pale yellow, bright and brick red and a pink-tinged shade of orange. Borders were made of blue fabric. Men could wear orange, light green or royal blue scarves. Etruscan garments also featured bold, lively patterns; a circle-and-cross pattern and a zigzag-and-dot motif were among the most popular. Different patterns could be mixed together in an outfit; a woman might wear a tunic with the zigzag-and-dot motif, a *peplos*-type jumper (see page 43) with folds of zigzags and a shawl with more zigzags. They also used embroidery to decorate clothing. Floral motifs were embroidered on to *chitons* while scarves could feature dot-patterned needlework in contrasting shades.

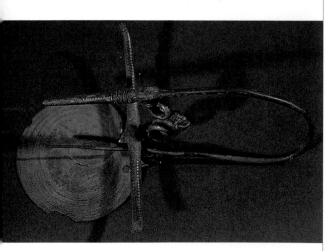

above: The Etruscan upper classes took great pride in their jewellery and wore lots of it, such as this *fibula* (brooch) from Necropolis of Cavalupo (8th–7th century BC).

right: Preferred by kings and aristocrats, the *tebenna* was sometimes worn over a white embroidered tunic. A terracotta sculpture of Apollo from Veii (510 BC) wears a tunic and a *tebenna*.

Make-up and grooming

Etruscans lined their eyes and possibly painted their eyebrows. Toilet boxes, mirrors, rouge, lip paint and face-colour have been discovered in women's tombs. It is also assumed that some men applied face-colour. The Etruscans looked after their health. Studies of Etruscan skulls reveal traces of dental work, crowns and bridges of tight, light gold fittings, sometimes with animal's teeth in place of missing human teeth. Women exercised but did so while naked. They waxed their bodies to make their skin smooth and hairless.

Etruscan women adopted a number of hair styles, and these changed frequently. Hair could be parted in the middle with plaits or curls falling down at the back, or waving down each side of the face in a windswept look. Another popular style had a frizzed fringe while the rest of the hair was braided or gathered in a snood at the back. The hair could be gathered by a net at the nape of the neck with curls falling over the forehead, or enclosed in a sheath. Women bleached their hair and adorned it with bronze and gold spirals as well as bone, ivory or metal-topped pins, metal jewels or leaves.

Men wore their beards curled and their hair in ringlets over the forehead, but sometimes the fashion called for short hair. The statue of Apollo from Veii has long hair twisted in curls from the back of his head in much the same way as Archaic Greek male sculptures.

Hats and head-dresses

A typically Etruscan hat was the *tutulus* – a sturdy, pointed tiara-style head-dress with a brim at the front. But hats were not an integral part of the Etruscan wardrobe. They were more generally worn outdoors by peasants and warriors. Etruscan men wore beret-like hats that varied in height. The *petasos* (see page 53) was worn by peasants for protection against the sun and is seen on some Etruscan sculptures of men.

ANCIENT

ROMAN EXTRAVAGANCE

ROME

S. Harding. Del.

E. Harding Jun.r Sc.

Background

According to legend, Rome was founded on 21 April, 753 BC by Romulus and Remus, twin sons of Mars, although archaeologists have found traces of Bronze Age people there, dating from perhaps 1500 BC. Rome was a village in a favourable position, on the Palatine hill on the east bank of the River Tiber some 16 miles (25 km) from the sea. The two brothers ruled jointly for a while, but Romulus killed his brother and reigned by himself until 715 BC. His successor, Numa Pompilius, is said to have founded Roman law and its religious practices, setting up the College of Priests, and to have been the first to divide the year into 12 months.

In the 7th century the Romans were believed to have been united with their near neighbours, the Sabines, and became the most powerful village in Latium (western central Italy), until the Etruscans conquered them in about 616 BC. The third Etruscan king was expelled in 510 BC and the Roman Senate decreed that Rome would become a republic. The Senate (made up of patricians – members of ancient noble families) had originally been set up as an advisory body to the kings, but now took over control and the Republic was to last some 480 years.

With time, Roman power, influence and property grew to proportions unprecedented in the ancient world. By the end of the Republic (31 BC), Rome controlled the entire Mediterranean, from Palestine to Gibraltar and beyond. They had defeated their most powerful rivals, the Carthaginians, and taken over many of the lands ruled by the Greeks including Egypt. Its success was due to the strength of its army; conscription was a duty for every property owning male citizen. The end of the Republican era saw struggles for power between various men, including Julius Caesar, Pompey, Mark Antony and Octavian. Eventually, Octavian was the victor and became 'princeps' – first citizen, rather than king, in 27 BC although he was, in effect, a dictator.

After more than 40 years Octavian was succeeded by Tiberius, an adopted stepson, who was followed by his great nephew Gaius (Caligula), Claudius (Caligula's uncle), who conquered southern Britain, and Nero (Claudius's stepson), a lavish spender who is alleged to have burned a large part of central Rome in order to build a huge palace. After his death in AD 68 came Galba, Otho and Vitellius, who each reigned only for weeks, then Vespasian (reigned AD 69–79), followed by his sons Titus (AD 79–81) and Domitian (AD 81–96).

The Senate then tried to reassert its authority over the army, and elected Nerva, an elderly statesman, as the next emperor. He adopted the Spanish soldier, Trajan, as his successor. Conquests in the east during his reign (98–117) expanded the empire to its greatest extent, but his successor Hadrian (r. 117–38) had to abandon most of these territorial gains. Antoninus Pius (r. 138–61), Marcus Aurelius (r. 161–80) and Lucius Verus (co-emperor 161–9) kept the empire stable and defended its borders, but Marcus Aurelius' son Commodus (180–92) was unfit to rule and his reign marked the beginning of the decline of the Roman Empire. Economic crises, corruption, inflation, revolts, attacks on the empire's borders, civil wars and power struggles within government all contributed to the eventual decline of the empire.

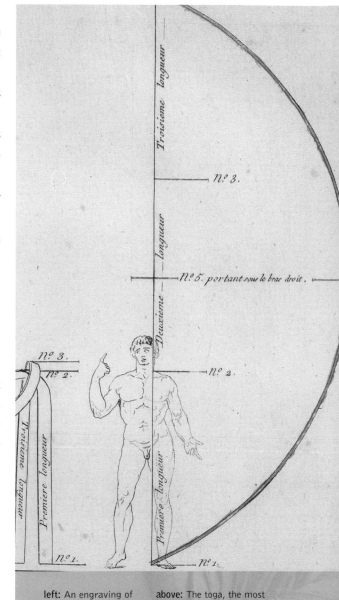

left: An engraving of Gaius Julius Caesar on a coin dating from the 1st century BC. Only Roman emperors wore any type of hat: the imperial crown, a solid gold wreath of laurel leaves.

above: The toga, the most renowned Roman garment, traces its origins back to Ancient Greece and Erturia. The image here shows the cut of a toga, illustrated by Jean Racine in Volume II of *Research on the Costumes and Theatre of All Nations*.

Diocletian (r. 284–305) divided the empire into four regions, with himself in overall control. After years of struggle between the rulers of the four regions, Constantine (r. 306–37) emerged in overall control. He moved the imperial capital to Byzantium, which he renamed Constantinople in 330.

By 395 the empire was permanently divided between two states – east and west – and the western empire continued to crumble. The Visigoths invaded Rome in 410, the Vandals in 455 and the last western emperor was deposed by the German Odoacer in 476. The eastern empire lived on until 1453. Today, it is referred to as the Byzantine Empire, the subject of the next chapter.

Roman power had brought a long period of peace to a substantial territory, but the Romans were often tyrannical masters – enslaving some of their captives, exploiting conquered lands and taxing their occupants heavily. Many subjects embraced the Roman way of life, and worshipped Roman gods, but the Romans were tolerant of local culture and religions, so long as they did not perceive them to be a political danger. Any perceived threat, however, was dealt with ruthlessly: if political means failed, cities and towns in revolting states would simply be razed to the ground.

In conquered areas, they built towns on the same plan, with a forum for public meetings (often with a basilica, or hall, in larger towns), public baths, theatres and a temple. Bridges, sewers, aqueducts and public monuments were built throughout the empire. Towns and frontier areas had garrisons of soldiers, with the famous straight, paved Roman roads between them, so that armies could travel swiftly and safely regardless of weather conditions and goods could be moved easily. The empire also had a vast maritime trade network – ships transported olive oil from North Africa, glass from Syria and wool from the British Isles.

Roman culture and thought were heavily influenced by those of Greece, but law and government were of purely Roman genius. All aspects of Roman society were heavily regulated by the government – politics, arts, culture and costume. Different laws applied to different classes, and citizens had more rights than non-citizens. Social status was usually inherited; the children of slaves would themselves be slaves.

Women

Roman women shared much the same life as those from other ancient cultures. Arranged marriages were the norm, and at the age of 12 a girl was considered to be of marriageable age. Women spent their days preoccupied with housekeeping chores, including making clothes for their family. But a rich woman had slaves to depend on.

Restrictions were placed on the freedom of Roman women. Roman law decreed that the head of the family – the *paterfamilias* – had absolute power over his wife and children. A father could sell his children into slavery and control the affairs of his son even through adulthood.

Upper-class women did not leave their homes unaccompanied: they would always have slaves and servants in tow. On journeys, women would travel together, resting on the way

above: The Colosseum (c AD 75) reflects the grandeur of the Roman empire and is a magnificent example of Roman engineering.

left: Three's company: upper class women did not leave their homes unaccompanied. Like these Roman noblewomen (left and centre), they would always have a slave or servant (right) in tow.

in tents or in the home of a public official. Although women were not kept in seclusion, they would spend time at home in the women's apartments, the *gynaeceum*. No woman could participate in public life, but in time rich women were allowed a limited degree of financial independence. Both Augustus and Claudius initiated laws that prevented wives from becoming guarantors for their husbands. In this way, in the event of a husband going bankrupt, a wife's estate and assets could remain untouched.

Although Roman women were not liberated, evidence suggests that some were progressive, and educated. Beyond housekeeping, they busied their intellects with interests such as philosophy — some women are known to have had their own personal philosophers with whom they discussed a wide variety of subjects, including astrology and mathematics. Nero's wife, Poppaea, for instance, is known to have travelled accompanied by her own personal mathematician.

Costume

What we know of Roman lifestyle is largely how the upper classes lived. As poorer Romans did not write books, much of what we know today of Roman costume concerns what the upper classes wore. At the height of Roman power, their wardrobe influenced the Spanish, British and Germanic peoples. But Roman costume was, in its turn, an amalgamation of that worn by its forerunners: it was influenced by clothes worn by the Etruscans and the Greeks, and to a lesser extent by items worn in states that it had conquered. The Romans divided their wardrobe into two main categories: *indumenta*, items that were slipped over the head and removed only for sleeping, and *amictus*, clothing wrapped or draped around the body. The wide range of climates in the Roman Empire led to a major step in the history of fashion: the concept of seasonal dressing — sartorial elements geared toward specific seasons and weather conditions. Early Roman outerwear included, among other pieces,

left: Women's clothing changed little throughout Roman times. This marble statue shows a woman wearing two tunics, a short undertunic which ends at the knee and a longer outer tunic, or *stola*, wrapped under the bust with a belt.

above: Like the Greeks, a Roman's wardrobe consisted of two main garments: a tunic and a cloak. The colour, shape and decoration of these items denoted the wearer's social rank. From left to right: a public orator, a senator, a citizen and an equestrian.

mitts, the poncho and trews or trousers, which were believed to have been adopted from the Germans. These pieces, first adopted by soldiers, later became wardrobe elements of Romans and other Europeans.

Women's clothing

Textiles and colours differentiated men's clothing from women's; the latter tended to be made of lightweight materials such as Indian cotton and silk and in a variety of colours such as deep blue, yellow and red as well as sea-foam green and light pink. Unlike men's dress, women's costume in Rome experienced few changes. Their wardrobe staple was the *stola*. Initially made of wool, it later became available in cotton or linen and rich women wore *stolas* made of silk. More ample than the tunic, the *stola* was an ankle-length garment with full sleeves. Not always stitched at the neck, it was usually fastened by clasps and girded in two places: below the bust with a girdle known as the *cingulum* and at the hips with a *succincta*, a wide belt. The *stola* appeared in a number of colours: red, blue and yellow and sometimes the cloth could be embroidered with gold thread. Under the *stola* women could wear a *subucula*, a sleeveless shift dress, as well as the *strophium*, a bust bodice made of unstiffened fabric. For warmth, women wore a *palla*, a square or rectangular piece of cloth that might have a hood and was fastened around the shoulder with a clasp.

Noblewomen wore a silk tunic decorated with gold fringe. As an outer garment they too opted for the *palla*, the *sapparum* – a linen outer garment with half sleeves – or the *olicula* – a short cape that covered their upper arms. Originally women would not accessorize their dress, but the use of such items as silk scarves, kerchiefs, fans and sunshades came into fashion from the 2nd century BC onwards.

Men's clothing

In the early days of the Republic, Roman men dressed simply, wearing just a loincloth. Known as the *subligaculom* or *licinium*, it was made of linen and knotted at the waist. By the time of the empire, only athletes and workmen were permitted to wear loincloths; workmen wore theirs under a tunic.

Like the Greeks, the Romans wore two main garments: the tunic and the cloak. The basic short-sleeved tunic – the *tunica* – was worn at home. Adapted from the Greek *chiton*, it consisted, in its most basic form, of two pieces of wool cloth joined at the shoulders and down the sides, with slits for the head and arms. It was gathered at the waist with a belt, but could also be worn in public places with a girdle, which could come equipped with a purse to hold money and valuables. During the Republican period it was worn knee-length, but grew to ankle-length during the Empire.

Certain tunic styles corresponded to a man's social rank and others were worn on specific occasions:

> • *Tunica angusti clavi*: Knights and magistrates adopted this style of tunic. It was decorated with two narrow purple stripes – one over each shoulder.

above: A marble statue (2nd century BC) of a veiled muse.

right: A fresco of the goddess Flora from Stabia near Naples.

Gallerie Justinienne.

above: Social status was inherited. Citizens had more rights than non-citizens. A Roman couple (6th Century AD).

• *Tunica laticlavia*: Worn by senators, this tunic featured wider purple stripes.

• *Tunica palmata*: Part of a two-piece ensemble, worn with the *toga picta*, this tunic was worn by victorious generals. Its two pieces were made of purple silk embroidered with gold thread. It was also decorated with scenes of a victorious military campaign.

• *Tunica recta*: An ungirdled tunic worn by young men and by young women on their marriage.

• *Subucula* and *tunica exteriodum*: Two tunics worn together, with the *subucula* underneath.

• *Caracalla*: An ankle-length tunic. The *tunica* was worn until the 3rd century AD except by the ultra fashion-conscious who wore one that fell to just below knee length. After this date the *caracalla* was worn.

While at work, at a festive occasion or at a religious ceremony, noble Romans wore a long tunic. Made of cotton, wool or, during the empire, silk, it could feature a weave of gold or silver thread as well as embroidery.

The toga – the most renowned Roman garment – can trace its origins back to the Greek *himation* and the Etruscan *tebenna*. It was adopted by the Romans in about the 6th century BC and was originally worn over a loincloth, and then over a *tunica*. Made of an oval piece of woollen fabric, it was initially quite small, but as time went on it gradually grew until, during the last century of the Republic and the beginning of the empire period, it reached about 5.5m (18ft) in length and 3.5m (11ft 6in) in width. Its enormous size meant that to fit it onto the body required the assistance of a slave in order to drape it properly. The imperial toga of the 1st and 2nd centuries AD was even bigger, measuring roughly 6m (20ft) in length. This was an exceptional style, however, worn only by very prominent Roman citizens.

Slaves, women and foreigners were prohibited from wearing the toga. It was a garment reserved for Roman citizens, especially the leisured classes and the rich. As with the *tunica*, the toga's decoration, colour and shape denoted the wearer's social rank. A citizen's place in society – be he a candidate for public office, a general or an emperor – would be immediately obvious from the colour of his toga and how it was draped.

How togas were folded varied as fashions changed. They could also be folded differently on specific occasions to convey a certain meaning. For example, the *toga pulla*, which was worn during mourning, had a fold of material that covered the head.

The different forms of togas included:

• *Toga candida*: Worn by candidates for public office. It was similar to the *toga virilis* worn by young men except that the wool was bleached to remove the yellow shade of the natural fibres. Candidates often wore this toga without a *tunica* underneath. According to Plutarch, this fashion enabled them to show off their battle scars.

• *Toga picta*: A toga that was worn by Roman generals on specific occasions. The property of the state, the *toga picta* was loaned to a general for ceremonial wear, and it signified victory. Later it became the emperor's official garment and was reserved for his use only.

• *Toga pulla*: Worn by mourners, this toga was black, dark brown or grey. It included a piece of material that covered the head.

• *Toga trabea*: Appeared in three styles. A solid purple signified that the wearer was spiritual or was in touch with the gods, purple and white was worn by rulers of the Republic, and a purple and crimson striped pattern was reserved for *augurs* (interpreters of omens).

As the Roman Empire expanded northward, harsher climatic conditions than those in Italy made wearing warm clothes a necessity. The most commonly worn outer garment was the *lacerna*, a cloak made from a rectangular piece of wool with rounded edges, although in northernmost regions of the empire it was made of felt or leather. It was draped over the shoulders, fastened either there or at the neck with a clasp and sometimes featured a detachable hood. Originally uncoloured, with time it was dyed in a variety of colours. Augustus is said to have disapproved of citizens covering their togas with *lacernas* in public places such as the forum or circus so, as a mark of respect, citizens would remove theirs when he arrived.

Other outer garments worn by Roman men included:

• *Sagum*: This practical blanket-like wrap – in different shades of red wool – was copied from the Gauls by soldiers.

• *Pallium*: Similar in style to the Greek *himation*, this was a short rectangular cloak.

• *Paludanentum*: Worn by Roman generals, this was an enlarged version of the

• Greek *chlamys*. It was fastened over the right shoulder with a clasp.

• *Paenula*: A woollen rain cape, often with a collar and peaked hood, worn mostly by peasants.

• *Casula*: A poncho-style wrap.

Footwear

Like elements of dress, shoes worn by Romans were a badge of rank. The government decreed the style of footwear as well as the colour of shoes specific classes of Romans – including citizens, soldiers and members of the senate – could wear. At first shoes were extremely simple. The majority of citizens wore the *carbatina* – a sandal made of a piece of plain hide that covered the natural shape of the foot and was held in place by a thong. The shape evolved eventually into the more sophisticated *calceus*. In foul weather Romans wore buskins or closed boots. They were known as *gallicae*, so it is possible that the style might have been adopted from the Gauls.

The wardrobe of Roman women featured fewer shoe styles than that of the men. They wore sandals, *calcei* (ankle boots) and boots that extended beyond the calf. The wealthy wore shoes that featured lavish adornment such as gold trim, pearl embroidery, and other ornamentation.

above: This beautiful Roman mosaic (2nd–3rd century) depicts a young philosopher.

ANCIENT ROME

75

above: Gold, silver, lead, copper and other metals were hammered into shape to form intricate rings, earrings and necklaces. The gold jewellery shown here is from a Roman grave at Zara and dates back to the 1st century BC.

Jewellery

During most of the republican period, jewellery tended to be made by Greek craftsmen and so was in a predominately Greek style. Glass and semi-precious stones were used to add colour to gold jewellery. As the spoils of war became greater, more sophisticated stones were used, including pearls, diamonds, sapphires and emeralds from Egyptian mines. During the empire, fashion in jewellery became even more ornate. Gold, silver, lead, copper, iron and other metals were forged – or hammered – into shape. Women wore rings, bracelets, necklaces and earrings and the *fibula*, the almost universal brooch-fastener, became more and more elaborate. According to Pliny, Caligula's wife, Paulina, once appeared at a feast with her arms, neck and girdle dripping with pearls and emeralds. Hadrian's wife, Sabina, possessed a jewelled tiara which today would be worth in the region of US$1 million.

Make-up and grooming

Few Roman households except the very rich had a private bath. Visiting the *thermae* – the public baths – was a ritual enjoyed by both men and women and lasted several hours. But public baths served a purpose beyond hygiene: they were places where men met and relaxed with their friends after work. Women had their own separate baths or visited the public baths in the morning.

The heat for the baths was provided from outside by fires that were tended to by slaves. Hot air flowed under the floor and via hollow tiles in the walls and then out through chimneys in the roof. Inside the heat could be so intense, that those in the hot chambers wore wooden clogs to avoid scalding their feet. The hot chambers featured some rooms where dry heat provided a sauna and others that provided wet heat or steam for a Turkish style bath. Heat opened the pores but olive oil – not soap – was used to cleanse the skin. After being subjected to the heat for a while, the olive oil would be scraped off by a slave using a *strigil*, taking the sweat and dirt with it. To close the pores cold plunge pools were available. Slaves also splashed cold water onto their master with the help of a pouring dish – a *paterae*.

Traditionally, there were four stages to a bath: first, sweating in the *sudatorium*, where bathers could be massaged with scented oil, before moving on to an even hotter chamber, the *calidarium*, with its hot plunge pool. A rest break followed in the *tepidarium*, a warm room, to prepare the body for the cold water treatment – the *frigidarium*.

After bathing, they exercised by training with weights, running, playing with hoops or taking part in ball games, using a heavy ball similar to today's medicine ball. The less active played board games or gambled with dice.

The Romans also developed the use of hot springs such as that in Bath in southwestern England, where they built a medical bathing complex. People from around the empire visited spas, bathing in or drinking the waters, which they believed could cure a range of illnesses.

Cosmetics, perfume and skin care products were widely used in Rome. Like the Greeks, women applied a white foundation to their skin – a toxic formula of lead, honey and fat. To achieve a pinker tone, they added dye – made from ochre, saltpetre foam or wine dregs – to the mixture. Soot was applied to the lashes and brows for dramatic effect and they also used rouge and fake beauty spots.

Although natural materials were used as the ingredients of Roman skin care, we would consider the elements quite putrid today. Face masks could be made from plant extracts, but sheep fat and breadcrumbs soaked in milk was another formula favoured notably by Poppaea, Nero's wife. This mixture often produced a sickening odour if it was left to sit for more than a few hours. Butter and white lead were applied to spots; cow placenta was used to treat sores and boils.

Another horrendous-seeming formula – a paste made from calf genitals dissolved in sulphur and vinegar – was also employed. Anti-wrinkle treatments were mixed from ass's milk and could be applied as many as seven times in a single day. Poppaea is credited with

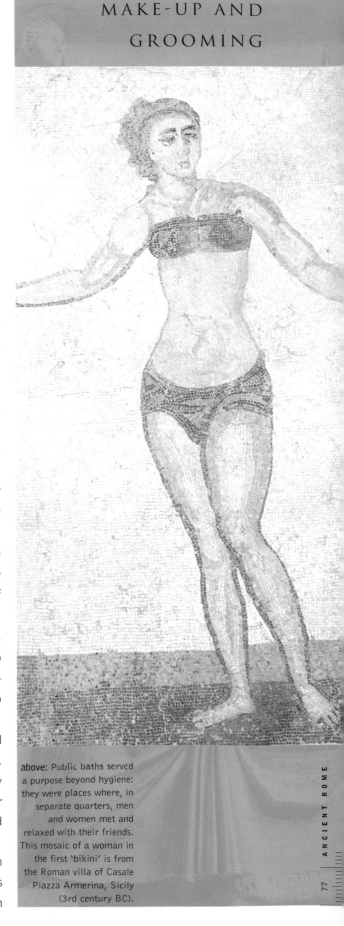

above: Public baths served a purpose beyond hygiene: they were places where, in separate quarters, men and women met and relaxed with their friends. This mosaic of a woman in the first 'bikini' is from the Roman villa of Casale Piazza Armerina, Sicily (3rd century BC).

ANCIENT ROME

77

MAKE-UP AND GROOMING

popularising this skin care formula. She is also known to have bathed in ass's milk and is reported to have travelled with a herd of the beasts so that she could allow herself this indulgence while on journeys.

Ovid prescribed a few complex formulas for healthier skin, one of which combined barley, vetch, ten eggs, powder from a stag's antlers, narcissus bulbs, gum and honey. Pimples, he claimed, would disappear with the help of a mixture of lupins, broad beans, white lead paint, red nitrate, orris root, kingfisher guano, myrrh, tree sap, honey, dried rose petals, ammonia salts and barley infusions.

Hair and head-dresses

To the Romans, hair had a meaning that transcended style; many rituals to do with hair were based on ingrained superstitions. For example, on 13 August, the birthday of the goddess Diana, women washed their hair. However, if a spirit interrupted this ritual, it was considered dangerous to then have the hair cut. In any case, washing the hair too often could, they believed, disturb the spirit watching over their heads. Soldiers thought that hair should not be cut on board ship, except during storms.

Most Roman citizens wore their hair short and combed forward. Some fashionable men curled their hair and even sprinkled gold dust or coloured powder through it. Ovid relates that baldness was regarded as a deformity, so bald men wore wigs or false hair pieces glued to the scalp. Some men even had their bald heads painted to give the impression of having hair and Julius Caesar is reputed to have worn his laurel wreath to conceal his baldness.

Slaves wore their hair long and did not shave, as signs of their plight. Freed slaves, on the other hand, shaved their heads and wore a wool cap – a *pileus* – as a mark of distinction.

Citizens only grew their hair and beard long during times of mourning until the reign of Hadrian, when long hair and trimmed beards became fashionable. It is believed that Hadrian wore a beard to conceal facial scars. At this time, slaves started to shave off their own beards. Sometimes depilatories were used to remove facial hair. Beards were also clipped and plucked. Rich men were shaved by slaves; some even kept slaves whose only job was to work as a hairdresser. But the average Roman citizen visited a barbershop, where the barber would use flat, straight razors.

At times, Roman women seem to have made up for their plain wardrobes with the flair of their hairstyles. Originally, they wore their hair quite simply, parted in the centre, gathered at the nape and worn in a bun or ponytail. During the Republic, hairstyles remained simple but there were variations as some married women began to wear their hair coiled on the crown. By the time of the empire, hairstyles had become rather more sophisticated. The hair was still parted down the centre but it could be waved, curled or worn in a loose roll that sat low on the back of the neck. A fringe of tight curls was another popular look.

During the Flavian era women wore piles and cascades of curls. Julia, the wife of Emperor Titus, wore her curls high on her head. A tiara held her style in place. At the back of the head fell a soft knot of braids. The accessories and tools necessary to achieve these

above: Cosmetics, perfume and skin care products were used by men and women in Ancient Rome. This 1st century case shows a selection of make-up tools.

above: Women had their
own separate baths or
visited the public baths in
the morning. This mosaic
of the so-called 'Domina of
Sidi Ghrib' at her toilet
depicts a grooming ritual.

complicated looks were discovered by archaeologists. They include bronze, ivory and bone combs, curling tongs that would have been heated in a brazier, hairpins, ribbons and nets.

Roman women also wore wigs – often made of goatskin – simply because they were an easier way to achieve and maintain a sophisticated hairstyle. Sometimes women would incorporate a veil – a *flammeum* – into their hair.

Dyeing the hair was a common practice. Originally only prostitutes did this, colouring their hair yellow. But with time, women of all classes began to do so. Women also dyed their hair blonde, making a bleach from various plants, elderberries, nutshells and vinegar, while some women wore blonde wigs. Black was another popular hair shade. Pliny passed on a nauseating concoction for black hair dye: leeches mixed with vinegar. Once this formula had fermented for two months women would apply it to their hair, sit in the sunlight and simultaneously rinse their mouth with oil to prevent their teeth turning black. Neither Roman men nor women wore hats. Only the emperor wore an imperial crown, a solid gold wreath of laurel leaves.

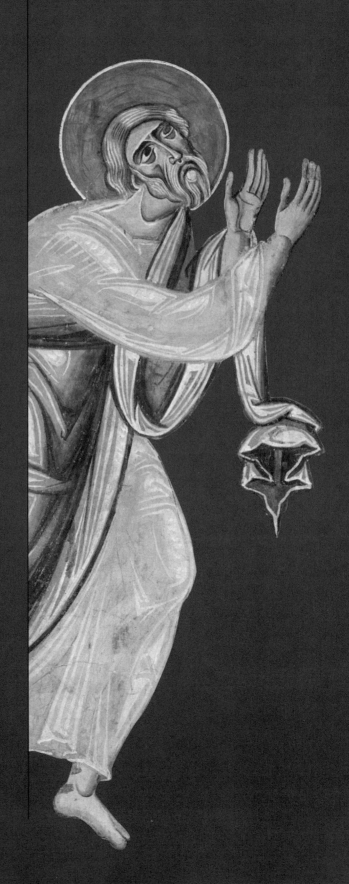

THE

BYZANTINE

LAVISH IMPERIALISM

PERIOD

Background

Between the 5th and 12th centuries the Byzantine Empire – with its capital, Constantinople – was the global seat of commerce, culture and fashion. Originally a colony of reed huts founded in about 660 BC by a community of immigrant Greeks from Megara, Byzantium was renamed Constantinople in the year AD 330 when the Roman Emperor Constantine the Great (r. 324–37) re-founded the city and named it after himself. It was officially known as Konstantinoupolis near Rome – 'the City of Constantine which is the new Rome' – and eventually developed into the most opulent city in the world. Located on the European side of the Bosporus, the waterway dividing Asia and Europe, the new capital was positioned to strengthen the Roman Empire. Constantine realized that this site – with its spectacular harbour – would in time become a vital link, by both land and sea, between western and eastern civilizations.

Theodosius (r. 379–95) was the last emperor to rule over both the eastern and western territories of the Roman Empire. During his reign he introduced one major change to Byzantine society: the Roman Catholic form of Christianity became the official or state religion. This completed the rise of Catholicism from an underground religion practised by common folk to a devotion of the elite, a process started by Constantine.

On his death, the empire was divided between Theodosius' two sons. Honorius received the western empire and Arcadius the eastern. When Rome fell to Germanic invaders in 476, Constantinople became the capital of what was left of the empire. The papacy eventually re-established itself in Rome.

After the fall of Rome, Constantinople's position as the crossroads into Europe from the east became increasingly important. The finest luxury goods – most notably silk – were brought into the city from Asia, initially by sea. Later, silk, perfume and spices came overland via Persia, although after the secret of silk production came to Constantinople in 552, the Persian silk trade diminished. In turn, Constantinople exported a host of Byzantine goods – works of art, silk vestments, papyrus, porcelain, glass ware, incense and perfumes – to churches, monasteries and the courts of western Europe. Byzantine furniture and ceremonial robes are still found today in Russian churches.

The city's thriving bazaars were the meeting point for Constantinople's multiracial population. There, a range of exotica was swiftly traded: Chinese silk, sandalwood from Indo-China, pepper from Malabar, Sindu musk as well as precious and semi-precious gemstones.

Justinian I (r. 527–65) and his wife, Theodora, are the most famous rulers of Byzantium, both for who they were and what they did. Their rise to power was phenomenal. He was a peasant, a Balkan farm boy, who rose via diligent service in the army. Theodora was the daughter of a bear feeder at Constantinople's amphitheatre. Later she became an 'actress' and dancer (possibly a euphemism for a prostitute). As we shall see later, their eventual meeting and marriage had a substantial impact on the direction of the empire.

Justinian's reign is regarded as the apex of Byzantine culture. He sponsored a compilation and recodification of Roman law, which formed the basis of legal theory in

left: This ceiling fresco from the palace of Constantine and Helena at Trier (4th century) shows a lady with her jewel box. Gemstones were widely traded in Byzantium.

above: A detail of a mosaic in the Hagia Sophia cathedral, Constantinople, showing Emperor Constantine in imperial regalia (11th century).

THE BYZANTINE PERIOD

above: Ivory leaf of diptych showing relief of Byzantine Empress Ariane (c AD 500).

Europe until the 19th century. He commissioned the architects Anthemius and Isidore to construct the spectacular church of Santa Sophia, which they did between 532 and 537, after the original had been destroyed by fire, and he encouraged the making of enamels, mosaics and objects of gold and silver as well as the manufacture of silk fabrics.

Justinian and Theodora – with their love of ceremony and taste for opulence – personify the ornate Byzantine style. Historians have painted a picture of their era which is rich, elegant and elitist. Their everyday clothes were flowing silk and brocade robes embroidered with oriental pearls and gemstones. They sat on golden thrones and had courtiers to attend to their every whim.

The great imperial palace in which they lived, which was built in the 5th century, was another of the city's focal points. Under Theodora's direction, the palace contained every luxury made by the finest Byzantine craftsmen as well as those imported from the east. The doors were made of solid silver and the walls were covered with mosaics. Her taste has been described as both decadent and imperious. Inside there were pure silver columns, silver tables featuring mother-of-pearl inlays, gold furniture, lush imperial purple curtains and marble floors. Guests invited to the palace trod on a fragrant carpet of rose petals, rosemary and myrtle. Outside, the imperial garden featured a marble footpath upon which ibises, peacocks and pheasants wandered. Meanwhile, fountains jetted scented water.

Justinian's cultural patronage and lifestyle at court may have been impressive but less successful was his military prowess. His re-conquests of North Africa and Italy were short-lived, and the end of his reign was fraught by war with the Persians, invasions by Bulgar and Slavic tribes and the outbreak and spread of bubonic plague. The Byzantine Empire never achieved the same heights again.

In the 8th and 9th centuries the emperors and church were split over the question of whether the use of icons amounted to idolatry. Tension was also caused by the presence of the popes in Rome, some of whom were inclined to interfere in matters that should have been referred to the emperor in the east. Another problem for the emperors was the rise of feudalism, which concentrated land and wealth in the hands of a few wealthy families.

But it was the Crusades, from the late 11th century on, that led eventually to the crumbling of the Byzantine Empire. Seeking protection from the onslaught of attack by the Seljuk Turks, in the late 11th century Emperor Alexius I Comnenus requested help from Venice and the pope. The Crusades were a series of plundering expeditions – fought with the help of dubious allies – against the Turks, with the aims of regaining the Holy Land for Christianity, gaining access to the trade routes in the east and reuniting the eastern and western empires under the western papacy. The empire was crushed during the fourth Crusade, with Constantinople falling to Venetians and Crusaders in 1204, but was regained by the Greeks in 1261. In 1453, Byzantium's last emperor, Constantine XI Drageses, died defending this once great capital against the Turkish army of Sultan Mehmet II. Although Byzantine territory still remained in the Peloponnese, no other emperor was crowned. Considering the fall of Byzantium, the 18th-century French philosopher Montesquieu later rightly declared that it was a tragic epilogue to the glory of Rome.

Women

Outside of the court, in all other echelons of Byzantine society, women were restricted and secluded. Their family came first and daily life was dominated by domestic issues.

The obvious exception was Theodora, who commanded respect and wielded a great deal of power. While she held court, her inner circle led a pleasurable existence. Much of what is known about Theodora has come from the *Secret History of Procopius*, the memoir of court historian Procopius who is said to have loathed Theodora and Justinian, so it cannot be taken as accurate.

Hecebolus, the governor of Pentapolis in North Africa, was the first to discover Theodora's charms; he liberated her from her humble circumstances and she became his mistress. For a time they lived together in North Africa but after a quarrel they parted and Theodora made her way back to Constantinople, where she worked as a wool spinner. Eventually Justinian spotted her.

At the time Justinian sought Theodora's hand in marriage, the law forbade a wedding between a patrician and a courtesan. But Theodora managed to persuade her lover to have the law repealed. In 525 Theodora married Justinian and two years later she was empress of the Byzantine Empire.

Theodora rode in a coach that was pulled by four white horses and she ruled from a solid gold and gemstone throne. Its purple cushions matched her slippers. She was a complex woman, and although her rule was harsh and unfeeling (she murdered her enemies – having them poisoned, drowned or tortured), she was shrewd. During the Nike riots of 532 when rebels attacked the palace, Theodora refused to leave the premises, telling her husband that she would rather die in the purple of an empress than run away. Historians believe that her courage saved her husband's crown. As empress, she was certainly politically influential, supporting her husband's vision of the empire, helping to plan his great building schemes and with his legal reforms. Her public role was far more prominent than was traditional for an emperor's wife: she took an active part in councils of state and received ambassadors and envoys.

Theodora could also be charitable: she donated gold to churches and in one act of goodwill liberated Constantinople's prostitutes – buying the women's freedom and then inviting them into the palace where she presented them with a change of clothes. Her intervention into the plight of prostitution made an impact. In 535, an edict made pimping a crime and brothel keepers were forbidden to set up operations in the empire's major cities.

Costume

Byzantine style merged Greek and Roman influences with Asiatic and oriental opulence. In time it proved to be highly influential on both medieval and Renaissance costume. Like the Greeks and the Romans, the Byzantines wore clothing that was simple in shape. The most important garment of the time was the T-shaped tunic. The toga, too, was worn by Byzantine consuls until the middle of the 6th century. But the incorporation of brightly coloured fabric, fringes, tassels and jewelled embroidery, all of eastern origin, lent a

above: The Empress Theodora with her attendants. The garments are made of patterned silk with embroidered coloured borders. The women are dressed in long tunics with cloak and *tablion*.

COSTUME

above: Christianity had a strong influence on Byzantine costume. In a fresco from Basilica Saint Angelo, Formis Capua, Italy, Noah is shown wearing a long-sleeved, ankle-length tunic over which is draped a cloak.

spectacular edge to Byzantine dress. The embroidered motifs could be religious – depicting the figures of the Magi, for example – or they could be floral and eastern-influenced geometric shapes.

Clothing was symbolic of stature and rank. Constantine's meeting with the Nicaean Council in 325 underlines this point. His attire at the crucial meeting – planned to quell religious unrest throughout the empire – was sweeping and grand. He wore gold-embroidered, jewel-encrusted purple robes, high-heeled red buskins and a spiked tiara. Throughout Byzantium from this moment on, clothing became a symbol of stature and rank.

Emperors – who occupied the dual roles of heading the state and the church – lived lavishly, although their lifestyle was highly regimented and governed by ceremony. Every detail of what an emperor would wear on a specific occasion was prescribed – his garments, crown and jewels. Only royalty could wear the royal purple, for example. This choice of colour was inspired by the Roman Emperor's purple *toga picta*. The manufacturing techniques for purple dye was a secret, jealously guarded by its imperial manufacturers.

Opulence and splendour aside, Christianity played a large part in Byzantine clothing styles. For both men's and women's clothes, a Christian-inspired modesty prevailed, so the body was concealed. Women covered their faces and their hands and men wore trousers beneath their robes. In these heavy layers and the long billowing tunics that were worn by both men and women, the physical shape of the two sexes became indistinguishable.

Religious scenes culled from Christian faith were embroidered on to garments as symbolic motifs. The mosaics of the church of San Vitale in Ravenna reveal that the emperor was dressed in what we would think of as an ecclesiastic fashion. At first there was no distinction between the dress of clerics and the rest of the population, but government officials instigated bans prohibiting clerics from following the latest fashions. From this point on a distinct style of vestments emerged and today's Catholic and Orthodox priests wear vestments which look almost unchanged.

The ceremonial attire of Byzantium's emperors contributed to the empire's reputation for sartorial excess. However, unlike in Rome, restrictions on dress were not set by the government; the choices of material and decoration were purely a matter of economics. Wealth and status were displayed by wearing ornate clothes: Justinian is known to have conducted the empire's day-to-day business wearing a richly embroidered tunic, a second tunic with a gold border, a huge, sweeping cloak, a pair of purple silk hose and a crown.

Women's clothing

Women's clothing shared the main characteristics of men's costume – they were both shape-concealing and had a number of layers. The first layer that was slipped on consisted of an ankle-length, tight-fitting chemise. Next came a shorter tunic gown, which revealed the chemise underneath. The tunic gown could be either fitted or girded just above or at the waist. Byzantine women wore the Roman *stola*, sometimes two at the same time. A *palla* (mantle) could be worn over the *stola*. Some women wore veils made from a long piece of

MAXIMIANVS

above: Emperor Justinian
and his entourage shown
in a mosaic from San
Vitale, Ravenna, first half
of the 6th century. The
emperor is wearing purple
robes embroidered with
gold. The Archbishop
Maximian (3rd from the
right) is dressed in *pallium*
and *stola*, his two deacons
(right) in *tunica laticlavia*.

material which could be allowed to fall behind the head, or folded forward and draped over the arm.

Theodora's long, high-necked tunics were entirely in keeping with the era's obsession with concealing the body's shape. Her rich silk dresses were enhanced with precious stones and lavish gold embroidery. She wore a gold collar around her neck, and just like her clothing, her jewellery was draped over her body. Ropes of pearls, emeralds and rubies graced her slender neck and for ceremonial purposes, she wore a heavy crown of gold featuring dripping pearls and emeralds that cascaded down to her chest.

Men's clothing

In early Byzantium upper-class men wore clothes with a Roman influence. The clothing was layered for concealment. First came the undergarment – a long sleeved, tight-fitting, ankle-

or knee-length white tunic. A *dalmatika* – a tunic with long, wide sleeves – could be worn over the tunic or instead of it. So named because of its Dalmatian origins, the *dalmatika* was made of red and gold material.

Until the 6th century AD the toga was worn by most Byzantine citizens, but later only consuls could wear it and it was replaced by a cloak. There were three styles of cloak, all of Roman origin. Justinian is depicted wearing the first – a simple rectangle of fabric, floor-length when wrapped around the shoulders – on the mosaic in the church at San Vitale, Ravenna. A semi-circular cape which fastened at the shoulder was also worn. A circular cape – very much like the Roman *paenula* – was sewn up the front with an opening for the head, sometimes with a detachable hood. Another alternative to the toga was the Greek *chlamys*, which was often worn with a square piece of embroidered fabric called a *tablion*.

By the 5th and 6th centuries middle-class men wore the *tunica*. This featured a decorative neckline and was longer than the tunic worn by courtiers. Priests and noblemen also wore a *pallium*. Although this shares the same name as the Roman cloak, it was completely different, being a band of exquisitely decorated cloth, approximately 20cm (8in) wide, that was wrapped around the neck.

Under their tunics men also wore *hosa* (woollen or fabric hose) or *braco* (breeches). From the 6th century onwards men wore drawers or trousers. Labourers wore breeches that they tucked into their knee-length boots, covered by a thigh-grazing tunic and an ankle-length cloak, both made of simple, plain wool.

Textiles

Silk, taffeta, damask, velvet, tapestry, brocade, linen, wool, cotton – Byzantines worked with an array of fabrics to produce imperial clothes. The use of rich materials is what sets their costume apart from other civilizations.

The introduction of domestically produced silk was one of their major contributions to the history of fashion. At first, silk was imported into Constantinople along the enormously long trade route that stretched all the way from the Middle East to China. The manufacture of silk remained a mystery for so long because, to many, it was inconceivable that this most luxurious fabric was in fact produced by worms. But in 552 the mystery was finally solved, and all doubters convinced, when two Persian monks smuggled back a hollow bamboo staff in which were hidden hundreds of silkworm (*Bombyx mori*) eggs and the mulberry seeds needed to grow the leaves on which the worms feed. Once silk manufacture became established in the empire, the eastern monopoly on the silk trade ceased. The Byzantines manufactured a type of silk which has become known as samite. This had a texture which was thick and strong, similar to what we know today as brocade. Its heavy feel suited the dramatic cut and imposing mood of Byzantine imperial style.

Silk could also be embroidered with gold thread and it was sometimes meshed through sheets of gold fabric. Mandarin silk robes, featuring embroidered dragons, were occasionally imported into the empire. Because silk was the fabric which signified rank, it was always in demand.

left: The Byzantine period's major contribution to fashion was the introduction of domestically produced silk. This piece of 8th-century Byzantine silk shows a horseman with a chariot.

above: This detail of the mosaic in Hagia Sophia cathedral, Istanbul (11th century AD) shows the opulence of Byzantine clothing, with its use of rich materials and exquisite decoration.

Footwear

Men's and women's shoes revealed a strong eastern influence in the colours and materials used. They could be of embroidered silk, and decorated with gold and gem stones, in shades varying from black, grey and brown to vibrant hues of green, blue, red, plum, violet. Calf-length boots were worn as were jewelled slippers. Theodora sometimes even wore gold shoes. Labourers wore knee-length boots.

Jewellery and ornaments

Early Byzantine jewellery was influenced by Greek and Roman styles, but oriental and Middle Eastern influences came to prevail. Heavy jewelled collars were worn by both men and women of high rank. Earrings, rings and brooches were made of gold, pearls and precious stones – rubies, emeralds, sapphires, diamonds. A pair of 6th-century Byzantine boat earrings – an Egyptian-inspired style consisting of a hoop with a thick, upward-curving lower rim shaped like a boat – are in London's Victoria and Albert Museum. The cuff bracelet – an inflexible armlet that tapers towards one end – appears to be of 9th-century Byzantine origin. An original 9th-century Byzantine gold and enamel cuff bracelet can be found in the Archaeological Museum in Thessaloniki, Greece.

The art of enamelling spread westward to Byzantium from Persia and its production flourished between the 9th and 11th centuries. From here, Byzantine enamelling techniques spread into Europe. Theophano, a Byzantine princess, introduced enamelling to Germany when she married Otto II in the mid-10th century. A particularly popular style was cloisonné enamelling. Invented by Greek goldsmiths, the cloisonné style featured a thin coating of white or pale blue enamel inlaid between slightly raised gold wire. They also enamelled images such as flowers and other delicate patterns. The Byzantines invented techniques for producing coloured glass which they used to make small mirrors. These were regarded more as ornaments than functional tools.

Make-up and grooming

Like the Romans, the Byzantines had public baths. During the century after Constantinople was founded the city had 53 private baths, eight of which were open for public use. The Byzantines, it seems, believed that cleanliness played a part in a person's health and well-being, as Constantinople's hospitals prescribed twice-weekly baths for their patients. At Easter, the sick were given an extra bar of soap.

Cosmetics were not a huge concern for the Byzantines, but they are well known for their contribution to the art of perfumery. Because of its pivotal position for sea and land trade, the craft thrived throughout the eastern empire. Ingredients from China, India and Persia made their way to Constantinople, where perfumers occupied a prominent place in society as craftsmen, enjoying equal status with other vital trades such as candle- and soap-making, silk-working and tanning.

Among Constantinople's great bazaars, spicers and perfumiers had their own special place – a market between the emperor's palace and the church, Santa Sophia. This position

left: Ordinary Byzantines rarely wore hats, whereas in court circles elaborate crowns and head-dresses were worn. This intricate gold crown belonged to Emperor Constantine IX Monomodus (c 1042–1050).

above: An arm band (9th–10th century) made from two hinged pieces of gold set with cloisonné enamelling, an art which flourished in Byzantium.

HATS AND
HEAD-DRESSES

reflected Indian tradition, where the perfume market was set up in front of the mosque. Perfumes were important to both men and women: Constantine VII (r. 945–59) took perfume with him on campaign, and Empress Zoe (978–1050) has been singled out as a scent lover. In her *gynaeceum* could be found scent burners and servants who bottled perfume for her own personal use.

Just like clothing, Byzantine hairstyles for both men and women shared both Roman and oriental influences. Women wore their hair long and adopted elaborate hairstyles – perhaps wearing an oriental-style turban to hold their locks in place, or weaving a string of pearls into it.

Men wore their hair in a short, cropped bob with a fringe on the forehead – a similar style to that worn by men during the empire in Rome. Another popular style was for the hair to be cut medium short and brushed away from the crown. Before the 9th century men were clean-shaven, but later they wore short, trimmed beards and moustaches. To mark their religious dedication, church dignitaries shaved the crown of their head – a mark still known as a tonsure.

Hats and head-dresses

With the exception of a farmer's straw *petasos* and the *zucchetto* – a Greek skull cap – hats were not commonly worn by ordinary Byzantines, and until the 12th century priests and bishops conducted religious functions bareheaded. But head-dress did become an intricate part of court and church dress. In court circles men and women wore crowns and head-dresses designed by skilled jewellers. The pearl markets of the east provided a rich stock of raw materials and Byzantine pearl-encrusted head-dresses are said to have provided the inspiration for the pearl-sewn costumes which appeared later in the Middle Ages. Church dignitaries wore the *infula* – a knotted fillet of white wool which, as time progressed, became more elaborate, ornamented with jewels and gold embroidery. Although pomp and ceremony dictated the style of hat worn by different members of the church, necessity played a part, too. Because of the dank and cold atmosphere inside churches, bishops and cardinals wore the *zucchetto* in distinct colours that signified their rank. Monks, meanwhile, wore robes with a cowl that could be pulled over the head.

above: Emperor Constantine the Great renamed Byzantium after himself in AD 330.

right: This group of Byzantine women, shown on an early 14th-century mosaic, are wearing costume typical of the period. Their garments are made of heavy, richly decorated materials, covered in pearls and precious stones, and decorated with golden borders.

meum in
sti saccum
ne leticia.

THE

MEDIEVAL EUROPE

MIDDLE AGES

dist listoire que longuement parlere
enssamble von le Roy de gascoigne man

Background

The Germanic tribes who swept through and destroyed the western Roman empire from the 4th century – including Visigoths, Vandals, Ostrogoths, Huns, Angles, Saxons, Jutes and Franks – wiped out, among other things, the shipping and highway networks that had enabled centralized government and allowed communication between places at opposite ends of the empire. One result of this was that the artistic and cultural life of Rome was obliterated and replaced with the customs of these warring groups. This period is today known as the early Middle Ages or, somewhat inaccurately, the Dark Ages. Throughout this time, the one unifying factor in western Europe was the church, the only organization that could form the basis of social unity.

There was a brief period of respite during the reign of Charlemagne (742–814), king of the Germanic peoples known as the Franks. His reign, as first king of the Carolingian Dynasty (771–987), and first emperor of the revived western Roman Empire (800–14), was a time when the arts, letters and fashion flourished. Historians see this revival of learning as the first seeds of the Renaissance. Because Charlemagne and his son, Louis, ruled over most of western Europe, it was once again possible for people to travel more easily. Germans, for example, went to Italy and France to study. In the beginning the empire and the church co-operated, but increasingly there were struggles as the church tried to interfere in the emperor's secular concerns.

At this time a new social structure began to emerge in parts of Europe – the feudal system. Nobles swore allegiance to the king and undertook military service and provided soldiers for him in return for land. In turn, vassals would swear allegiance to a noble in return for protection and housing. The system extended down through various grades of peasants (ranging from freemen to serfs) who worked their overlord's land and fought for him in return for protection and food. The clergy were answerable to their own hierarchy.

Life, for most people, was harsh during the Middle Ages; living conditions – even for the nobility – were uncomfortable. In homes, heating was often inadequate. By the 11th century large homes featured huge fireplaces, whereas peasants' cottages and even manor houses had central open hearths right through the Middle Ages. These did not heat the home efficiently, and as there was no chimney, the smoke was left to find its own way out through gaps in the walls and roof.

A more modern Europe was developing. In France, England and Spain national monarchies were formed. From the middle of the 11th century, another economic and cultural revival took place. Towns flourished as prosperous communities. Travel became more frequent as a result of transportation becoming increasingly faster and safer. Better food became available and so people became generally healthier and the population of western Europe increased. The large number of Romanesque and Gothic churches, abbeys, monasteries and cathedrals that were being built around this time was an indication of the increasing wealth of the church, which is itself a reflection of a general increase in prosperity throughout society. Universities were also being constructed as centres of learning in France and Italy.

left: Fashionable costume in the Middle Ages displayed a distinct Byzantine influence such as the garments seen here in Loyset Liedet's *The Marriage of Renaud of Mantauban and Clarisse* (Flanders 1460–78).

above: This early 15th-century illustration shows peasants – barefoot and simply clad – haymaking.

The capture and, more particularly, the plunder of Constantinople in 1204 had a profound effect on the medieval world, shifting the global balance of power away from the eastern Mediterranean towards western Europe. It also prompted the development of a new, flourishing civilization in the west.

The 13th century witnessed the progression of social organization away from feudalism and the emergence of a middle class, or bourgeoisie. Guilds of artisans and labourers were set up. These functioned by regulating prices and salaries and, with time, ensured that all craftspeople were specially trained. In most places, a craftsman could only practise his trade if he was a member of the relevant guild. Many were connected with the textile industry. In Italy and the Low Countries, in particular, the guilds became rich and powerful, taking an active role in the running of the town. They were also charitable institutions, helping the widows and children of members, and contributing large amounts of money to the church.

But life was still hard for the majority of people. Throughout the Middle Ages man battled against nature, hunger and sickness, and in two years the Black Death (1348–50), brought to Europe from the east by fleas on infected black rats, succeeded in wiping out one-third of Western Europe's population.

England and France had spent much of the medieval period at war. As a result of the Hundred Years War (1337–1453) the English empire – which had claimed half of France at the beginning of the century – shrank so that it included little more than England, Wales and Gascony, and France became hugely powerful. Its government was centralized, its monarchy was strong enough to be regarded as the most autonomous in Europe and its reputation as the world's capital of fashion had begun. Italy, on the other hand, was still divided into independent city states, which grew stronger as they grew richer. During the 15th century the Medici family built Florence into a world-class centre for the arts and learning, spurring on the new age and spirit of optimism.

Technical introductions that the Middle Ages can claim include the metal-rimmed wheel and horse shoes (which further eased transportation), gunpowder and cannons (which led to a dramatic change in the way wars were fought and to the end of the feudal system) and – in the mid-15th century – printing, which historians classify as the most important milestone in the history of civilization.

Women

Were the Middle Ages a time of oppression or the first true period of women's liberation? There are conflicting opinions, but there is little doubt that women of the time were oppressed: St Thomas Aquinas' opinion that women were created only for procreation sums up the medieval man's attitude towards women.

While men dominated household and government, women were subjected to hard domestic and agricultural work. The prevailing notion perpetuated by Aquinas and other influential thinkers of the day was that a woman did not possess a soul. Women were chattels and could not improve their own situation as they belonged to either their father

above: This 13th-century map shows the world as a circle, with Jerusalem in the centre.

right: The fight against the Black Death affected people of all social status during the Middle Ages. This illustration, *The Triumph of Death*, illustrated a volume of poetry by Petrarch (1304–76).

WOMEN

above: Despite their lack of freedom, some medieval women made great strides. Joan of Arc, Maid of Orleans (1412–31), shown here wearing a suit of armour, is still remembered for her extreme bravery defending her country. Illustration on parchment c 1420.

right: An elaborately dressed courting couple lead the dance in this illustration depicting court life in Bruges (c 1500).

or their husband, but by the 10th century women in most countries had achieved the right to refuse an arranged marriage. Women did not even have rights over their own children. Just as husbands could sell their children, in Norway, they could sell their wives to relieve their debts. Prostitutes were the worst off. They had no control over their wages. They were segregated from other women and they were prescribed a dress code which forbade them to wear certain clothing and jewellery. In London, for example, prostitutes were not allowed to wear striped hoods and aprons.

Conversely, in courtly circles women were appreciated for their beauty. The Age of Chivalry is known for improving men's attitudes towards women. A strict code of honour prevailed during the time and most prominent in a knight's ideals was to honour and cherish women. But some historians claim that the principles of chivalry were all show. Although chivalrous games elevated women to the role of lady and dame, women still knew their place. Among the elite, men were far better educated than women.

Among the lower classes, women did have occupations – repairing armour, baking, brewing and concocting herbal remedies. Some even progressed to the position of innkeeper, ironmonger, butcher or tailor. Poor women helped their husbands with farming.

Despite their lack of freedom some medieval women made great strides – seeking roles outside the norm to attain personal satisfaction. Eleanor of Aquitaine, wife of Louis VII of France and then of Henry II of England, was a powerful, political force. Catherine of Alexandria was highly regarded for her religious devotion, Joan of Arc for her courage and Hildegard of Bingen for her intellect. Hildegard was a German abbess, composer, playwright and theologian. In 1141, she experienced a vision, during which a voice told her to say and write what she saw and heard. The experience prompted her to write 15 books in which she recounted her visions and thoughts on philosophy, science and medicine.

Some women had access to study. As well as convents, women joined communities called beguines, where they could live an austere contemplative life without taking religious vows. In one particular incident, a woman dressed up as a man for years in order to enter a university and gain a degree. Women book owners are known to have carried books with them in order to increase the spread of knowledge.

Because the prevailing medieval notion was that a woman's health was a woman's business, they became midwives and also seem to have treated men. One study has found evidence that in the Kingdom of Naples between 1273 and 1410 there were some 24 female surgeons who cared for both men and women. There may have been more similar stories, but because information about the lives of women in the medieval period is often limited to such resources as wills, property transfers and court records, details relating to their progress are sparse.

Men

The highest order a nobleman could rise to in Britain was knighthood, which took years of long, hard preparation. At the age of ten, a youth would go to live at the court of his feudal lord or prince and then spent four years as a page, performing household tasks such as

above: The art of cloth dyeing in the 15th century.

lighting the fires, hanging tapestries and cleaning floors, as well as completing the necessary physical training and education involved. This included riding, swimming, archery, fencing and hunting as well as poetry and chess. After this time, the young man would become a squire, at which point he was able to follow his lord into battle. By the age of 21, when all of these duties had been fulfilled, he could be knighted. The knighthood initiation ritual – usually held at the lord's castle – demonstrates the medieval taste for pomp and ceremony. To show his godly devotion the knight was tonsured. He was also bathed, a ritual symbolizing purity, and then dressed in three layers of coloured robes: white (to symbolize grace), red (the colour of blood), and black (to indicate the acceptance of death), and then given his armour and weapons. The ceremonious aspect to knighthood paints a rather romanticized image of the brave medieval man, but this historical image is probably misleading, and medieval knights were probably simple, coarse men, trained to fight in bloody battles.

Costume

Much of the fashionable clothing worn during the early Middle Ages displayed a distinct Byzantine influence derived from costumes imported from the east, but fashions in the west could lag as much as 25 to 30 years behind. By the late Middle Ages, Western Europe had evolved its own unique clothing styles. A major introduction from the east during the Crusades was the use of buttons to fasten clothing.

Another important sartorial development which dates back to the Middle Ages was the appearance of the professional tailor. Clothing, formerly a woman's job, became increasingly dominated by men. By 1300, 700 tailors were operating in Paris.

Fashion historians trace the emergence of distinct national styles to the Middle Ages, and for the first time individual preferences for a range of sartorial elements including colour, textiles and accessories can be seen. Socially prominent people began to wear clothes featuring patterned crests – motifs or personal emblems which served to identify a family. The origins of heraldry could be traced back to the 12th century when soldiers wore a crest on their helmet or shield to identify themselves in battle. In the 13th century a soldier's shield featured his family's coat of arms on the right while that of his wife's appeared to the left.

Fashion, however, was not really a consideration for most people. Dress served the functional purpose of protection against the often harsh climate. Even though Charlemagne's ceremonial attire was sumptuous, including jewel-encrusted shoes, a cape fastened with a gold clasp and a diadem, he would usually wear simple clothes, even wearing sheepskin and rabbit rather than richer furs such as ermine or mink.

Until the 14th century, men and women of all classes shared similar attire. In summer and winter, they wore long, flowing clothes. The body was completely covered at all times, and people probably wore more layers in winter for warmth. Just as in Byzantium, the choice of fabric distinguished clothing worn by those of different social rank. Both sexes wore a long cloak as an outer garment.

above: In this illustration
(c 1500), showing Dame
Nature giving her orders
to Genius, the woman
wears a rich cloak,
typical of the period and
the man is wearing a belt
with a pouch affixed to it.

Throughout the early Middle Ages both men and women wore an undertunic and a short overtunic belted at the waist, which is believed to be the predecessor of the modern shirt or blouse. Another garment that was worn by both sexes was a fur overtunic. In the 15th century, it was somewhat longer, was belted high under the chest and fell loose to the ground.

The rich wore cloaks which were lined with fur, silk or gold cloth. Peasants, serfs and labourers wore shorter gowns for ease of movement while they worked, and men sometimes wore practical breeches. Church officials wore ecclesiastic robes that have changed very little since that time. Guildsmen would often wear costumes that indicated their craft.

Women's clothing

Throughout the Middle Ages, women borrowed men's clothing styles, gradually adapting their shapes to suit the female form.

WOMEN'S CLOTHING

Eleanor of Aquitaine is said to have brought the flowing gown into fashion. Rich women wore elaborate clothing – flared, floor-dusting skirts made of heavy fabric like brocade. The waist climbed high to just under the chest, at which point a decorative belt was added to emphasize this particular area of the body region. Tops were delicate and most featured a high neckline. Sleeves could be simple and fitted or elaborate; they could be lined with fur or cut so wide and long that they reached the floor. By the 14th century sleeves featured serrated edges and some fashion historians claim that this effect inspired the later invention of lace.

The arrival of the Black Death in 1348 had a profound effect on fashion in the west, as a result of the political and social crises it provoked. People began to dress flamboyantly, just as they have done ever since in times of crisis (such as the relationship between the oil crisis and the disco era in the 1970s). Hemlines rose and clothes fitted the body closely and became more flattering to the figure. Costume became increasingly elaborate, for instance, sleeves and hemlines featured a jagged edge, a technique known as slittering.

Towards the end of the Middle Ages, more modest clothing styles returned for women, and their clothing became increasingly functional – if not somewhat severe. Skirts ceased to drop to the floor and no longer trailed on the ground, necklines rose and sleeves stopped at the elbow.

Men's clothing

Class and occupation determined the clothes worn by medieval men. During the 13th and 14th centuries the male wardrobe featured a few staples: a long-sleeved tunic with a hem falling just to the knee, worn under a wide-sleeved, loose gown, which could be belted. Over this, an ankle-length, sleeveless *surcote* hung loose around the body. This garment had open sides and a slit at the front. The *cyclas* was another form of surcoat, which was again worn over the tunic.

Several other outer garments were known. The *ganache*, was a loosely tailored gown, with side seams split from shoulder to hip. The *berigault* was the name for a style of cloak-gown. Long cloaks made from a semi-circular piece of fabric were also popular.

The period also saw a shift in the centre of fashion after the fall of Constantinople. The Flemish were expert weavers and certainly the best woollen fabric – sought after by the nobility of western Europe during the 14th and 15th centuries – was produced in Flanders and so it is likely that the Flemish had an influence on what was being worn.

In France, Paris was beginning to establish itself as a capital of men's fashion. An inventory of the best robes belonging to the French King Charles V (r. 1364–80) includes seven six-piece suits furred with ermine; seven three-piece suits trimmed with miniver and 16 parts of suits also furred with miniver. The French taste for luxury was so influential that it spread throughout Europe.

Generally, men wore shorter gowns and a doublet with hose as well as a *cotehardie* – an outer garment which featured laces and a low neckline, which was flared out from the hips or waist. By the 15th century the *cotehardie* was so short that it merely reached the length

above: These women wear high-waisted gowns with decorative belts. The woman on the left is wearing a conical head-dress or *hennin* from which trails a veil.

right: The appearance of extravagant costume, such as that shown here, was a direct reaction to the Black Death crisis. The burial of the dead from the plague is shown on the left.

Florence

uc du trainflateur du
s Cent nouuelles de

MEN'S CLOTHING

above: Eleanor of Aquitaine, Queen of England, Queen of Henry II (1122–1204) was a powerful political source. She favoured dresses made of samite, a stiff silk made popular in Byzantium. This illustration of her is by E. Hargrave from a contemporary portrait.

right: 14th-century fresco showing medieval costumes.

of a frock coat. The *houppelande* was another fashionable garment, worn by both men and women, which dates from about 1400. This long, loose tunic was belted and featured fitted shoulders, a high collar and ample, loose sleeves. Women also wore a long *cotehardie* as well as long, flowing gowns. Shape also emerged as a distinct element of dress. Clothing had become even more of a mark of social rank.

Textiles

Wool was the most important fabric of the Middle Ages. By the 15th century in England looms were developed specifically for weaving wool. There were several variations of woollen fabric, including camelot, a fine, woven wool, which was produced in France. Jersey was made in Italy, and linen was also manufactured and worn in several weights from heavy to sheer. Silk weaving also became popular in Europe and as a result, the price of silk was reduced greatly. Heavy matte silk was used for expensive mantles and their linings were made from velvet and satin.

The nobility wore clothes made of fine, lightweight wool, linen from Reims and imported silk. Eleanor of Aquitaine favoured dresses made of samite – the stiff silk produced originally in the Byzantine Empire. Her dresses often featured gold embroidery and hand-sewn pearls, which were used to conceal the hems. Meanwhile, peasants wore clothes made of coarse fibres – rough linen, duffel and lindsey wool. All classes wore fur, although social rank did determine which fur an individual wore. Ermine and sable were worn by the rich, while peasants wore the skins of sheep, badgers and foxes. People wore fur no matter what the season, with the actual fur next to the body, to insulate, while the pelt was shown.

Fur was popular because it was functional. Outer garments were lined with fur because it was lightweight, waterproof and it breathed. Fur also suited the demands for modesty that prevailed throughout the Middle Ages as it cloaked the body, making the curves and shapes of a man or a woman's body indistinguishable. So fur was fashioned into long robes, such as the fur-lined *pelisson*, which were worn by both men and women.

Fabric fairs became important meeting points. There were several held in France: at Champagne, Bar-sur-Aube, Provins and Troyes. These attracted an international group of fabric traders from Scotland and Russia, Egypt and Constantinople. Fabric and made-to-order clothes were sold at these fairs and the international clientèle which they attracted ensured that similar trends spread across Europe and beyond.

Rich fabrics were used in the Middle Ages both for clothes and for domestic purposes. Although sumptuary laws were passed to regulate the use of extravagant fabric, as in the time of Henry III in England, they went largely unheeded. English and French households used fine linens and wools for tablecloths, sheets, clothing and hangings. Thomas, Duke of Gloucester (1354–97), one of Edward III's sons, had 16 sets of silk and embroidered gold bedding in his household. Rich fabrics – like silk velvet – were draped over thrones. In European castles windows were draped with silk curtains, three of which can be found in the Metropolitan Museum of Art, the Cooper Hewitt Museum in New York, and the Cleveland Museum of Art.

TEXTILES

above: The Middle Ages introduced a shoe with a pointed toe (those seen here are dated c 1350), a style, that, though modified, remains with us today.

Commoners showed an appreciation of fabric. For village celebrations and processions, the streets were decorated with textiles. Fabrics were used for banners and to hail royalty and the nobility, and townsfolk draped their homes with large decorative swatches.

Tapestry can be traced to the Middle Ages. As well as being used for hangings, tapestry was incorporated into costume in decorative elements such as borders. However, fashion historians believe that tapestry is an unreliable source of information about clothing as weavers often depicted their subjects in costumes that were more fantastic than accurate.

Medieval fabric was used to distinguish social classes. Costume worn by the clergy and the elite were made with rich borders and trims. Noble families such as the Viscontis of Italy had their own signature bands and borders, of which stripes of silk were a popular type. These were often teamed with diamond and chain patterns: a crown cap with a stripe and a geometric band was found in the tomb of Henry IV.

Colours were personal – certain families wore specific colours to battle, so colourful dress became associated with soldiers and was thus considered unsuitable for civilian dress. When the Emperor Frederick III visited Rome in 1468 he appeared dressed dramatically in black velvet. From this point on soldiers and women could wear colourful dress.

Textiles and clothes were stored carefully in chests. Made of oak, chests were the most functional and known piece of domestic furniture, with others also used to store all sorts of domestic tools. They were also used as luggage – for rich families on the move between their country estates.

Jewellery

Early medieval jewellery has been labelled clumsy by comparison to Byzantine styles, although some examples of Irish jewellery are exquisite. Later, workmanship became more skilled. Gold was the material worked with most frequently – used for bracelets, necklaces and rings.

Footwear

A shoe with a pointed toe, the *poulaine*, was introduced in the medieval period and provided a style which is still with us today. Initially, footwear featuring pointed toes was considered a status symbol. Consequently shoe toes grew to be unnaturally long, sometimes up to 45cm (18in), and eventually an English law set in 1363 assigned toe lengths to specific classes: commoners could wear shoes with 15-cm (6-inch) toes; the toe of a gentlemen's shoe could extend a further 37.5cm (15in) and nobility were permitted to wear shoes with extremely long toes – stretching up to 60cm (2ft). But the church considered the extremely long, pointed toe to be perverse and so the pointed toes eventually spread wider – producing what became known as a 'duck's bill'.

Make-up and grooming

Bathing was a Roman tradition that survived into the Middle Ages. Some households featured a sunken bath made from wood while others used a bowl of copper, brass or tin.

Sophisticated water supply systems were known in the Middle Ages. At Christchurch Monastery at Canterbury, for example, plumbing was set up after 1153. And it was probably this water system that saved all but four of the monastery's inhabitants from falling victim to the Black Death in 1349.

Hygiene was upheld more strongly in the monastery than in the domestic environment, where fingers were used as forks and a piece of bread served as a plate. It then comes as no surprise that the custom of washing the hands developed at this time. Books on etiquette dating from the Middle Ages instructed readers to wash their hands and face and brush their teeth every morning. But not much was written about bathing the body. King John, it is believed, bathed once every three weeks while his subjects washed less frequently.

In Paris, just as in Ancient Rome, there were public baths which were open 24 hours a day but closed on Sundays and holidays. In England, communal tubs – sometimes built out of doors – were known and bath-time was often a social occasion. Lovers bathed together and medieval doctors prescribed against drinking too much while in the tub.

The stigma of nudity dissolved somewhat during the course of the Middle Ages. Tubs and sleeping chambers were shared and until the 16th century night clothes were not worn. Despite the unhygienic conditions which dominated the domestic environment, health and well-being were prominent considerations among the upper classes. Medical prescriptions – eccentric though they were – existed for ailments such as fever (a green frog hung around the neck) and migraines (a hangman's rope tied around the head). For epilepsy the patient was instructed to wear a medal engraved with the names of the Three Wise Men: Gaspar, Melchior and Balthazar.

Women employed equally strange concoctions in their quest for beauty. To achieve a pale complexion some women applied leeches to their skin. Quicklime was applied to areas of the body to remove unwanted hair. To lighten the hair a mixture of henna, gorse flowers, saffron and calf's kidneys was applied to the scalp. To scent the hair, it was rinsed with dried roses, spices – nutmeg, caraway and cardamom – and vinegar. Honey was applied to the lips as a gloss to make them look full, and people rinsed their mouths with warm wine for healthy gums.

Slimming remedies were commonly used by women. Some believed that a svelte figure could be achieved by bathing regularly in sea water and using a deodorant of bayleaves, calamint, absinthe and hyssop. Women with a more substantial frame adhered to much the same slimming methods as today. To encourage circulation, women applied friction to their body by using a body brush and then they retreated to a sweat chamber, following this with a cool bath.

Make-up customs varied from country to country and shades of make-up were specific to social rank. Some women used water-soluble paint to enhance their skin tone. In Spain during the 6th century, for example, prostitutes used pink cheek paint. Three centuries later, poor German women also applied pink paint to their face. In Britain, women used white paint, whereas Italian women attempted to simulate a natural look by applying flesh-pink paint in a shade slightly darker than their natural skin tone. Rouge was the favourite

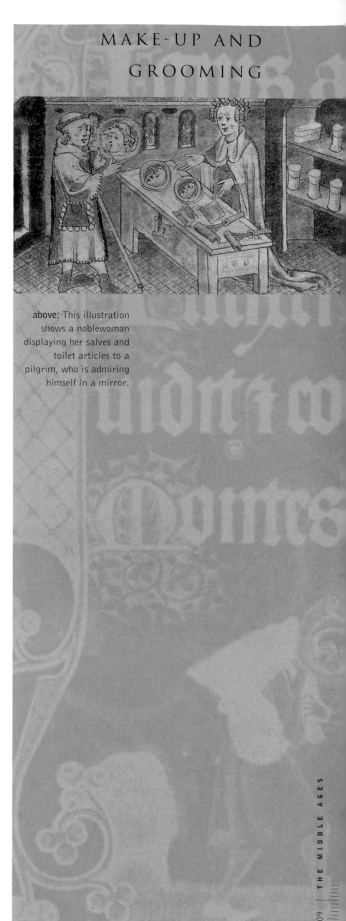

MAKE-UP AND GROOMING

above: This illustration shows a noblewoman displaying her salves and toilet articles to a pilgrim, who is admiring himself in a mirror.

cosmetic of prostitutes, but it was also used by Anglo-Saxon women, and in the 6th century Spanish women applied a cream rouge to their lips. In Germany and England rouge in orange shades was popular. During the 13th century in Tuscany, rich women began to use a bright pink blush.

Full lips were also a beauty ideal in the Middle Ages, as Chaucer observed in *The Court of Love*: 'With pregnant lippes thin, not fat but lean.' Between the 6th and 15th centuries the use of green, blue and grey-brown eye shadows was known. Black liquid eyeliner was also applied to the upper lid with the help of a stick.

The biggest change in women's grooming habits in the Middle Ages involved eyebrows. In 13th-century England, women altered their brows so that they became pale and narrow. Sometimes they shaved them to resemble the effigies of classical sculpture. In France, women tinted their brows brown and plucked them so they appeared delicate. This caught on and throughout the 14th and 15th centuries women plucked their brows into thin lines.

Perfumes were not commonly used in the Middle Ages. By the 14th century, saffron was seen as an acceptable light scent, but nothing as exotic as the fragrances of Byzantium was worn. The Crusades brought some oriental perfumes into the west, but they were most popular in Italy and France.

Both men and women used mirrors. These were made of silver or glass suspended from their girdles and sometimes men wore them in their hats. Mirror cases were often intricately crafted and carved from ivory.

Sculpture, mosaics, stained glass, carvings of stone, ivory and wood all provide clues to what we know today about medieval hairstyles, which were mostly natural. Some men wore their hair shoulder length while women wore theirs in one of two styles: loose and flowing or in plaits. There were, however, variations over time. The church, as so often, had an opinion. One early medieval English bishop was renowned for carrying a knife with him. If he spotted a man with long hair, he would make him stoop to have it cut and then throw the locks in his face. The church's attitude toward beards was permissive: Roman Catholic priests of the 9th century wore long beards, as did Charlemagne from time to time.

Clergy in Britain were divided on the subject of the tonsure: some wore a circle while others shaved one in a semicircle, although for monks this may have been related to the order they belonged to. Italian, Spanish and German priests all wore a circular tonsure – known as the tonsure of St Peter.

Initially men wore their hair in a short bowl cut. By the 13th century men wore their hair much longer and often curled it using irons, and having either a fringe or a middle parting. By the 14th century long hair was common for men. The fashion for long hair and beards started with the upper classes and was soon copied by men of all social ranks. Edward II wore his hair long and curled his beard and moustache.

A centre parting was common for women's long hairstyles in the Middle Ages. But long hair was hard to manage, so women began to divide it into a number of sections, lacing it through ribbons. From this emerged the style most commonly associated with medieval women – braids or plaits.

left: This portrait by Jan van Eyck of Arnolfini and his wife shows the couple wearing cloaks made of fur – a very popular fabric during this period. The demands for modesty throughout the Middle Ages is shown in the way the silhouettes are made indistinguishable by the cut of the clothes. Arnolfini's wife is shown with the medieval predilection for a slightly protuberant belly.

above: An elegantly clad 15th-century couple. The man sports a short bowl haircut and the woman a fashionably high-waisted gown and a heart-shaped head-dress.

Braiding her hair into plaits signified a girl's passage into womanhood and marriage. In Britain, by the 12th century, braids could be coiled around the head and were sometimes put up in a chignon. In the 13th century, a common style was to wind the plaits at each side of the head just above the ears. By the 14th century women began to alter their hairline by plucking it to give the illusion of a higher forehead.

Hats and head-dresses

Throughout the Middle Ages the taste for adorning the head fluctuated. Initially throughout Europe the approach towards headgear was cautious. However, as time went on, there were experiments with new ideas. In the second half of the 12th century the hood became separated from the mantle, and was combined with a small, shoulder-length cape. This was a practical innovation, keeping the head warm and dry without impeding movement. Various styles of hats emerged, including the pointed Phrygian cap as well as an early attempt at a beret. Hats featuring wide brims were known and often worn over a hood by men on journeys.

By the end of the 13th century women began to wear a hairnet or *crespine*. At first it was worn in conjunction with a *barbette* (a band of fabric worn horizontally round the temples) and the fillet. In earlier times, wearing a hairnet alone had been considered shocking and immoral. But by the 14th century, attitudes had changed and wearing the *crespine* on its own was considered permissible. Women also wore veils, made from a semi-circular piece of linen and draped to frame the face.

During the late 14th and early 15th centuries a cushion head-dress became popular. This was a padded roll which was worn over the hairnet and held the hair coiled above each ear in small curls known as templers. By 1410, the horned head-dress, or *bicorne* – made from wire upon which was draped a light veil – and a heart-shaped head-dress both emerged. Head-dresses reached new heights. The conical *hennin* or steeple head-dress with a veil trailing from the point was popular in France, and its height was determined by the rank of the woman wearing it. Evidence suggests that by 1428 it had reached a height of 120cm (4ft). The most lavish creation of the time was considered to be the butterfly head-dress – made from wire on which a cap or caul was imposed to hold the hair in place.

left: This illustration by Joseph Strutt (1842) shows the wide range of headwear worn by men in the 14th century.

above: Ranging from the 11th to the 13th century, the costumes of these Medieval women are all made of rich fabric and accompanied by ornate headgear.

THE

EARLY RENAISSANCE STYLE

RENAISSANCE

Background

Western Europe emerged from the hardships of the Middle Ages in a spectacular cultural flowering – the Renaissance, literally, a rebirth. It had its roots in the early 14th century, reached its height at the end of the 15th and continued well into the 16th century. The Renaissance started as the interest in the forms of classical sculpture and architecture, especially in Italy, grew and became a broad cultural and intellectual movement which gained impetus toward the end of the 14th century, as society became increasingly modern and more prosperous. A money economy replaced the feudal system, and consumer goods – with fixed price levels and values – became available on an open market.

The Humanists – new, worldly Italian thinkers – rediscovered ancient Greek and Roman writings on science, government, philosophy, mathematics and art and allied them with contemporary Christian ideas. They advanced Cicero's premise that man was a dignified rational being and, as a result, during the Renaissance individuals became more self-aware and extrovert. Artistically, the most influential writings were those of Vitruvius, a Roman architect from the first century BC, who highly regarded the disciplines of proportion and symmetry. His descriptions of Roman building types led people to study those still standing and to an immediate revival in the use of their forms. Vitruvius also wrote that the human body represented the beauty of proportion in nature and this had immense repercussions on the form of clothes, which sought to conform to his proportions.

The Renaissance spread right across western Europe, but the main centres of activity lay in the rich states of northern and central Italy, particularly Florence, Rome and Venice, and in Flanders which became an important centre for trade and the arts. Antwerp, Bruges and Ghent were Europe's busiest port cities and thriving textile centres. Using imported wool from England as raw material, Flemish weavers created the continent's most luxurious textiles. The 'Flemish Renaissance' was not concerned with the architectural forms, but more with intellectual achievements, philosophy and painting.

In Italy, prominent families – like the Gonzagas of Mantua and the Estes of Ferrara – lived in stately homes, wore splendid clothes, engaged their minds in intellectual pursuits with like-minded people, and lavished their personal wealth on works of art, for both private and public collections.

In addition to the papal court in Rome, the most influential patrons of all were the Medicis who, though they held no official title, dominated politics in Florence. As bankers to all of Europe's royal families, they held offices across the continent in Lyons, Antwerp and London and used their immense wealth to patronize culture and the arts in northern Italy. Great artists – Leonardo da Vinci, Andrea del Verrocchio, Antonio and Piero Pollaiuolo, Michelangelo, Sandro Botticelli and Filippino Lippi – whose works dominate the best museums worldwide were beneficiaries of the Medicis' philanthropy. Under the leadership and patronage of Lorenzo de Medici, who became known as 'Il Magnifico', Florence became the artistic centre of Europe. He oversaw the extension of his family's eponymous library, opened the Platonic Library of Philosophy and spent both public money and his own funds on buildings, festivals and art to be enjoyed by the citizens of Florence.

left: Vitruvian Man (study of human proportion) by Leonardo da Vinci 1451–1519.

above: The man shown wearing ornate gold embroidered garments, riding at the front of the procession, is thought to be Lorenzo de Medici. It was partly due to his patronage that Florence became the centre of Renaissance art and an equally important centre for fashion.

right: During the Renaissance, clothes were made from new, heavier materials. Velvet was particularly popular in northern Europe. The women and children shown here are all wearing ruffs at the neck and wrist and some have slashing on their sleeves.

The guilds which had been set up in the Middle Ages were also patrons of the arts, particularly in cities like Florence and the cloth-towns of Flanders where they paid for alterpieces, statues and buildings. They also continued to increase in power. The most powerful and wealthy guilds were associated with the textile trade. Members of guilds were subjected to strict rules. Any member who betrayed the confidence of his association – making the secrets of his guild known – could be hunted down and killed. Guild members were prescribed a uniform for the job and sometimes even wore one in their leisure time. Guilds also perpetuated standards of quality and set fixed prices for merchandise.

Literature flourished across Europe right through the Renaissance. Italy played home to Petrarch (1304–74), Machiavelli (1469–1527), Ariosto (1474–1533), Bandello (1485–1561), and Aretino (1492–1556). In France, the poet Pierre Ronsard (1524–85) founded the Pleiade – a poetry group that produced hymns and elegies with the dominant theme of love, and in Spain, Cervantes (1547–1616) satirized in *Don Quixote* the whole notion of romantic chivalry.

The most important innovation of the era was the printing press. Invented in 1452 by Johann Gutenberg, it increased the spread of knowledge and evolved thought from being dominated by the Roman Catholic theologians to a more progressive range of eclectic ideas. The printing press increased the pace of communication. Previously books had been printed by hand and written in Latin – the language of scholarship. But the new educated middle class – the bourgeoisie, who could afford to buy books – wanted them written in their own language. So the trade for all types of books – almanacs, travel books, frothy romances, poetry and Greek and Roman philosophy as well as books on etiquette and dress – began to flourish.

The Renaissance was a time of trade, invention, communication and discovery. Cartographers (Portuguese map makers), broadened the knowledge of the world. Ships powered by sails sent explorers further afield. Trade with Asia – funded by private investors – continued bringing luxuries like spice, silk and perfume back to ever increasing demand.

In 1492, Christopher Columbus – the son of a Genoese woolcomber – discovered the New World, landing in San Salvador, Cuba, Haiti, Guadalupe, Puerto Rico, Jamaica, Trinidad and the mainland of South America, among other places. On his second voyage he founded Isabella – named after Queen Isabella of Castile who, with her husband, Ferdinand of Aragon, had given him financial backing for the first voyage – the first European city in the New World. These great voyages brought exotica back to Europe – food such as corn and potatoes, items such as tobacco, cola, gold, silver, parrots and brightly coloured feathers which were used to accessorize men's hats.

From the last years of the 15th century Portuguese explorers, such as Vasco da Gama and Ferdinand Magellan, travelled further and further to the east, reaching first China, and then Japan in 1517. They returned to Europe with sartorial luxuries such as the folding fan, an accessory which quickly caught on among court circles.

The period between 1484 and 1520 is known as the High Renaissance. It was during this era that the cultural, artistic and scientific advances made in the early Renaissance were understood and accepted. Modern medical ideas began to gain wider acceptance: at the Paris hospital – the Hotel Dieu – Ambroise Paré, a former barber who became surgeon to four French kings from Henri II to Henri III, made great advances in the practice of surgery.

But eventually Rome replaced Florence as Italy's artistic centre. Pope Julius II (r. 1503–13) began to attract the best artists to the city. Michelangelo painted the ceiling of the Sistine Chapel, where the Flemish composer and singer Josquin des Prés resided as choir master. From Umbria, via Florence, Raphael arrived to paint frescos throughout the Vatican palace. By the time Leo X, son of Lorenzo Il Magnifico, asserted his place on the papal throne, Rome was Europe's pre-eminent artistic and cultural seat.

Europe looked to Italy. England and France embraced Italian ideals of art, architecture and fashion. The king of France, François I, became the last patron of the painter and thinker Leonardo da Vinci. He gave him a yearly allowance and in 1516 installed him in the Chateau Cloux, near Amboise, where he lived until he died in 1519. He is regarded as the all-round genius of the Renaissance; his notebooks reflect a huge knowledge and foresight of a vast range of subjects including biology, anatomy, mechanics, and aeronautics. His belief that the circle was the purest, most perfect form pushed further the prevailing notion of symmetry and proportion that dominated aesthetics during the Renaissance.

Two years before Leonardo's death, in 1517, a German Augustinian friar called Martin Luther attacked the corruption prevalent within the Catholic Church, publishing a list of

above: The Renaissance was a time of great discovery. The expeditions eastwards opened up trade and made sartorial luxuries, such as folding fans, silk and feathers, more accessible to Europeans.

above: Colour was an important feature in both men's and women's clothing, as illustrated in this painting of a court ball. The female silhouette, with the narrowly shaped upper-body and the billowing effect of the farthingale below, is typical of the Renaissance period.

grievances called *The Ninety Five Theses*. The printing press aided the spread of Luther's ideas of reform and the resulting Reformation spread across Europe, ending ultimately in a north/south split: the northern countries, roughly speaking, becoming Protestant while the south remained Catholic. Initially in England, Henry VIII defended the Catholic church, but when the pope refused to grant him a divorce from his first wife he broke from Rome, declaring himself Supreme Head of the Church of England. Once again, Europe was about to be plunged into political turmoil.

Women

Although true equality between the sexes was still several centuries away, the Renaissance heralded an era where women enjoyed unprecedented freedom. Women, such as Elizabeth I of England (1533–1603), the second daughter of Henry VIII, were as well educated as men in a wide range of subjects. Other prominent women of the time, such as Alexandra Mancini Strozzi and Isabella d'Este Gonzaga, Marchioness of Mantua, were recognized for their intellect. Isabella of Castille, the patron of Christopher Columbus, co-governed Spain with her husband Ferdinand of Aragon, oversaw a war against Portugal and succeeded in

above: The so-called *Armada Portrait* shows Elizabeth I with the Spanish Armada visible behind her on the left. She is wearing a stiff lace collar and a dark garment with satin sleeves which are decorated with ribbons, gems and pearls.

driving the Moors from her country. On 7 November 1558 Elizabeth I acceded to the English throne at the age of 25. Through her 45-year reign she proved to be a shrewd monarch. Her country grew prosperous and thrived on a cultural level – two years before she died, Shakespeare's *Hamlet* was performed for the first time on stage. Her greatest victory lay in saving Protestant England from Spanish Catholic domination – her army's fire ships defeated the attempted invasion of the Spanish Armada in 1558. 'I know I have but the body of a weak and feeble woman,' she proclaimed to her troops gathered at Tilbury before the battle, 'but I have the heart and stomach of a king'.

Despite the inspiring examples of powerful womanhood, the feminine ideal during the Renaissance had little to do with intellectual ability, political acumen or might. As Victoria Griffin rightly observed in *The Mistress* (Bloomsbury, 1999), it was the courtesan who had become the image of ideal womanhood. Most famous of the kind was Diane de Poitiers, the mistress of Henri d'Orléans, the future King of France and the son of François I, the country's great Renaissance king and the creator of Fontainebleau. De Poitiers' talents were legendary. After Henri's wife, Catherine de Medici, complained about her inability to conceive, Diane set to work to solve the situation – a decision, which Griffin claims, was

probably prompted by the thought that the possibility of an infertile queen could mean an annulment for the royal couple. And this could threaten her own position at court. On Diane's advice Henri sought an operation (probably circumcision), and Catherine tried a few new lovemaking positions. A new routine was also introduced to the Royal's sex life whereby Henri would spend the first part of the night in bed with Diane before going to Catherine's bed. The result? Ten years into their marriage Catherine produced a son, following which she spent more than a decade being pregnant, making her, Griffin claims, one of the most prolific royal wives in history. After Henri's death and that of his son François II, Catherine became the force behind the throne for both Charles IX and Henri III.

Costume

As people grew more self-aware, clothing, and in particular fashionable clothing, became of increasing importance during the Renaissance. Fashion, once purely a pastime of the rich, also became a preoccupation of the thriving middle class. During the Middle Ages clothes had become distinct from country to country, but the Renaissance had a more unifying effect on fashion. As communication and transportation became faster and more sophisticated, the spread of luxury goods became regular and people began to hanker for the same merchandise. In England, as Jack Cassin Scott has observed, a range of sartorial ideals were accepted – elements were taken from different national styles and mixed up, often in one outfit.

Made by tailors – whose standards were set by the powerful tailor's guilds – clothes were made to match a customer's requests and it was common for a client to pay several visits to a tailor just for a single item of clothing. Tailors began to form business networks of closely related trades in specific regions of towns and cities. In London, the area of London Bridge housed the first haberdashers. A tailor's shop, work rooms and home were all located on one site. Travelling tailors serviced country folk who did not have access to urban centres.

Clothes were regarded as an investment and time was spent on their upkeep and repair. Courtiers required an extensive wardrobe and often sold their garments on to second-hand shops in order to recoup some of the cost.

In terms of sartorial influence and innovation there were two major centres of importance – Florence and the court of Charles the Bold, Duke of Burgundy, in Flanders. Among the most influential and long-lasting styles to emerge from Flanders was one that came as the result of the defeat of Charles the Bold in 1477. As the Swiss descended upon his troops in Nancy they celebrated their victory by cutting up the tents, lavish banners and luxurious costumes belonging to the Burgundian army and lacing these shreds through the tears in their own costumes. From this moment on a style known as slashing – where the seams were left open or slits deliberately created in a garment so as to make the lining visible – caught on. It was a form of ornament used by both sexes but was rather more popular in men's costume and was certainly one of the most characteristic fashion motifs of the later Renaissance.

left: Diane de Poitiers, mistress of the French king Henri II, was one of the most famous courtesans of her time. Her hair is simply adorned and arranged to make her forehead appear higher, a look that was fashionable among women. She is wearing simple drop-shaped earrings that were also popular in the 16th century.

above: This illustration shows Henry, Duke of Saxony, wearing a stunning outfit that demonstrates the style known as slashing on his doublet, cloak and hose.

COSTUME

The ruff was another sartorial development to which the Renaissance can lay claim. A prominent feature of both male and female costumes, it started off as an effect created by pulling the edge of a shirt or shift close to the neck with a drawstring so that a frill appeared, but it eventually became an independent item of clothing. Its correct name was the 'band' because it was made from a band or strip of linen, as much as 5.8m (18ft) in length. It was able to grow to such elaborate proportions because of the introduction of starch — which was originally manufactured in Flanders, reaching England in 1560. Starch tinted the colour of the white ruff, adding a blue or yellow shade to it. Supports such as an underpropper or *supportasse* — frames of silk-covered wire pinned underneath the ruff — were used to keep them in place. The frills of a ruff progressed to pleats, which were spread out and pressed into the shape of figure eights. Later, ruffs could be made of gauze and sometimes featured edges of gold or silver lace and could be tacked to the high collar of a gown's bodice or used to decorate a man's shirt. Ruffs might look uncomfortable, but fashion historians claim that if the wearer held his or her head high this was not the case.

Middle-class men and women wore garments featuring detachable sleeves or double sleeves. First was the narrow sleeve which could be attached to a dress and then a wider sleeve could also be fixed to a gown's bodice (or a man's doublet). These sleeves were an affordable method of changing the style of a garment. The practice was favoured most by Italian women, who with two dresses and ten pairs of sleeves could obtain a number of different looks. Historians note that this habit for detachable sleeves predated the modern custom of buying skirts and blouses to mix and match.

Points were another prominent characteristic of Renaissance dress. Points resembled shoe laces and were used to fasten trunk hose to a doublet waist, or a detachable sleeve to the armhole of a doublet or bodice. This process was known as lacing or trussing. Though points served a purely functional purpose, the rich used those with decorative motifs at their tips. Points also made it possible for costume to be even more lavish and ornamental. They also enhanced a looser, casual attitude toward clothing.

Fans and handkerchiefs were quintessential Renaissance accessories. Voyages of discovery — to China and the New World — brought fans back to Europe. Christopher Columbus presented Isabella of Castile with a feather fan when he returned from his second voyage in 1496. Later, Queen Elizabeth — who appears in several portraits holding a fan — was said to have popularized their use in England. She preferred fans made from feathers featuring elaborate jewelled handles and these were made to compliment her lavish ensembles. Elizabeth's inventory counted as many as 31 fans, some of which cost as much as £40. Outside of court circles fans became popular — they were a part of a well-to-do bride's trousseau. In the warmer climate of Venice, Milan, Genoa and Siena, the personal fan made a handy fly swatter in summer, but they were really more fashionable than functional. Some featured a mirror centre while others were garnished with pearls. The wives of rich Venetian merchants carried fans made in flag shapes. Catherine de Medici introduced the folding fan to England. She had her own company of perfumers, who were also skilled fan makers. A portrait showing her brandishing a finely constructed fan hangs

above: The sleeves of this low-cut bodice are detachable. They are attached to the armholes by points, by a process known as lacing.

in the British Museum. Folding fans could be attached by a chain or ribbon to the girdle to leave the hands free.

Handkerchiefs were used by both men and women. They served several purposes — from blowing the nose to decorative use. They were also worn as head scarves and around the neck. Some were simply carried in the palm of the hand or held tightly in the middle so as to reveal their fine edges. The pocket handkerchief popularized in Venice in the mid-16th century became a favourite ornament of European royalty — particularly Catherine de Medici. The handkerchief was considered as a definite item of luxury which the poor were prohibited from using by law. Henry VIII instituted laws governing how they could be decorated. Most handkerchiefs were made from linen and silk and, with time, became increasingly decorative. The 16th-century handkerchief is known for being more decorative than that made in the 15th century. Edged in lace, it could also feature needlepoint work, tasselled edges or embroidery.

Although clothing styles remained more or less constant in the 15th century, changes did occur at the beginning of the 16th century and the styles that emerged can be seen in the paintings of Michelangelo and Raphael, among others. Following Leonardo's theory that the circle was the perfect shape, appearance for men and especially women became rounder and clothes took on a sensual aspect. Sleeves and skirts became full. Clothes were made from textiles which were thick, luxurious and soft, like velvet, brocade and damask. Embroidery and ornamentation were frequently employed to add to the richness of a garment and the beauty of the human body began to be accepted.

Women's clothing

At the beginning of the 15th century women wore a soft, billowing version of the *houppelande* — a long, wide gown with long full sleeves and high collar. In the middle of the century clothes became fuller. A woman's wardrobe staple was an ensemble composed of a white linen undergown with long, hanging sleeves over which was worn a high-waisted dress in a contrasting colour.

By the century's end gowns featured a V-shaped waistline, a stomacher filling in the gap at the front of the dress, and sleeves that opened at the shoulders, elbows and at the back all the way to the wrist so that the undergown's sleeves were revealed. By the 16th century, the shift became the most important item of a woman's wardrobe.

The most noted Renaissance sartorial invention for women was the farthingale — a narrow under-structure which held out the skirt, and was first worn at the Spanish court in 1468. But as different nationalities picked up the custom, the farthingale began to increase in width. In 1530 a wider type of farthingale appeared in France, where it was known as the *bourrelet*.

A farthingale added a swing to a woman's skirt. This movement was further accentuated if she wore heels. The farthingale hoop was made from willow twigs, cane or whalebone, which were sewn into fabric. There were three main shapes: the narrow Spanish farthingale, a drum-shaped structure popular with French women and a bell-shaped

above: This sumptuous outfit features velvet and brocade. The rectangular neckline is decorated with pearls, a style which is mirrored in the head-dress. The woman, Eleonora di Toledo, is holding a handkerchief, an accessory of Renaissance fashion.

WOMEN'S CLOTHING

above: The family of Philip IV of Spain. Margarita Maria stands in the centre, wearing a Spanish-style farthingale which is narrower in shape than most other styles.

farthingale. They greatly increased the width of the woman who wore them and skirts required a lot of material as a result. Laws and edicts were issued to curtail their use but to no avail. As Jack Cassin Scott has pointed out, no royal edict ever controlled fashion.

Although women's clothes were very heavy in the later Renaissance, the desired silhouette was well-defined. Clothing emphasized wide shoulders, a long, narrow waist and full hips. A woman's upper body was narrowly shaped by the *basquine*. Made from rigid cloth, this corset type undergarment hugged close to the body and gradually shaped it into a funnel, suppressing the soft natural shape of the chest and forcing it upwards. This silhouette complemented the billowing effect of the farthingale below. Stays made of whalebone were an alternative that also gave women a flat-chested look, and the effect was added to by the stiff, triangular stomacher reaching a point below the waistline, and curving out over the skirt.

In Renaissance Florence, skirts initially trailed on the floor, but the leg soon began to peep out from under the skirt, especially when women rode, hunted, took part in sports or danced. This desire to show the legs led to a concern to have stockings and drawers that fitted perfectly.

Catherine de Medici was one of the first women to wear drawers. They gave women greater freedom, enabling them to ride side saddle – a custom which originated during the Renaissance – but still cover their knees if their skirts did get displaced. Initially drawers were made of cotton or fustian but as they gradually gained acceptance they were made of finer fabrics such as brocade and gold and silver cloth. But drawers were not adopted by all European women, and they did not become popular in either England or Germany.

Women wore long, pleated cloaks as overgarments. Some featured a round, narrow neckline and a frivolous touch of a slit under the arms which revealed a woman's dress.

Elizabeth I remains famous for her love of lavish clothes. Though she is not remembered as a great beauty, Elizabeth was considered a woman of great style. A typical Elizabethan look was stiff. She wore a Tudor ruff, epaulets, a jewelled wig, a body-hugging corset and a farthingale. Both her forehead and brows were plucked. Elizabeth so loved her clothes that she parted with nothing in her wardrobe. Upon her death her personal wardrobe included 3,000 dresses and head pieces. In 1998 her life was illuminated on screen in *Elizabeth*, in which the Australian actress Cate Blanchett starred in the lead role. Alexandra Byrne, the film's costume designer, was nominated for an Oscar for her work.

Men's clothing

Wearing colour – a marked characteristic of men's clothes during the Middle Ages – continued unabated during the Renaissance. Adding a further element of flamboyance to men's garments was the habit of wearing clothes featuring brightly coloured fabric patches as well as stripes, squares and triangles. The heads of certain elite families showed a preference for wearing certain colours: Amadeus VI and Amadeus VII of Savoy became known as the Green Count and the Red Count respectively because of their preference for these colours. People would dress their servants in uniforms of the same colour, and

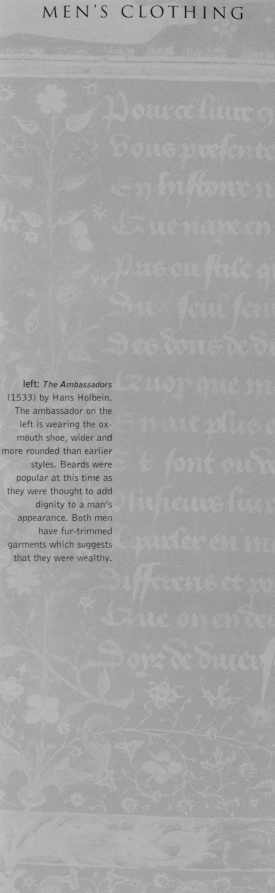

left: *The Ambassadors* (1533) by Hans Holbein. The ambassador on the left is wearing the ox-mouth shoe, wider and more rounded than earlier styles. Beards were popular at this time as they were thought to add dignity to a man's appearance. Both men have fur-trimmed garments which suggests that they were wealthy.

particular colours were reserved for specific activities: russet was often worn for rural pursuits, for example. Young men often wore bright colours.

The silhouette for men's clothing at the time accentuated the physique. To make their shoulders and chest appear more broad, men padded their coats with hay and fastened a belt at their waist. Stockings replaced narrow trousers and the crotch area became a prominent body zone through the introduction of the codpiece and other ornamentation such as ribbons. Pointed shoes were replaced by the ox-mouth shoe which was very wide and rounded at the front of the foot.

The leaders of male fashion in 16th-century Europe were Henry VIII of England, François I of France and Charles V of Spain and the Netherlands. They were all men of learning and culture: they patronized Holbein, Leonardo and Titian, respectively. They rivalled each other for the sumptuousness of their clothing: Charles, for example, wore a doublet of silver brocade and a gold, sable-lined robe. But of the three, it was Henry VIII who has been considered Europe's leader of the time. Ruthless, handsome and athletic, Henry dressed in sumptuous attire. His clothes were made of rich brocades, which were

MEN'S CLOTHING

above: Henry VIII was a leader of fashion in 16th-century Europe. His padded doublet, accentuated shoulders and codpiece were worn to project an image of authority and masculinity.

right: Portrait of Charles IX, shown wearing a doublet, breeches and a short velvet cape. It was thought to be masculine to have shapely legs, so hose were worn to show them off to best effect.

embroidered and encrusted with jewels.

European men used books to give them ideas on how to achieve a stylish appearance. Castiglione's *The Book of the Courtier* became the handbook for gentlemen. Among the details of ideal courtly behaviour, it also gave advice on what to wear for manly pursuits — fighting at war, hunting and playing sports.

Everyday men's clothing displayed signs of increasing modernity. A man's wardrobe was made up of a few indispensable elements:

- •Shirt: A man's white linen shirt became the symbol of affluence during the Renaissance and across Europe it replaced the chemise. Wearing a clean and freshly pressed shirt — made from white linen, silk or taffeta — distinguished a gentleman from a peasant worker. The cut of the shirt was ample, the neckline was normally low and, with time, a small collar and sometimes a frill — featuring black, red, blue or gold embroidery — appeared at the neck. This eventually evolved into the ruff.

- •Doublet: Until the 16th century the doublet was the main garment worn on the upper part of the body underneath a man's coat, eventually being replaced by the waistcoat. Stiffening gave the garment its shape, and padding was used for extra bulk, as this was believed to add a masculine element to a man's appearance, but by the 17th century the padding disappeared again. Most doublets had a pointed waistline. The sleeves were laced together so that the elbow, the back of the arm, the shoulder and the lace all showed through.

- •Jerkin: The equivalent to a modern suit jacket, a jerkin could feature either a high or low neck. No matter what the style, it was usually left open to display the doublet, shirt and codpiece. Originally the sleeves were detachable, but in the middle of the 16th century they were dropped and the jerkin became sleeveless and was finished by padded rolls or wing-like fabric effects at the shoulder.

- •Codpiece: A padded and protective triangle of fabric which appeared at the front of the hose to emphasize a man's groin, a codpiece was laced to the doublet.

- •Hose: Shapely legs were considered to be a sign of masculinity. But tights were not a style that was universally adopted. Because they were expensive to produce, tights were worn only by the rich. The staple of the sumptuous wardrobe, a fashionable man's attire was assembled around his choice of tights. Trunk hose went from the waist to just above the knee and were fitted at the hip and featured a degree of padding. They were made in several shapes but by the middle of the 16th century the padding was predominantly at the waist. Canions were tube-shaped hose extensions worn below shorter hose to reach to the knee. Venetians wore hose which fitted full at the hips and fell to below the knee and were either loose or fit snugly on the leg. Popular in northern Europe, pluderhose were made of fabric panels and also featured lining and stiffening. Slops was the term for a baggy type of trunk hose popular in England.

- •Stockings: Once a machine was invented to knit stockings, tights progressed from

a loose, tailored-fit garment to a form-fitting, comfortable item of clothing. Those which were knitted featured a clock — or ankle gusset, a feature of women's stockings until World War II. Garters — thin strips of material fastened around the leg above the knee — held up a man's stockings. The stocking could be rolled over the garter. Initially a garter served a purely functional purpose but by the 17th century they had become more ornamental.

There were, of course, local variations on these basic items of clothing. A rich Venetian might wear a pair of close-fitting knitted tights secured to a doublet with hooks or double pins. A *zipone* — a buttoned-up tunic which grazed the knee — was layered on top of the doublet and the ensemble was finished by an overgarment — a cape called a *zornea*, which featured a pair of wide sleeves and was secured around the waist with a belt.

Textiles

The textile industry contributed greatly to the development of Renaissance Europe. In Italy, the profits of the fabric trade funded many grand projects of art and architecture. Likewise in England, as Harold Nicolson pointed out: 'It was wool rather than individualism that first gave us our liberties.' Fabric merchants were prominent citizens. For instance, in the late Middle Ages, Duke Philip the Good of Burgundy had appointed Giovanni Arnolfini, who made his fortune selling silk, as his personal revenue adviser.

Throughout the Renaissance, fabrics became ever more elaborate and extravagant as textile workers — weavers and manufacturers — became more skilled. The precious silks that once had to be imported from the east were manufactured in Flanders — at Ypres, Bruges and Ghent — where some of the most lavishly decorated brocade was produced, as well as samite (Byzantine heavy silk), taffeta and velvet. Northern Europe had a particular taste for clothing made of velvet. Fur — ermine, squirrel, lamb, fox, muskrat and rabbit — continued to be used for trim. At this period, Paris alone counted 400 furriers.

Scarves, handkerchiefs and veils were made from thin silk, chiffon and crêpe. Outer garments could be made of leather. Travellers were encouraged to wear doublets lined with taffeta because the fabric was more resistant to fleas.

Debate surrounds the origins of lace and some fashion historians trace its invention to Ancient Egypt. Christopher Froschauer's book on fashion, which was printed in 1536, claims that lace was Italian, brought by Venetian merchants to Switzerland. In *Lace, History and Fashion*, Annie Kraatz stated that the Venetians and Flemish (around Antwerp) could take credit for perfecting the craft of lace-making by the end of the first quarter of the 16th century. The use of lace in the making of fine clothes was widespread throughout the Renaissance. In Italy lace was known as *merletto*; in Germany it was called *spitze* (points) and in France, *dentelle*.

Two types of lace-making were popular — bobbin-lace and needle-lace. Sometimes these methods were combined. Point lace, for example, was made of strips of bobbin-lace joined together with fine needle stitches. Lace was produced by family-based workshops, convents and orphanages, sold by the yard at haberdasheries and used regularly by both men and

left: Bright colours were a trademark of Renaissance clothing, as demonstrated in this Venetian scene. The men dressed in the red ceremonial robes with black sash and cap are members of the lay confraternity of the Scuola di San Giovanni Evangelista.

above: The beautifully decorated sleeves shown here are testament to the immense skill of the textile workers of the 15th and 16th centuries.

TEXTILES

women. Its popularity was partly due to the fact that it featured widely on ruffs. The finest lace was produced in Italy.

During the Renaissance the beauty of fabric was appreciated. As the era progressed rich fabric was left unadorned. Gone were the beads, braids and embroidery so favoured by the Byzantines. When motifs were used they showed an Oriental influence: Asian fruit, lotus and palm leaf patterns appeared periodically.

Wool, linen and cotton were the main fabrics used for everyday garments. England became Europe's wool supplier. The west country, East Anglia and west Yorkshire all produced wool of different weights, types and colours. Around 1560, Elizabeth I supported a band of refugees, fleeing from the Low Countries because of religious persecution, to settle in East Anglia, where they produced some of the finest yarn – light, soft wool which became known as the New Drapery.

Germany, Ireland and Scotland produced the finest linen. The highest-quality velvet, damask, brocade and satin were produced in Spain and Italy.

An array of strong colours were popular for clothes – deep red and blue, wine, gold and black frequently appeared. After 1550 rich, jewel-tone shades rose to prominence including scarlet, yellow, orange and emerald. Elizabeth I appeared in colour combinations, but particularly white and silver.

Footwear

During the Renaissance shoes were made of a variety of materials including leather, cloth and silk. Rich women, courtesans and prostitutes wore *chopines*. Colin McDowell claims that this shoe was one of the earliest fashion fads. Like a set of stilts, they elevated the wearer high off the ground and affected her way of walking, but this problem was alleviated by lowering the sole of the shoe, thus inventing the high-heeled shoe. Shoes were expensive items and *pantofles* – wooden platforms attached to the sole of the shoe with pieces of fabric – were used to protect shoes from hard weather by raising them from the ground.

The height of the heel, shape of the upper and toe cap changed from time to time, in accordance with the fashion of the time. By the 1580s shoe straps had evolved. These were fastened on to the foot with the help of a ribbon or a tie.

Jewellery

In the hands of Florentine craftsmen, jewellery surpassed the idea of being merely decorative. It was elevated to an art form in the Renaissance. By the 15th century, two young goldsmiths, Ghiberti and Brunelleschi, were establishing reputations for themselves as seminal craftsmen in Florence. But they faced stiff competition. Florence was the centre of jewellery making and several prominent craftsmen – among them Antonio Pollaiuolo, Francesco Francia, Maso Finiguerra, Caradosso, Michelozzo, Verrocchio and Lorenzo di Credi – were busy catering to the insatiable demands of noble families, as well as those of European royalty. Famous artists were also commissioned to design jewellery. Their designs were then completed by goldsmiths. The courts of Burgundy and Berry in France

above: Charles VII of France is shown wearing a velvet cloak trimmed with fur, both materials remaining popular during this era. His wide-brimmed hat is decorated with embroidery.

right: These leather boots were believed to have belonged to Elizabeth I. They would have been laced up the side of the boot and buckled across the top of the foot.

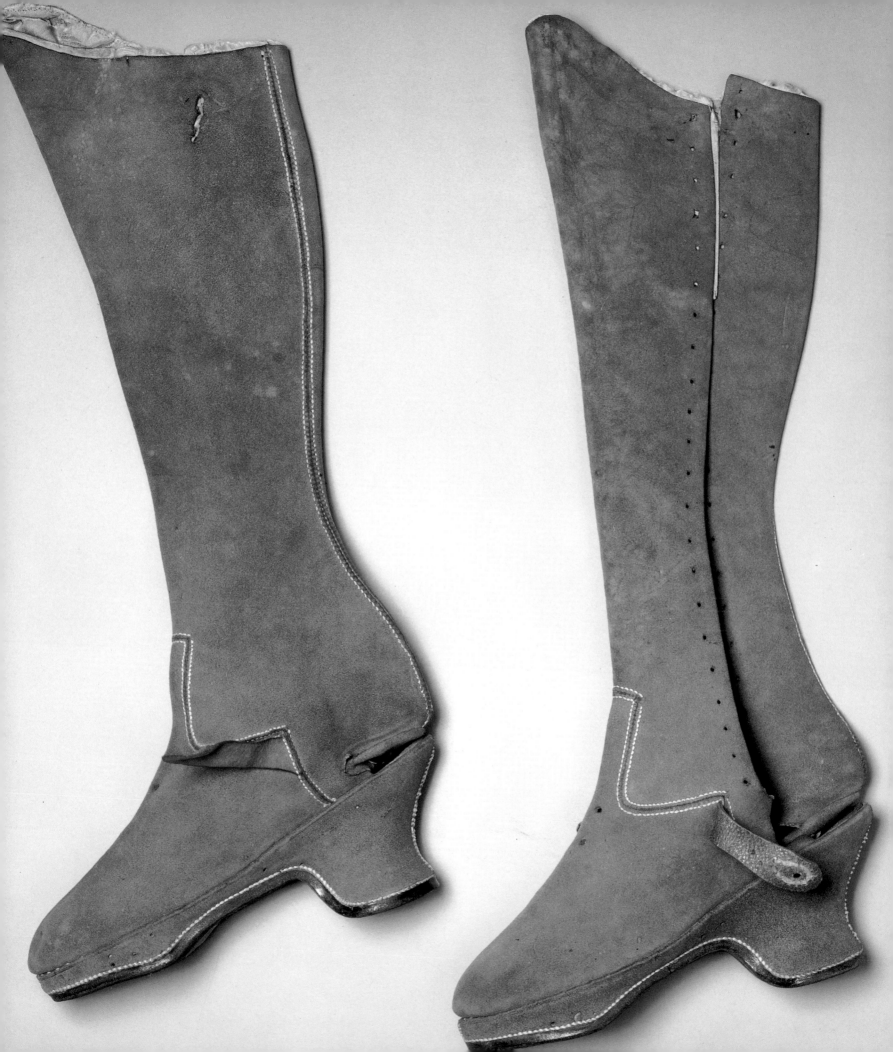

looked to Florentine jewellers for sumptuous, precious pieces.

For lavish items of adornment François I of France looked to Benvenuto Cellini. The Florentine sculptor, goldsmith and engraver is probably the most famous jeweller of the Renaissance both for his work (although only one actual piece displaying his skill exists, a necklace in the Desmoni collection in New York) and his reputation. After a duel, Cellini was banished to Rome where he set about his craft – establishing himself as an artist in metalwork. In his infamously self-promoting autobiography (1558), Cellini claims that in the Battle of Rome in 1527 it was he who slayed the Constable Bourbon and shot William the Silent, Prince of Orange. In 1537 he was welcomed into the Court of François I but he soon returned to Florence, where Cosimo I de Medici became his patron. It was in Italy that he completed his most famous work – Perseus with the head of Medusa – cast in bronze.

Florentine jewellery was extremely detailed. For example, the *enseigne* – a disc-shaped hat ornament worn by men – could contain a complete battle scene even though it was only 3cm (1¼in) in diameter.

Diamonds – cut in the shape of a pyramid or point – were made popular first in the 15th century by the Medicis and then taken up by French royals such as Henri II and rich noble families. The diamond ring became a symbol of power and it was worn during coronation ceremonies. A new way of cutting diamonds was discovered enabling the reflection of light on the cut and polished surfaces of the crystals to greatly enhance the brilliance of the gem and making greater perfection in the workmanship of the jewel possible.

Paintings provide the clues to the pieces worn at the time. In Van Eyck's altar piece in St Bavone in Ghent, a Madonna wears a white tunic with a brooch clasped at her bosom. A portrait of a woman by Durer displays a fashionable necklace made from amber beads which were set apart by four pairs of seed pearls at each side. In a painting of the de Sacrati family thought to be by Baldassare Estense (1443–1504) the mother is wearing a necklace featuring small beads held on light chains.

Men and women wore gold neck chains. The style was particularly popular in Germany. As philosophers looked back to Ancient Greece and Rome for inspiration, the nobility popularized another Classical art form, the cameo. The best cameos – displaying scenes and figures inspired by Greek mythology – were made in Milan. Lorenzo de Medici was a noted collector of cameos made by master gem-engravers.

Rings were perhaps the most important piece of Renaissance jewellery. The greatest innovations of 16th-century jewellery, Sylvie Lambert has claimed, were the new ring designs. Again, Gutenberg deserves the credit. The development of printing, as well as new engraving techniques involving wood and copper, meant that plates and models were passed back and forth between goldsmiths and jewellers.

Earrings and bracelets were not often worn in the 16th century in most of Europe. When worn, earrings were simple drop-shaped pearls or gemstones. In Spain, however, earrings were elaborate. Spain, because of the discovery of the Americas and its thriving trade with the Orient, had become the richest country in the world, and the taste for

left: François I of France rivalled Henry VIII for the sumptuousness of his clothing. He is shown here wearing lavishly decorated jewelled armour.

above: This German woman is adorned with jewellery. The gold chains around her neck were particularly popular in Germany. Rings, worn in abundance here, were an important item of Renaissance jewellery.

JEWELLERY

jewellery was demonstrative of its position of unrivalled economic power. Spanish jewellers favoured the techniques of filigree and enamel. They also made good use of the copious amount of emeralds gleaned from their new territories in South America, particularly Peru. Articles which date from this time include long, pendant-shaped earrings – which featured enamel, pearl and precious stones – and the brass or gold badge worn by the clergy. Jewellery favoured at court was ecclesiastic in style, with crosses and pendants adorning the neck of the king, queen and upper echelons of the court circle.

The concept of jewellery as art thrived throughout 15th- and 16th-century France, Germany and England. Henry VIII was known for wearing a parure: a suite of matching jewellery including jewelled buttons for his doublets and clasps to hold his slashed sleeves. At this time, European noblemen used jewellery to accessorize their rich velvet clothes with gold buttons and gold pendants as well as finishing their caps and berets with medallions. Elizabeth I carried on Henry VIII's tradition, some say, to the point of greed. Pearls, it seems, were a personal favourite of hers. Hundreds were sewn onto her dresses, cloaks, veils and ruffs. She wore them in her hair and at her neck. The monogrammed brooch is a style that was popularized by her court. Wearing a watch, which was introduced to western Europe in the 16th century, became during Elizabeth's reign a mark of elegance.

Germany, Augsburg, Nuremberg and Munich were noted centres of jewellery making. In Paris, Jean Duvet (goldsmith to Francis I and Henry II) and Etienne Delaune (famous for his ornamental engravings) produced some of the most sought-after pieces.

Masks

During the Renaissance, masks were considered an integral part of outdoor costume. They were worn by both men and women. Elizabeth I wore a mask while she was hunting and when she was riding in her carriage. Affluent women wore masks while walking and on special occasions, such as an outing to the theatre. French women wore masks to be stylish and also because they believed that they preserved their skin. Men often wore masks to conceal their identities.

Make-up and grooming

Women went to great lengths to look beautiful. While the plucked brow and forehead is today considered this era's beauty trademark, women also applied make-up. Along with other affluent women, Catherine de Medici was a member of a beauty society which experimented with new products and formulas. Meanwhile, books on the subject of beauty began to be published, notably *L'Embellissement et Ornement du Corps Humain* by Jean Liebaut, a Parisian doctor, in 1582. His book included recipes for cosmetic formulas, body lotions, hair care and hair treatment products. These were copied through the 17th century.

Catherine de Medici has been credited with popularizing make-up among European women. Rouge, paints and colour washes were popular with women of all classes. Eye shadows were not so commonly used. The desired effect of make-up was a more subtle enhancement of one's own natural beauty. However, the habit of applying white lead to the

above: Portrait of Anne Boleyn, second wife of Henry VIII. She is wearing a monogrammed pendant, which was a favoured style. Pearls also adorn her bonnet, neckline and dress.

right: Elizabeth I had extremely extravagant taste in clothing. Her dress is encrusted with jewels and her hair is decorated with hundreds of pearls, a personal favourite of hers.

face to attain a pale complexion continued during the Renaissance. Sometimes women painted a number of layers on to their face and since bathing was not a common practice the paint remained on the skin despite its toxic formula. Women disregarded the warnings given by doctors and experimented with other hazardous formulas like mercury sublimate, which was applied to the skin to achieve smoothness, banish blemishes and disguise other facial imperfections.

Elizabeth I was an avid user of cosmetics. Richard Corson claims that she can take credit for the prominent use of paint, powder and patches. She applied both red and white paint to her skin. Patches were small black beauty spots, which were influenced by the use of rich black fabrics such as taffeta and velvet. The idea was that the dark patch or spot would further emphasize her pale complexion – the feminine ideal of the time. Corson claims that a Renaissance women's grooming regime focused attention that should have been spent on the care of their teeth in favour of perfecting a patch.

As bathing was not a common practice, the production and use of perfume proliferated during the Renaissance. So prevalent was its use that it was not only applied onto men's and women's skin, it scented the air, and was often doused onto pets. In 1508, Dominican monks at the convent of Santa Maria Novella in Florence established what remains today the world's oldest perfumery. The popes and the Medicis were clients and through the centuries each new director of the Farmacia has provided a recipe for a 'cure'.

Meanwhile, the small southern French town of Grasse began to establish itself as a centre for perfume. The initial motivation for perfume making in Grasse came about because the town was a centre for the tanning industry. Urine was commonly used during the tanning process and leather gloves were perfumed to cover up the smell. According to Susan Irvine in *Perfume: the Creation and Allure of Classic Fragrances*, the glove-makers also made and imported perfumes, which they sold. When the leather industry collapsed in the 18th century, they continued to sell perfume.

As in medieval times, it was popular for women before marriage to wear their hair loose, long and flowing with a centre parting, from which the locks cascaded down. Upon marriage women covered their hair and continued to pluck the hair line and eyebrows. But they began to experiment with braids – twisting them over the head and incorporating thick strands of unbraided hair over the crown of the head – a popular style in late 15th-century Flanders. Women also styled their hair by using curling irons, although often hair was worn in a simple style, leaving the head-dress to give the decorative touch.

Wigs and false hair pieces were also worn. The best wigs were made in Italy and France, from silk or real hair, supplied by peasants and nuns. It was bought and sold at public hair auctions. Blonde was still considered the ideal hair shade and women applied bleach and dye to their hair to obtain this colour. It seems that formulas for hair dye had become more sophisticated, as it was possible to achieve different shades of blonde – smoky, golden, tawny, honey or a combination of tones. Bathing in the moonlight was also considered a method of beautifying the hair.

At the start of the 15th century, older men wore beards but fashionable younger men

left: *The Courtesans* by Vittore Carpaccio shows two women wearing false hairpieces with their curly hair brushed forward onto the face. The dresses feature low necklines and slashed sleeves, revealing their undergarments.

above: Portrait of Simonetta Vespucci, 1500, by Piero di Cosimo. It illustrates the typical Renaissance hairstyle of rich women, with high shaved forehead and hair braided with pearls and gemstones.

THE RENAISSANCE

139

MAKE-UP
AND GROOMING

above: This portrait (c 1535) of François I shows the court dress of the time. He is wearing a doublet of patterned brocade, an embroidered jerkin and a fur-trimmed cap.

right: This late 16th-century English linen bonnet is intricately embroidered with fruit and flowers, using brightly coloured and gold thread.

were clean-shaven. A century later, beards were back in vogue. Much time was devoted to their grooming, and they were trimmed and waxed so that they could be shaped and curled. False beards were sometimes worn: at the Duke of Burgundy's funeral, the Duke of Lorraine wore a waist-length false gold beard.

Short hair styles were favoured by men for much of the Renaissance. A bowl type of cut was worn – most prominently by Henry V. His portrait hanging in London's National Portrait Gallery typifies the look. Shoulder-length hair and the long fringe both became popular in the 15th century. Louis XI of France wore his hair long and flowing. But short hair became popular once again thanks to Duke Philip of Burgundy: in 1461 he fell ill and was forced to shave off his hair, so some 500 noblemen followed his example. A flamboyant, Florentine style known as the *zazzera* – a shoulder-length bob frizzed at the sides – caught on with fashionable men across the continent. In London and Paris it became known as 'the Florentine cut'.

Hats and head-dresses

Portraiture reached a peak during the Renaissance. Royalty and members of prominent families posed for great artists and it is from their work that historians have gleaned information on hats and hairstyles. Van Eyck's portrait of Arnolfini shows him wearing a straw hat that was popular with men. It was made from woven straw and was probably the handiwork of peasants. The *chaperon* – a turban style hat – evolved from the hood. Portraits of Henry VIII and Edward VI show other sumptuous styles worn by rich men. These were beret-shaped with a narrow brim which turned up from the face.

Hats were also adorned with jewels and feathers. Through the 15th and 16th centuries Italian women often wore turbans. Hoods were common in the Low Countries, while French women wore velvet caps. Bands were worn across the forehead. Head-dresses also featured luxurious embroidery and precious gemstones.

BAROQUE

THE AGE OF FRENCH DOMINANCE

PERIOD

Background

'*L'État, c'est moi.*' These three words are the most memorable of the 17th century, uttered by Louis XIV, the Sun King, an absolute monarch who ruled France from 1643 to 1715, believing that there was no limit to his power. Not only did France, under his guidance, reach its zenith as a European superpower, Louis also set the tone for culture, economy and politics across Europe. Recognizing the influence art and architecture had on society, he used both as tools to project and control his idea of centralized government on his subjects. All things decorative – clothes, interiors and furniture – were designed to capture his spirit of an ordered, disciplined and controlled government and lifestyle.

The 17th century belonged to France. A new era of refinement had dawned across Europe. Privileged society had become more sophisticated and it was France that led the way in this new grand age. At table, for example, the knife and fork were now commonly used – such etiquette measures had been introduced by the French. Their language was also spoken by the Continental upper classes.

But privilege came at a price. The Thirty Years War (1618–48) brought religious tensions to a head, dividing northern and southern Europe roughly into a respective Protestant and Catholic split. Germany and Spain fell into decline and England exploded into civil war. The issue was the monarchy – the medieval concept of the divine right of kingship was challenged by a faction who believed that the king should listen to representatives of the people. The ensuing troubles sent England into cultural decline – theatres closed and the king was decapitated. Puritanism and repression spread throughout the country.

Because of Spanish domination, Italy, too, experienced decline. Gone were the days of Renaissance Florence. However, Rome had already spawned the century's dominant artistic and cultural style – the Baroque. The term is of Italian and Portuguese origins: a *barroco* describes an irregular pearl. Baroque painting and architecture were used by Italian Catholics as Louis XIV later employed them – as a propaganda tool in the Counter Reformation. The idea was that because art directly influences the senses it could be used to typify and display the beauty and richness inherent in Catholicism. At the forefront of the Roman Baroque artistic movement was the painter Michelangelo Merisi da Caravaggio (1573–1610). Caravaggio's paintings typify the Baroque style in the way that they concentrate the viewer's attention on the essential drama of the moment, ignoring or softening irrelevant surface detail and portraying the human form to correspond as closely as possible to its natural form.

Today the term Baroque is used to describe the art and culture which thrived throughout Europe from 1600–1750. This artistic movement involved three main styles. Flamboyant or operatic Baroque describes the taste of Italy and Flanders and signifies the invention of opera, which happened at the start of the century, and the overblown style of the churches built in Rome. Realistic Baroque grew from a painterly approach developed by the great European artists of the time: Caravaggio in Italy, Velázquez in Spain and Rembrandt in Holland. Classical Baroque grew from the rounded forms of art and architecture favoured

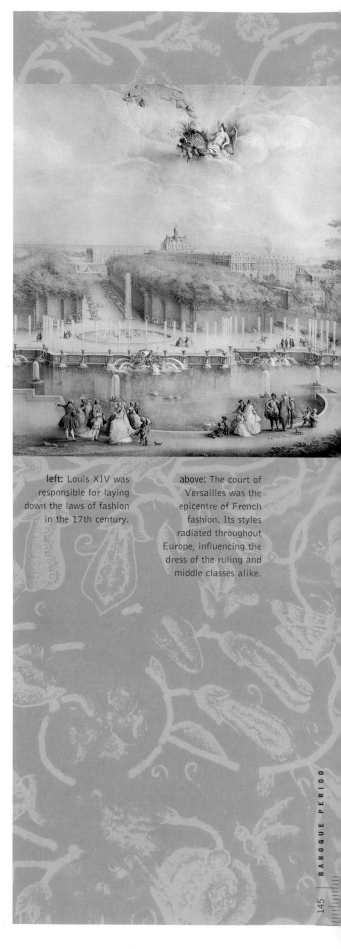

left: Louis XIV was responsible for laying down the laws of fashion in the 17th century.

above: The court of Versailles was the epicentre of French fashion. Its styles radiated throughout Europe, influencing the dress of the ruling and middle classes alike.

above: Portrait of Madame de Sévigné, one of the most famous salon organizers. Her dress, with its simple decorations, reflects the new Baroque style – more natural, sober and elegant than the extravagance of the Renaissance.

by the court of Louis XIV, as typified by the cool, severe spirit of Perrault's design for the façade of the Louvre or the entirety of Louis XIV's château at Versailles.

Built between 1660 and 1680 by Le Vau, J. Hardoin Mansard and Le Nôtre (who designed the garden), Versailles was the place to be for fashionable Europeans. Louis' court counted 10,000 permanent inhabitants: 5,000 lived at the court while an additional 5,000 serviced their needs. A continual spate of fêtes and festivals celebrated the glory of the King and were watched by throngs of his adoring public. Nancy Mitford compared the château to a glorious shop window. But Louis kept firm control of the whole situation: rigid regulations and rules of etiquette kept the court in check and spontaneity was discouraged. The whole way of life at court was a grand theatrical ritual led by the Sun King.

Court dress reflected the king's classical taste. Courtiers appeared in great, curled wigs, high heels and perfectly tailored lace-accented garments dripping with ribbons. Women at court wore lavish dresses of silk and brocade and their flowing trains were attended to by young servant boys.

Like all fashionable centres, society would eventually tire of the opulence of Versailles. But at the time, the decadent life lived by Louis and his inner circle provided Europe with aesthetic inspiration. Continental courts and nobility sought to imitate it in all its glory. England's Restoration in 1660, for example, saw Charles II return home after a decade in France to set up a court reflecting the style of the Sun King, but in a comparatively understated fashion. Exiled courtiers returned to England from France and Holland wearing European clothing, but Restoration culture remained much more pragmatic, eclectic, comfortable and even domestic, according to Douglas Russell.

But despite the overpowering reign of Louis and Europe's monarchies, the power of the new middle class must not be underestimated. A new urban, literate, merchant class developed during the 17th century and their hard work and commerce built Europe's capital cities into places of great cultural and economic force. After the Glorious Revolution of 1688, when William and Mary were invited to rule instead of Mary's father, James II, Parliament produced a bill of rights, specifically limiting the sovereign's powers over Parliament and the population. This was the early blueprint of a modern democratic system of government. Society, in general, had progressed a long way. Gone were the prevailing notions of superstition which governed everyday life. People turned to science for pragmatic answers to universal questions. By now the theories of the universe according to early scientific thinkers like Galileo, Kepler and Copernicus, as well as those of the mathematician Isaac Newton, had begun to circulate.

Women

Although they were becoming more liberated, women could still not take an active part in political or commercial life. However, women began to be encouraged to express their ideas freely with the introduction, in the 17th century, of the 'salon', a meeting of a group of like-minded people in a domestic setting. Jane Mulvagh has described salons as power bases where writers, politicians, journalists and others could hear the latest gossip, exchange

above: During the Baroque
period, women's dresses
featured two skirts. The
outer one, which normally
ended in a train, was made
of heavy material to allow
it to 'fall' better.

ideas, sharpen their wits and further their careers. Salons were usually established by rich women, like Lady Caroline Holland, Madames de Staël, de Chevreuse and de Sévigné.

Women's opinions and ideas were given increasing consideration. Philosophers such as René Descartes and Poullain de la Barre had introduced new theories on gender. Descartes proposed that the soul and the body were separate and therefore no longer dependent on biological considerations. De la Barre believed that the soul was genderless. If women were given the same education as men, he believed that their 'female vices' would fall away. Though these ideas were all hotly debated in drawing rooms and salons of the court and better households they did not penetrate every strata of society – one 17th-century male feminist stated that women should defer to their husbands not because men were always right but to keep peace in the household.

If women worked, they were paid less than men. Lesbian couples lived as husband and wife through the 17th and 18th century, although usually one of them would cross-dress as a man. Conventional marriage and child-rearing were still considered to be a woman's chief occupations. For the rich, the conditions of pregnancy began to improve. Wealthy women could have their babies delivered by a male surgeon. A better food supply meant that children survived longer, so married couples also began to exercise birth control,

COSTUME

above: The men are dressed in the cavalier style – wearing doublets, wide trousers, turned-down boots and Rubens hats adorned with feathers.

considering the size of their families and setting a limit on how many children they would like to have.

Costume

The emergence of the new middle class accelerated the pace of fashion. Richer than ever, people began to experiment with clothing and clothing styles began to cross social boundaries. And as the middle class adopted styles the upper classes enjoyed, this forced the upper classes to seek out new styles to distinguish themselves from the masses. Mila Contini notes that in just two years (between 1672 and 1674), sleeve ornaments changed at least seven times. At first they were buttoned to the wrist. Then they were turned up and featured colourful ruffs. Next followed an open sleeve which revealed the entire length of the arm. Another variation produced a sleeve which was awash with lace and ribbons and yet another which featured two circles of lace at the forearm and the wrist.

Fashion also reflected the spirit of the Baroque artistic movement: clothing – like the architecture and sculpture of the time – moved and flowed and the basic costume silhouette for both men and women became more natural, sober and elegant. Gone was the Renaissance excessive use of decoration; women wore flowing skirts unencumbered by heavy braid while their bodies were lightly adorned with simple jewellery. Comfort also

Coffee houses were popular places for men to meet and discuss the issues of the day. The men are wearing lace cravats, *justaucorps*, breeches and coloured silk stockings.

became a consideration, with the looser lace collar replacing the restricting ruff and padding gradually disappearing from men's trunk hose. Dress, in the 17th century, began to reflect an individual's personality. A client's opinions played an integral part in the making of garments.

From approximately 1650 on, French fashion dominated Europe, replacing the Spanish influence. As the Baroque style spread to the Court of Louis XIV from the middle of the 17th century, clothes – which were carefully constructed and tailored, though adorned with bows and lace – also reflected a taste for uniformity. Clothing began to be made more like a modern-day suit or ensemble. This style has been referred to as *en suite*. Unlike the mix-and-match clothing of the 16th century, a bodice, petticoat and gown would be made of the same fabric and all were meant to be worn simultaneously.

The French had also begun their unending quest to become the world's leading producers of luxury goods. The impetus behind this may originally have been financial. Cardinal Richelieu had set up a lace-making industry in Alençon, which meant that lace no longer had to be imported from Italy. Additionally, France's minister of finance from 1665, Jean Baptiste Colbert, organized the economy in a way that placed importance on exports but avoided imports, and all the raw materials for clothes worn in France were produced domestically. Lyons became the centre for the manufacture of both silk and brocade.

French fashion became exported widely throughout Europe via mannequins which were sent across the continent so that they could be viewed by other monarchs. Approximately half the size of a human and dressed to replicate the styles worn at Louis XIV's court, these dolls were made in Paris by specialists on the rue St Honoré. News of changing fashion trends – such as the new cut of a man's doublet – began to appear in the French newspapers

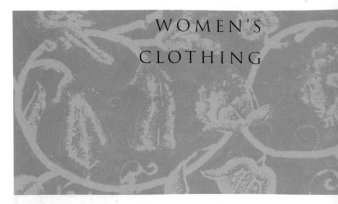
which were seen across Europe: *Le Mercure Galant*, for instance, was read in Vienna, Venice, Berlin, Madrid, London and Brussels.

The late 17th century witnessed a marked definition between men's and women's clothing. And seasonality, a theme which emerged in early Rome, began to reappear, with lighter materials favoured for summer, and soft, warm fabrics used for winter clothes. The 17th century also gave rise to the fashion designer. Under the auspices of Louis XIV, a dress-maker's guild was formed with the profession attracting men and women (before this, dresses had been made at home or by tailors). Monsieur Regnault and Monsieur Gautier became famous for their work, as did Madame Villeneuve and Madame Charpentier. They encouraged their clients to experiment with shapes, skirt lengths, materials and colours. Madame de Sévigné bragged about the work of her tailor Langlée, while Molière discussed the work of Perdigeon. The playwright Sir George Etherege gave a detailed account of the skilled makers of his character Sir Fopling Flutter's attire for a trip to London: 'The suit – Barroy; the garniture – Le Gras; the shoes – Piccar; the periwig – Chedreux.'

Women's clothing

Women's costume in the 17th century displayed a new dramatic freedom of form. The plunging neckline, which became known as the décolletage, exemplifies the fact. Gone was the heavy Spanish ruff. In keeping with Baroque principle, which stressed natural proportion and freedom of form, the upper bodice of a woman's dress now featured an expansive, open neckline displaying the heaving chest in full view. Sometimes it was covered by a lace collar.

This greater sense of sartorial freedom not only reflected new cultural taste, scientific discovery played its part in the development too. In 1628, William Harvey had discovered a new bodily function – blood circulation. His discovery was the impetus for new debate on whether the tight-fitting corset accounted for women's complaints of aches and pains, and this led eventually to the rigid wood and iron stiffeners which had been used in the making of women's clothes going out of use. A few innovations followed. The suppressing upper garments gave way to short, waisted silk jackets. The waistline of dresses rose up to reach a bodice which could be laced lightly at the front with a full skirt falling below. The stomacher was still worn, but it became shorter and less stiff. The hips were still padded but the sweeping, exaggerated shape of the farthingale had disappeared. Instead, the skirt featured underpinnings and underskirts were worn. The transition from bodice to skirt became less dramatic; in mid-century, women began to wear a busk – a metal, wooden or ivory stay which fitted snugly into the corset or the bodice of a dress to stiffen it. Sleeves became shorter, stopping at the forearm and finished off with a cascading lace cuff.

As the century progressed, women's dress became elegant and restrained. By 1670 the *robe de chambre* was introduced. A T-shaped garment, it was constructed from two pieces of fabric, a back and a front piece, and was tied at the waist with a sash. This was worn as a casual substitute to the formal gown. When it was worn with a light-fitting bodice underneath, the ensemble became known as a mantua. This outfit featured elbow-length

left: Portrait of a noblewoman by van Dyck (1599–1641). It shows the new style of the period: the plunging neckline revealing the chest, the high waistline of the full skirt and the shorter sleeves with lace cuffs.

above: Mademoiselle Fontanges was a favourite of Louis XIV. Her dress has two skirts, the outer one, featuring a train, made of heavier fabric. The colours, scarlet and dark blue, were particularly popular during the Baroque period.

cuffed sleeves and remained fashionable for another century. By 1680 its skirt had expanded and added to it was a padded roll.

Another looser-fitting dress was known as the French sack. With a silhouette influenced by a maternity gown, the sack – which was also called the *Adrienne* or the *robe volante* – was cut open in the front and cinched lightly at the waist. Underneath it could be found a hoop skirt and a bodice or negligée (at this time the term was applied to day wear rather than night-time lingerie).

At Versailles, women wore three skirts, one under the other, and the final one often featured a train so long that a page was required to walk behind and carry it. Each skirt had a name. The first that was put on was called *la fidèle*. It was decorated with ribbons and embroidered with thread in the favourite colour of the woman's beloved. The second skirt, *la frippone*, was made of gold and silver cloth. The third skirt could be called either *la modeste* or *la secrète*.

Men's clothing

Men's costume was of a quite sober style at the beginning of the 17th century. In France Henri IV wore simple clothes. He appears to have given little thought to his attire and often appeared at court in garments patched at the elbows. During his reign, 16th-century styles prevailed at court. But by the 1620s signs of change began to appear. The unstarched ruffs and the flat collar replaced the stiffened ruff, for example.

In England, Charles I, too, displayed a taste for simple, elegant clothes. His portrait painted by Anthony van Dyck in 1635 displays the point. Gone is the rich, imperious style of Henry VIII. Charles wears a wide-brimmed beaver hat, plain suede breeches, a smooth satin doublet, a lace collar, hose gartered below the knees and knee-high boots. The luxury – evident from the fine fabric of which his garments were made – and the sharp cut of each of his garments is almost anonymous and demonstrates a casual flair. The image marks the restrained beginnings of the Baroque style known as the cavalier.

Slashing proved to be a passing trend. Shirts – now of voluminous cut and cuffed at the wrist – featured a single slash down the front. Trunk hose fell below the knee so they resembled breeches, and fuller breeches began to be worn which fell loose, meeting the top of the boot at the knee.

But with the ascent of Louis XIV to the throne, particularly after 1661, men's fashion displayed a new flamboyancy. Colin McDowell has written that French fashion in the reign of Louis XIV was characterized by reckless extravagance. Men's clothes were lavish creations made of brocade, gold and silver embroidery and expensive silks. Fortunes were spent on them and good taste was swamped by the desire for magnificence. Louis XIV was considered the best-dressed man in all of Europe; his taste for fine clothes influenced monarchs and noblemen across the continent.

Nothing was considered too lavish – sometimes up to 300 ribbons could adorn a single jacket. So extreme were men's sartorial indulgences that the French government issued an edict preventing the use of gold and silver on clothes. Gold and silver was, at the time, used

MEN'S CLOTHING

left: Louis XIV had a love of lavish garments. He is shown wearing a coat, waistcoat and breeches, all of which are extravagantly embroidered with gold thread.

above: Portrait of Charles I by van Dyck (1635). This more casual style, known as the cavalier look, is far removed from the flamboyance of the French court. He is dressed in a satin doublet, breeches and knee-high boots.

both on clothes and coaches, incurring huge debts for the indulgent individuals who lavished themselves with luxury. But legislation had little effect. So violent were the protests of the artisans who made the clothes that the government was forced to repeal it.

King Charles II can take the credit for introducing Persian style to late 17th-century men's fashion. The look – a three piece suit composed of a coat, waistcoat and breeches – proved so popular that it formed the foundation of modern men's formal attire. Other innovations in men's dress included Rhinegrave breeches (wide breeches resembling modern culottes) which take their name from their place of origin, the Rhine. Outerwear included the Brandenburg greatcoat – a sweeping coat worn initially by Prussian soldiers. For the next three centuries, its design provided the model for the man's overcoat.

Textiles

Although men and women's fashion grew ever more distinct in the 17th century, clothing for both was made from much the same materials. Lace, for example, featured on the clothes of men, women and children. Children's clothes, such as bonnets, gowns and aprons, featured lace accents and women's collars were edged with lace. A fashionable type of sleeve, called *les engageants*, was made from three layers of lace, and robes and shirts made especially for bathing, were adorned with lace, as the bath itself could be.

France became the unrivalled centre of lace production in Europe. Calais, Lille, Sedan, Arras, Normandy, Le Havre, Dieppe, Rouen and Honfleur all supported thriving lace-making industries. Oise, just north of Paris, produced fine silk lace as well as lace made from metal. In addition to manufacturing silk, factories and workshops in Lyons made gold and silver lace. Jean Baptiste Colbert followed Cardinal Richelieu's lead in maintaining the lace-making industry: he had the foresight not to copy lace produced in other regions in Europe, such as fine Venetian lace, but to lead the way by producing 'French lace' – new, unseen lace designs. To do so, he consulted the highest artistic minds: Louis XIV's court painters and designers all contributed design ideas for the production of lace.

Despite French dominance, lace was still produced in other regions of Europe. Italy still manufactured it, however, demand lessened as the work produced there lacked a modern edge. Flemish lace was exported to Italy. It was sought after because of its high quality. Made from linen, it appeared in a distinctive shade of pearl-toned white.

In general, textiles were appreciated for themselves during the 17th century. Sometimes small cuts were slashed into fabrics and spangled beads were applied, but these added texture to the cloth rather than excessive decoration. When braid was used, it became less distracting by often appearing in the same colour as the cloth and embroidery featured in neat, compact clusters. Brocade was also used but to a lesser extent. However, later in the century gold and silver metallic brocades were used along with satin, velvet and lace. The sartorial ideal, Geoffrey Squires has argued, was for an ensemble to produce a total impact.

Along with lace, satin and velvet were popular fabrics in the early 17th century. People of middle and lower classes also wore garments made from wool and linen. Men's outer garments were often made from Spanish leather.

above: France became an important centre for lace production in the 17th century. Men's and women's necklines featured lace collars. This stunning example's so wide that it conceals the woman's shoulders.

Near the end of the 17th century the demand for lace decreased. Replacing its popularity was Indian muslin imported by the East India Company. Corresponding to the new seasonality apparent in the 17th-century clothes, light, printed calicoes were used for summer garments. Block printing – a technique which originated in the east and India – became a method that replicated popular Persian and oriental patterns on fabrics produced in England. Ribbons, braid and fringe came from Italy, Spain and France.

Jewellery

A taste for simple, elegant jewellery prevailed in the early 17th century. A single strand of pearls, drop-shaped diamond earrings and precious stones pinned in a neat row across a lace collar were the pieces a rich 17th-century woman would choose as accessories. Jewellery was merely part of a sartorial ensemble, enhancing the wearer's natural beauty instead of distracting from it. As France became the centre of luxury goods, the finest jewellers could now be found in Paris (instead of Florence), where they were kept busy by the French royal family, initially catering to the demands of Marie de Medici and Henri IV and then later to their grandson, Louis XIV, and Madame de Maintenon, whom he married in a secret ceremony in 1684. Madame de Maintenon considered wearing jewellery to be hugely important for a woman. She advised the Duchess of Burgundy 'to wear jewels so as to draw attention to the clearness of your skin and the neatness of your figure'.

During the 17th century the demand for pearls increased substantially. Women wore pearls through their hair, around their wrists, as simple drop earrings, pinned at their shoulders and fastened to thick strips of dark velvet around their neck. Diamonds remained popular. Supplied by Indian diamond mines, they were perfected – cut, polished and faceted – in Antwerp, Amsterdam and later, Paris. Precious and semi-precious coloured stones, such as topazes, sapphires, rubies, emeralds, turquoise and coral, became other court favourites. Rings and bracelets adorned the hands of rich women. At the beginning of the century, Flanders produced stunning rings of enamel and gold. Popular for women at the Spanish court was the cluster style of ring. Made of several precious and non-precious stones, it could be worn on the index finger or attached to the wrist with a black ribbon.

Only royalty and the fabulously wealthy could afford to wear jewels, and some did so to excessive proportions. Madame de Maintenon, for example, explained that the collapse of the Duchess de Maine was due to the weight of gold and gems she had adorning her hair. Women of all classes often made do with fake jewellery – the best of which was made in Spain. Anne of Austria wore fake ruby earrings, and jewellery in England was made from crystal which was mined in Cornwall and near Bristol.

Make-up and grooming

Smells – from foul to pleasant scents – are always associated with the 17th century. Water, it was believed, was harmful for the skin, so most people avoided bathing very often. Instead, they thought that they could diminish unpleasant body odour by applying friction to the skin (by rubbing the body with dry towels) and changing their clothes frequently:

MAKE-UP
AND GROOMING

above: Portrait of Madame de Maintenon who believed jewellery was a very important part of a woman's appearance. She is seen wearing a single string of pearls and simple drop earrings.

MAKE-UP AND GROOMING

above: Hairdressers became prominent in the 17th century. This elegantly dressed barber indicates that he had a fairly high standing in society. Men were clean-shaven at this time, only the court elite were permitted to wear a moustache.

right: Portrait of a woman at her dressing table. Pearls are prominent, she has them in her hair and there are strings of them in her jewellery box. A perfume bottle can be seen on the table – pefume was widely used by men and women alike to disguise body odour.

wearing a clean white shirt, some people believed, would serve to absorb sweat and dirt from the skin.

Perfume was another substitute for cleanliness. To disguise body odour people wore pomanders, made from ambergris and benzoin, fastened to belts and neck chains. They also carried sweet bags – purses made from light silk taffeta in which scented powder and perfume sachets were placed. Some stately English homes featured distilling rooms where perfumes were made and bottled and in some households, servants were employed solely to scent rooms.

Scent was used on the body and as medicine. Aromatic lozenges were sucked to clean the teeth. Under the guidance of Colbert, France established a thriving fragrance industry. Louis XIV surrounded himself with pleasant smells at Versailles. The perfumer Maritial, a court favourite, had his own chambers to mix scents. Orange-flower water gushed from fountains and scented cushions were scattered throughout the palace.

Both men and women used scented handkerchiefs and wore scented gloves. According to Susan Irvine, everything – from pet dogs, snuff and tobacco to precious stones – was scented with heavy fragrances of spices, musk and ambergris.

In terms of make-up, face patches, introduced in the 16th century, continued to be popular facial adornments for women and men. Made of velvet and silk, patches came in different sizes and shapes such as circles, diamonds, stars and crescents. They were carried in the handbag or kept in specially designed boxes. Like other cosmetics, patches were sold by travelling salesmen.

Make-up was worn by both men and women throughout Europe during the 17th century but it was frowned upon by both the clergy and influential thinkers. Full, red lips, dark, groomed eyebrows and clear, bright eyes were the desired feminine ideal. But for once, blonde hair went out of fashion, in favour of either black or brown hair.

Women, during the time of Louis XIII, often wore their hair in tight, neat plaits. A popular hairstyle was launched by Mademoiselle de Fontanges – a favourite of Louis XIV. On a hunt with the king, she appeared with a glorious coiffure adorned with feathers and ribbons. While on horseback, her hair became tousled so she simply tied it up with a silk ribbon or a garter. From that moment on, women at court tied up their curls – which had fallen to the shoulders until then – in a similar fashion which became known, appropriately, as a *Fontanges*. The style reached great heights falling in tiered ruffles which were fastened to a wire frame. These could add 15–20cm (6–8in) to a woman's height. Meanwhile, young women wore their hair in soft, loose curls which fell about an inch below the ears.

Just as fashion designers rose to prominence in the 17th century, so did hairdressers, causing consternation among the clergy, who threatened to excommunicate women who allowed their hair to be styled by men.

Men wore their hair long. Louis XIII introduced the love lock – the practice of tying a curl or a strand of hair with a ribbon as a symbol of affection given by a man to a woman. But by 1660 men had begun, like women, to wear wigs. In England, by 1665, most men had started to wear wigs. For Queen Margot of France, who was bald, a wig was a

necessity. Louis XIV, who had a full head of hair, wore wigs to increase his height. He popularized the peruke – a towering, peaked, voluminously curled wig – a fashion that lasted for at least another century. Colbert picked up on the growing popularity of wigs, imposing a tax on the trade. Imported hair was used to make wigs – which appeared in natural hair shades – but a profit was made by their export. Louis XIV was also clean-shaven, which set another precedent for men across the continent.

Footwear

High heels were a 17th-century invention. Before that time, soldier's riding boots featured heels, but these served the function of keeping the foot secure in a stirrup. But when men began to incorporate the boot into their daily attire, the heel became a permanent feature, and both men and women began to wear high-heeled shoes. As Geoffrey Squire has written, this new sense of elevation, initiated by the heel, suited the 17th century's Baroque spirit: the altered posture fell in line with the flowing lines and affected manners of the period.

Heels, it seems, made a man feel important. Louis XIV, who was short, sometimes wore shoes with 12.5-cm (5-in) heels. He had a marked preference for high, red leather heels and this fashion caught on with his courtiers and also spread to England. James II wore high-heeled, red leather shoes as did the men of his court. The 17th century also saw the introduction of the decorative shoe. Louis XIII is believed to have introduced shoe roses made from ribbon and stiffened lace (which appear in Rembrandt's portrait of Marten Soolmans). Pom-poms also adorned shoes worn by royalty and the rich.

Until the 17th century, men's and women's shoes were of similar design. But, as the century progressed, the design of shoes for both sexes began to diverge: women's shoes were simple in design compared to the lavish – some might say pompous – creations men wore. Women wore mules and slippers made from satin and silk. Boots – a symbol of masculinity – were worn more often by men than women, who wore them only when riding.

Bags

Purses and pouches were used by men and women throughout the century. There were several styles and each served a specific function. Sweet bags, as discussed earlier, were used to infuse a pleasant smell around their owner. There were also bags designed specifically to cater to the trend of gaming, which had become a leisure pursuit of the rich. Dice, counters and cards were all kept inside drawstring pouches. Another type of game bag was the sporran – a small leather pouch carried by Scottish Highlanders. A sporran used by James I is today a part of the Burrell Collection, near Glasgow. Pouches were also used by the elderly to carry their daily necessities. Women carried drawstring handbags. But rather than display their use they hid them under their skirts. Inside they kept useful items such as a fan, a compact mirror, a watch and perhaps a few needlework tools. Men also hid their pouch in the deep pockets which became a feature of 17th-century breeches.

Bags were often exchanged by people as gifts. And, again, France produced the finest items made from woven silk, brocade, silver thread, silver metal mesh and embroidery.

left: This 17th-century tapestry purse depicts birds, squirrels and flowers made of coloured silks and metallic threads. It is a drawstring purse that may have been used to carry cards and counters for gaming, or perhaps perfume.

above: High-heeled shoes appeared for the first time in the 17th century. They were often of ankle height (as here) and could feature decoration such as ribbons, lace and roses.

BAGS

Some featured embroidered inscriptions such as 'Voilà mon trésor' ('Here is my treasure') and 'Au plus fidèle' ('To the most faithful').

Gloves and muffs

Gloves were worn for decorative reasons rather than for a functional purpose. Made from leather, satin, velvet or silk, their gauntlets could be decorated with gold and silver thread as well as featuring spangled beads and embroidery. Gloves included in the Victoria & Albert Museum's costume collection bear intricate embroidery of flowers such as borage, pinks and lilies as well as motifs of insects, fruits and foliage. Seed pearls, ribbon and lace were other decorative materials used on gloves. Ann Hart and Susan North have noted that through the century the design of the glove altered as both the gauntlet and fingers became shorter. Gloves were also perfumed.

Both men and women wore muffs to protect their hands from the cold. Made of various sizes and shapes, men preferred small muffs while sometimes women's muffs were large enough to conceal their lapdogs. The origin of the muff can be traced back to 15th-century Venice, where they were a favourite accessory of courtesans. Louis XIV made the muff a popular accessory for men. His muffs were made of exotic skins – tiger, panther, otter and beaver. Muffs for women were also made from bead-flecked silk and brocade, lined with fur, and could be fastened together with crystal and gold buttons.

Ties and cravats

The origin of the tie can be traced back to approximately 1650. Bands, cravats and a neck cloth known as the *steinkirk* (it takes its name from the 1692 battle of Steenkirk in Flanders) all became an intricate part of the attire worn by the distinguished 17th-century man. Neckwear was considered an important wardrobe item because its proximity to the face enhanced the natural good looks of the wearer. Initially, 'band' was a generic term applied to any neckwear that was not a ruff. The cravat – a folded strip of fabric wrapped around the neck – came to Paris via Croatia, but opinions on its origin vary. Some fashion historians believe that the cravat was directly introduced by the Croatians or that it was a style picked up by French officers from Croatian troops during the Thirty Years War. Some cravats featured bows, while others were tied in a knot. Cravats were often made of French and Venetian lace. By the 1680s the popularity of the heavy look of the lace cravat had diminished and it was replaced by a trimmed neck cloth. In comparison to the cravat it was of simple design – a long narrow strip of linen or muslin with lace or fringe at the ends that could be tied once around the neck in a loose knot. The neck cloth became known as a steinkirk once the ends were twisted together and tucked neatly into a buttonhole.

Hats and head-dresses

By 1690 the tricorne – a three-cornered broad-brimmed hat featuring plumes – appeared and remained a fashionable addition to a man's appearance for another 100 years.

above: Portrait of William of Orange showing the use of muffs by gentlemen in the 17th century. He is also wearing a *steinkirk*, a scarf-like cravat, with one end tucked through a buttonhole.

right: These two gentleman are lavishly dressed in richly decorated doublets and breeches. One of them is holding a pair of satin gloves, worn more for decorative than practical reasons.

EIGHTEENTH

THE ROCOCO

CENTURY

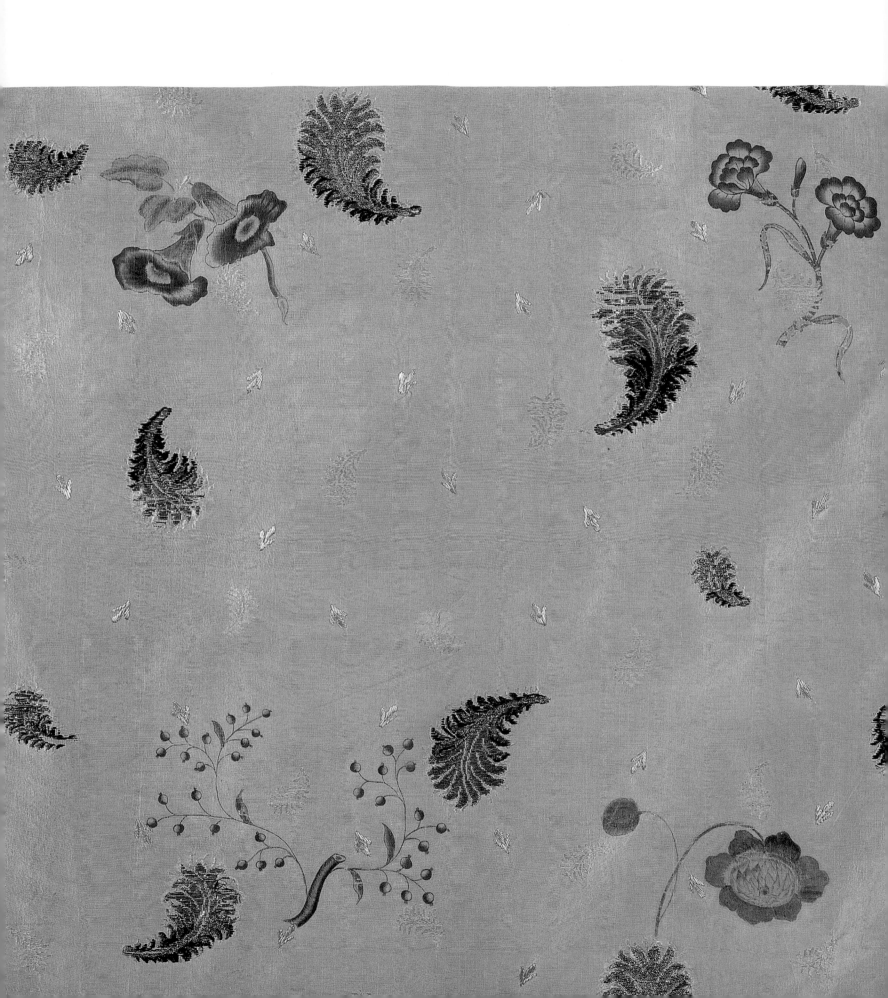

Background

The beginning of the 18th century saw Europe at war once again. The War of the Spanish Succession (1701–14) involved just about every country in Europe. In France, Louis XIV reigned at Versailles and France was at the height of its power. But as the century progressed change was on the horizon.

Industry and global trade thrived but this was in no way due to the input of European monarchs or the nobility. Across the Continent, an urban middle class or bourgeoisie was making things happen. In France, the sphere of influence for art, culture and fashion shifted from Versailles to Paris. There, in salons and *hotels particuliers*, the intelligentsia mingled with the upwardly mobile, discussing philosophy and world news.

As the bourgeoisie rose to a new position of influence, out went the imperialist style of Baroque. It was replaced by Rococo, a sumptuous style which influenced interior design, fashion and architecture between 1715 and 1775. Derived from the French word 'rocaille' (meaning 'rockery' or 'shell encrustation'), Rococo (sometimes referred to as 'Louis Quinze') championed ornament, sinuous scrolls and curvaceous shapes. Just as the Baroque influenced the dress of Louis XIV's court and European sartorial style, Rococo extended its reach to fashion. Throughout Louis XV's reign the global textile trade thrived. Ribbons, lace, ruffles, ruchings, silk flowers and butterflies decorated the costume of the rich.

As Louis XV settled in to his new position as monarch, his affair with Madame de Pompadour flourished. It was her taste for the Rococo – the art of François Boucher, painted in pretty pastels, chinoiserie décor, and the porcelain produced at Sèvres (a factory she set up in 1736 to produce French china in the 'Saxon' style) – that transformed the look of Versailles and swept through the drawing rooms of Europe and beyond.

Until the French Revolution, the world still looked to France for aesthetic inspiration. Spain, Italy and Portugal had fallen on hard times. More prosperous were the Germanic principalities of Austria, Prussia and Russia. Amid the War of Austrian Succession, Prussia captured Silesia and set her sights on Vienna. Maria Theresa, empress of Austria and queen of Hungary (and the mother of Marie Antoinette), defended her land by forming an alliance with Russia and the Bourbons. Her autonomy became stronger later when her daughter married Louis XVI and became queen of France. Meanwhile, Peter the Great, the czar of Russia, elevated his country to new ranks of global prominence, and encouraged his subjects to adopt western dress. His successor, Catherine the Great, would pick up where he left off. Frederick the Great had transformed Prussia into a world power. A Francophile, he rewarded himself with the palace of Sans Souci at Potsdam, his answer to Versailles.

During the 18th century England rose to become a world power. The American colonies had made the English rich and soon Canada was won from France. India was England's next conquest. Buckingham House – designed by William Winde in 1702 for the Duke of Buckingham – was acquired for £28,000 in 1762 by George III king of England, becoming his official London residence. In 1820, the architect John Nash was commissioned by George IV to design a new palace on the land. But since its original acquisition in the 18th century, Buckingham Palace has served as the official residence of the British monarchy.

UNITÉ
INDIVISIBILITÉ
DE LA
RÉPUBLIQUE
LIBERTÉ
ÉGALITÉ
FRATERNITÉ

OU LA

MORT

left: This bodice of a braided silk jacket with its whimsical pattern of leaves and flowers, *Pet en l'aire*, reflects the sinuous feel of the reigning 18th-century style, Rococo.

above: The French Revolution was one of the most significant events of the 18th century. As the bourgeoisie rose to prominence, it's influence on the fashion of the time became stronger.

BACKGROUND

above: After the French Revolution, fashion became a political issue. Here Louis Leopold Boilly (1761–1845) captures the singer Chenard, a 'Sans Culotte' (1792). He is wearing a bicorne hat with cockade, a striped waistcoat with a jabot and a jacket.

Across the Atlantic, the American colonies had organized a new society and with it, a profitable pioneering lifestyle. By 1776, the United States declared independence, liberating their new nation from what they saw as the outmoded rule of George III.

The latter half of the 18th century saw the Age of Enlightenment dawn upon the world. A cultural movement of Germanic origin, the philosophy of Enlightenment championed reason over authority. The philosopher Voltaire (born François Marie Arouet) was its principal thinker in France and one of the founders of the French *Encyclopédie*, which was published in 1751 with the aim of bringing knowledge to the people. Voltaire's ideas were promoted in the courts of Frederick the Great of Prussia and Catherine the Great. Twice he was jailed because of his revolutionary theories, which attacked France's Ancien Régime. Underlying his essays, poems and plays was the theme '*Ecrasez l'infame*' (crush the abuses). Voltaire's targets were those in power: the leaders of the church, government and society's elite. With the Swiss-born French philosopher Jean-Jacques Rousseau – whose *Social Contract* (1762) stipulated that 'man is born free, and is everywhere in chains' – Voltaire helped sow the seeds of foment that led to the French Revolution.

Though Marie Antoinette advocated Rousseau and the freethinking philosophy of the times, she miscalculated its impact. While she toiled at the *Hameau*, her garden paradise at Versailles, the '*sans culottes*' – labourers and peasants – were revolting on the streets of Paris. In May 1789 Louis XVI gathered the Estates General (the French equivalent to a parliament) at Versailles invoking sumptuary laws which stipulated that nobles, clergy and the Third Estate (commoners) were to adopt 'appropriate dress'. His approach was top-down: nobles were to wear gold and brocades, white stockings and plumed hats; the clergy, purple robes, and the Third Estate, a dark, dreary uniform. It was a feeble attempt to control the situation. Six weeks later, the demands of the Third Estate – the need for fair taxation was one of several grievances – had overcome the monarchy, and in ten violent years France was transformed from an absolute monarchy into a republic. Louis XVI and Marie Antoinette were both beheaded. All churches were shut, and the property sold to benefit the state. The light, airy and lavish Rococo ideals which saw in the century were replaced by the gruff, practical and independent age of the Revolution.

Women

In the 18th century, women were able to achieve much greater autonomy. Rose Bertin was one of the more famous examples of the new breed of increasingly liberated 18th-century woman. She was Marie Antoinette's couturier and on terms with royalty, yet merely the daughter of a provincial policeman. In the 16th and 17th centuries, only the wives and daughters of some rich and powerful men could live their own lives. During the 18th century, however, as women became increasingly independent of men and their money, even women further down the social scale were able to move into such areas as running their own businesses, creating salons and writing books.

Empress Maria Theresa (1717–80) inherited the thrones of Hungary and Bohemia, served as the archduchess of Austria when her father Charles VI died in 1740, and successfully defended her subjects from the rest of Europe during both the Austrian War of Succession (1740–8) and the Seven Years War (1756–63). She shared none of her daughter's, Marie Antoinette's, sartorial concerns nor her taste for frivolity — her chief occupation was running the state.

Maria Theresa was not known for her beauty (as she aged, people called her 'the fat one'), and her husband, the Holy Roman Emperor Franz I (1708–65), strayed. After his death she warned a confidante against marrying a man who has nothing to do. Dress at her court was grand but prescribed: men wore a red coat with a gold gilet underneath, and women wore a red gown with gold and silver embroidery and lace trimming. The society over which Maria Theresa ruled was divided into five classes and each echelon was identifiable by their attire, which was set by the court.

German-born Catherine the Great (1729–96) became empress of Russia after her husband, Peter III, was murdered by one of his lovers, and reigned for 34 years. She was, in her own words, a self-made woman, and succeeded in expanding the Russian Empire, annexing sizeable territory in Poland in 1772. A liberal thinker but a conservative, not to say repressive, ruler, she was patron to both Diderot and Voltaire. Although Peter the Great looked to France for aesthetic inspiration, Catherine disliked its frivolity.

Conditions were more primitive in her beloved Russia than in western Europe. While on journey as a young woman, she was forced to camp out in tents, walk through puddles and dress herself in the kitchen. But when she ascended to the throne, things changed, including her attitude towards extravagance. Catherine the Great built palaces, country houses, parks, schools and hospitals in St Petersburg and Moscow and encouraged the education of the middle classes. She collected art, sculpture, jewellery and carpets, buying them from private collections across Europe.

Just like Diane de Poitiers in the 16th century, Madame de Pompadour, born Jeanne-Antoinette Poisson (1721–64), became the mistress of the king of France and, in doing so, the most famous French courtesan. Louis XV first saw the marquise while out hunting. After a lavish masked ball held at Versailles (such occasions were open to the public, the only stipulation was that guests were well dressed) — at which the marquise was disguised as the huntress Diana — she was installed at the palace as the king's official mistress.

At Versailles, the king gave her free reign to decorate as she saw fit. He also gave her several properties, including châteaux at Montretout, La Celle, Bellevue and Crécy. Louis also paid for her mansions at Versailles and in the Champs Elysées as well as hermitages at Versailles, Fontainebleau and Compiègne. Hers was a taste for the Rococo and its influence spread beyond the court through France. She commissioned the artist Boucher to decorate her residence at Bellevue, where he created a massive garden of perfumed china flowers. To counter the influence of the porcelain factory at Meissen — established earlier in the century by Augustus the Strong of Saxony — Madame de Pompadour established another, near Bellevue, at Sèvres. She had a passionate interest in the production of Sèvres porcelain. She provided it with models and instructed artists like Boucher to offer designs for the production to the Sèvres workmen. 'Pompadour pink' was created there for her. The

above: Portrait of Antoine Laurent de Lavoisier, French chemist, and his wife, by Jacques Louis David (1788). The manner in which de Lavoisier is looking up to his wife indicates, in a small way, the higher social standing women enjoyed in the 18th century.

marquise was also influential in affairs of state – Louis consulted her upon the nomination of ambassadors, among other matters.

Excessive extravagance was the most prominent trait associated with the last French queen, Marie Antoinette (1755–93). Her toilette bill alone amounted to 258,000 livres in one year. Thanks to Rose Bertin, her couturier, she became the leader of French fashion. 'Marie Antoinette preferred the title Queen of Fashion to that of Queen of France,' a lady at court said. She had married Louis XVI at the age of 15. At first he failed to consummate the marriage, so Marie Antoinette pursued pleasure elsewhere at fashionable Parisian salons, casinos, horse races and masked balls. But her independence was condemned. Her brother, Emperor Joseph II, eventually instructed the king on how to consummate the marriage, and soon the couple became the parents of two daughters and a son. For a while Marie Antoinette devoted herself to motherhood, but her self-restraint was short-lived. In 1785 she became involved in the scandal remembered as 'the Queen's Necklace'. She accepted as a gift from the Cardinal de Rohan, a necklace called a *rivière*. An engraving has revealed that it was a collar made up of 17 diamonds from which four diamond pendants hung as well as three festoons. Attached to this was another double *rivière* featuring four diamond tassels. But the necklace never adorned the queen's neck: its stones (it is said that there were 500 diamonds involved in its design), were sold off by the husband of de Rohan's mistress. When the fraud was discovered, the cardinal was arrested and Marie Antoinette suffered guilt by association. By this time the monarchy was close to bankruptcy and her reputation never recovered. Eight years later she was dead, guillotined before an applauding mob.

The French Revolution added momentum to the women's movement. Some women made public political speeches while others joined the army. In *Declaration of the Rights of Women*, Olympe de Gouges insisted that just as all men were equals women should be included among the ranks. But revolutionary men thought differently. A good female citizen was a woman who stayed home and looked after the children.

Costume

Just as history was changed irrevocably in the 18th century by the American and French Revolutions, men's and women's clothing, against this tumultuous backdrop, experienced a radical shift. The styles purveyed in France during the 18th century proved to be exceedingly influential. The fashionable world followed the example of dress set by Paris, and 20th-century designers including Christian Dior, Karl Lagerfeld, Vivienne Westwood, Jean-Paul Gaultier and the late Gianni Versace all derived inspiration from women's 18th-century sartorial styles. Karl Lagerfeld's spring/summer 1985 collection for Chanel featured a suit inspired and adapted from Antoine Watteau's painting, *Pierrot* (1718–19).

Until about 1675 clothing had been made for well-to-do men and women by tailors, or by servants, but from that date, rich people had their clothes made by dress designers and dress-makers. A woman's dress-maker was known as a mantua maker, after the mantua, the loose, everyday type of women's dress. Most mantua makers were women. In London,

left: Marie Antoinette was known for her sartorial extravagance. The ellipse-shaped skirt, adorned with ribbons, lace and artificial flowers was indicative of the Rococo style. Ball dress was always accompanied by a flamboyant coiffure.

above: During the 18th century, the rich commissioned dress-makers, such as the elegant one pictured here delivering her work, to make their clothes.

COSTUME

above: A French aristocrat is shown choosing fabrics chez Bertin, one of the most prestigious dress-makers of her time.

right: Portrait of Madame Seriziat by Jacques Louis David (c 1795). She is wearing a simple muslin gown, tied at the waist with a sash – a style introduced by Rose Bertin.

the mantua maker would work either from her own shop, her home or at the client's home. Some spent a day or, in some cases, up to a week at the client's residence, making or altering the clothing for the entire family. Clients often bought their own clothing materials in a shop or haberdasher, which were found in London and large towns in England. Travelling salespeople and markets provided fabric and other necessities to people living in small towns.

For a family with limited means sewing was still a housewife's job. It was up to her to repair and patch worn clothes and to make items like underwear and linen for the entire family. Because of the physical strength needed to pull them into shape, corsets – which women wore through the 18th and 19th centuries – were made by men. But in corset factories, the lighter labour was performed by women.

In France, 'the maitresse couturière' had carved a niche within the dress-making trade, providing garments for women. Milliners, too, began to move in on the previously male-dominated tailors' business. Fashion historians credit Rose Bertin for elevating the milliner from being a mere dress-maker to the more prestigious occupation of a fashion designer. Until Bertin's appearance, most fashion designers were seamstresses working in anonymity, but Bertin recognized the benefits fame by association could bring and soon she became a rigorous self-promoter, offering her services to society ladies. It was not long before she assumed a prestigious dual role, as both the queen's dress designer and Paris's Ministre de la Mode. Rose Bertin was a shrewd businesswoman; she set up and chaired an organization of fashion tradespeople. She also provided the forerunner of the designer label: from her time onward custom-made garments began to feature the monogram of the designer who made them.

Although her creations for Marie Antoinette corresponded to the frilly Rococo style, Bertin is thought to have introduced the masculine-inspired redingote gown – originally an English style – as well as the relatively simple muslin sashed gown to the French woman's wardrobe. Elegant women who learned of her work flocked to her shop on rue St Honoré. Among them were Madame Polignac and Madame de Guiche. But her self-assured style inspired jealousy among her colleagues (Mademoiselle Picot sued her after an encounter at Versailles when Bertin spat in her face), and rankled some of her grand female clients. 'Mademoiselle Bertin,' commented Baroness d'Oberkirch, 'seemed to me an extraordinary person, full of her own importance and treating princesses as equals.' The Revolution forced Bertin – like many other middle-class shop keepers and prominent designers who were left without a market for luxury goods – to flee Paris as the Revolution ruined the French fashion industry temporarily. The death of Andre Scheling, a tailor whose talent and direction Lyons textile manufacturers relied upon for guidance, caused a public sensation and brought the nation's fashion industry to a standstill. Meanwhile, Bertin landed in Vienna. But she then moved on and settled in London, only to discover that the Revolution proved to be a great leveller – she found that some of her former clients had become milliners, seamstresses and even servants.

above: *L'Enseigne de Gersaint* by Jean Watteau (1720). The pink dress on the left was known as the Watteau gown – a loose dress with a stomacher, plunging neckline and full underskirt. The woman on the left is wearing a street dress with laced bodice.

Women's clothing

Through much of the 18th century until the Revolution, for women, a distinct silhouette evolved, based on panniers – wide metallic hoops on which dresses spread out sideways from the hips (as much as 150cm (60in) at their greatest extent). Wide panniers were used for formal dress while smaller panniers were worn at home. The pannier was constructed by a series of three metal hoops, one placed over another, sewn to the material of the skirt and held in place by another hoop around the waist. Later, the pannier was made of two hoops and was fastened into place with a belt. Eventually the discomfort of panniers, and the way they made movement in such places as theatre boxes and coaches difficult, contributed to the outmoding of the style. Meanwhile, the waist, clenched in a corset, appeared slimmer than was natural and the décolletage plunged to reveal the crease of the bosom. The long skirt parted in the middle, revealing an underskirt and petticoat.

The look was captured by Watteau, a student of Rubens, who created lavish scenes of Parisian life in his paintings. *L'Enseigne de Gersaint* (1720–21), a shop sign commissioned by the art dealer Gersaint to rename his shop from *Au Grand Monarque* to *A La Pagode*, typifies the look. The canvas is dominated by Watteau's usual subjects: refined men in day suits, a woman reclined, revealing a plunging décolletage, while another, with her back

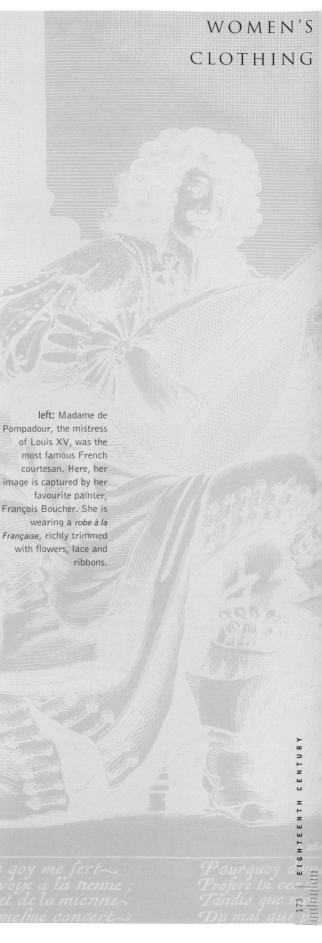

turned, wears powdered grey hair and a loose pink satin sack dress.

Watteau's work reveals the spirit of elegance which dominated the costume of the Regency and the Rococo, so much so that his name was applied to styles of women's dress. The Watteau gown, which appears in pink satin in Gersaint's sign, was a mainstay of the fashionable woman's wardrobe of the period. This loose dress, with a plunging neckline and a stomacher adorned with ribbons, was worn over a snug-fitting bodice and a full underskirt. At the back, folds fell from the shoulders to the hem of its floor-length skirt, obliterating a waistline. These folds became known as the Watteau fold, a style which remained a popular feature of 18th-century women's dress. The Watteau sacque – a gown designed for wearing at home – featured a hip-length blouson that opened at the front to display a stomacher, while pleats travelled down the back uninterrupted.

Madame de Pompadour was frequently spied in an elegant *robe à la Française* – a lavish style which reflected, in its superfluous trimmings, the prevailing taste for the Rococo. This complex creation featured a corseted waist and a panniered skirt. Its bodice was cut with a downward point, a plunging 'V' or square neckline and was trimmed with a border of pleated lace which was flirtatiously called '*tatez-y*' ('touch here'). Its overskirt was spread wide, opening in the front to display an underskirt. This was fastened to the bodice and

above: Marie Antoinette
in the Trianon park
(c 1775). She is shown
here wearing a simple
style of dress with a blue
redingote over the top.

featured *les garnements*, a border embroidered and decorated with frill, braid and flowers. Credit for Madame de Pompadour's dresses can not go solely to her dress-maker. Like the women of her time she picked the materials as well as the trimmings which adorned her lavish frocks.

Boucher's portraits of Madame de Pompadour reveal the styles of Rococo court dress which were worn by women in the mid-18th century. A typical court gown had slim sleeves that stopped just above the elbows with flared ruffles of lace, which could feature a few decorative touches: a lace bow or a sprig of fake flowers. Another ruffle appeared at the neckline and more bows and fabric covered a low-cut corset, which was known as the *modestie*. The skirt was open to reveal a *jupe* underneath it. The *jupe* involved more richly decorative touches such as flowers, ruffles and lace. With time, such a lavish style of female dress gave way to more practical styles like the negligée, a dress that was an all-in-one bodice and skirt. The actress Dancourt is said to have launched the style when she appeared in the play *Adrienne*. From this point on the negligée was often alternatively referred to as the *adrienne*.

The *robe à l'Anglaise* demonstrated the pre-revolutionary taste for English sartorial style. A short-cut, wide-lapelled, long-sleeved jacket was inspired by a man's redingote. A horse-hair underskirt replaced the cumbersome panniers and a tiny pillow that accentuated the size of a woman's backside – the *cul de Paris* – was fastened to the back underneath the skirt. The dress itself was made up of a form-fitting bodice, constructed on whalebone, that fitted snugly around the body. From this fell a skirt with a hem cut longer in the back, forming a train. Tied at the neck was a masculine-style *jabot*, a lace-trimmed, linen scarf which completed the look.

The fashion *à la Polonaise* was another prominent 18th-century female fashion style. The term was coined while France was at war with Poland and it applied to a robe or a gown which featured a draped skirt cut to reveal a petticoat underneath. This, an ankle-length walking skirt, was a comparatively practical style, often paired with heeled walking shoes and a caraco, a jacket made of soft silk.

Marie Antoinette hated wearing corsets and during her time hoop skirts disappeared. Women wore skirts which fell in soft pleats. When pregnant, she adopted a straight, loose-sashed dress known as *à la Levite*, which was inspired by costumes in a production of *Athalie* at the Théatre Française. From that moment on both men and women at court dressed in a similar fashion.

Her model farm, the *Petite Trianon*, inspired a new range of clothes. Simplicity soon became the new theme; white the *au courant* colour. Corresponding to it were the *chemise à la reine* and the negligée, made of muslin and Indian cotton.

Fashion was on the path of informality to which the Revolution added even more momentum. Already, peasant women had evolved their own simple style of dress: a bodice, fitted jacket and loose pleated skirt, often with a tricolour motif. The *negligée à la patriote* – a royal blue redingote worn over a white dress and red and white striped collar – was worn by women who took up the cause. Meanwhile, royalists dressed in black. The

left: These three women
are dressed in the fashion
à la Polonaise which was
popular towards the end
of the 18th century. The
ankle-length skirt was
practical for walking.

Revolution did away with clothes of silk, velvet and brocade and liberated women from restrictive clothes: corsets, panniers, tall powdered wigs, high heels, beauty spots and ribbons all disappeared.

Increasingly, austerity dominated women's fashion. Fashion had become a political issue and increasingly styles became more democratic. Women bought fabrics called 'Equality', 'Liberty' and 'Republican' and named their children after revolutionary ideas or people: République, Civilisation or Marat. As the boutiques on rue St Honoré shut, new shops selling ready-to-wear clothing opened – a trend followed in other European cities. Fashion

above: A scene from *The Suspicious Husband* by Francis Hayman, c 1747. The costumes used in this theatrical display show the hooped skirt to its full extent. The man is wearing a green velvet coat, decorated with silver thread.

was now established according to the wishes of a bourgeoisie anxious not to associate themselves with the Ancien Régime.

A green and white striped silk and linen *robe à la Française* (1770–80, a part of the collection of the Costume Institute in New York) depicts the change in women's dress. This dress features a more fluid skirt which has been tucked up through the pockets, a technique known in French as *retrousée dans les poches*. This idea, Richard Martin observed, corresponded to the philosophy of freedom and love of nature preached by Rousseau.

The Duchess of York in England launched a style which predated the Empire line. While pregnant she wore a false stomach, in effect, moving the *cul de Paris* from the back of the silhouette to its front. Once introduced to Paris from England, the look was adopted by both girls and expectant mothers. Fashion also took inspiration from older styles. Simple Grecian and Roman-inspired dresses – *à la Vestale* and *à la Diane* – arrived by the time of David's Directoire at the beginning of the 19th century. The light, flowing chemise dress and long linen, cotton and muslin tunics became popular.

Men's clothing

The 18th-century man was dressed in a waistcoat, or *gilet*, and breeches. The waistcoat was the decorative element of a man's wardrobe. Often made from damask, satin or velvet, it featured pockets, long sleeves, delicate embroidery, showing landscapes, flowers or animals, and gold, silver or enamel buttons. Only a few of the top buttons were fastened, leaving the waistcoat open, revealing the lace-collared shirt underneath. This collar – or *jabot* – was tied like a scarf. Breeches stopped short at the knee, where they were met with white silk stockings done up with laces. A man's collarless coat, a *justaucorps*, fitted closely to the body (the waist appeared slimmer because some men wore a corset underneath their garments), and flared slightly into a semi-circle at the hips (the tails might be stiffened with whalebone), with a slit running from the waist down to open the coat at the back. The coat was often lined with silk in a colour that matched the waistcoat.

In France, Louis XV was the only man permitted to wear a cloak of brocade. He stylized the garment by lifting one shoulder so that his costume underneath could be seen. Louis' attire was lavish. His breeches billowed, his stockings were made of silk and his shoes of the finest leather.

Men's clothing for much of the 18th century was dominated by English style. Lace and ribbon were considered frivolous in England so the lace *jabot* was replaced by a black silk tie. Next a white muslin scarf was tied at the neck. An Englishman's waistcoat was cut of coloured silk and stopped short at the waist, where it fell in two points.

The *frac* – a man's coat – fell to mid-calf and featured long, slim sleeves. Pale green, pale yellow or sometimes black, the *frac* also featured in the Italian man's wardrobe, where it was called *goldoniana*. By the end of the century, breeches were held up with braces. Breeches progressed down the leg so that they covered the knee and were met by stockings. By 1730 men had stopped wearing stockings under their breeches.

Although men's dress as a whole became more sober during the 18th century, groups of eccentrics emerged. The Macaronis surfaced by 1770 in England. They were young Englishmen fresh from their European Grand Tour, whose sartorial style had been affected by time spent in Italy. The Macaronis wore frilled collars, and soon a fringed lace cravat bore their name. To draw attention to themselves in the street, they wore iron heel clips which clinked while they walked. Their style was overtly feminine and fashion historians speculate that their extreme dress not only marked, but reaction against it caused, the end of the foppish male as a commonplace sight.

Les Incroyables were another rebel fashion group who appeared after the Revolution in France. They wore gold earrings, low shoes (which hardly covered the heels and toes of their feet) and breeches which were tied at the bottom with bright coloured ribbons. They had no political agenda. Fashion historians have brushed them off as a privileged group of young men who were acting up and never really represented the costume of their time.

After the Revolution, men's clothes – which now took their cue from English riding clothes instead of French frippery – moved closer to modern styles and became more sober. Gone were the silk knee breeches. Instead, an increasing number of men opted for ankle-

above: This image shows a member of *Les Incroyables*, a rebellious French fashion group that emerged after the Revolution. The broad cravat almost covering the mouth, the flowered waistcoat and the knee stockings with tassels are all items characteristic of their costume.

above: This Oberkampf
Toile de Jouy (c 1797),
bleached cotton printed
with engraved copper
plates depicts an array of
rural past times.

length trousers and pantaloons. Woollen frock coats, short waistcoats, stiff collars and folded socks were other wardrobe staples.

Jacques Louis David

Although the early paintings of David (1748–1825), display a tendency for the Rococo, he cast aside the frivolous style and became the leading artist of the French Revolution. A one-time protégé of Louis XVI, David became a Jacobin and a follower of Robespierre. He voted for the King's death and painted Marie Antoinette on her way to the guillotine. In the throes of the Revolution he also attempted to influence the way the French dressed. David was commissioned to design a national costume which corresponded to the Revolutionary ideals of liberty, equality and fraternity. His idea – breeches, a toga-style tunic, a round plumed hat and a blue cape – was no doubt inspired by a three year time period which he spent in Rome. But his austere costume never caught on with civilians and was worn only during public festivities organized by the painter. Dress did, however, derive from classical sources of inspiration such as Greek and Roman lines and its cut therefore became increasingly less complicated.

Textiles

Great progress was made in the global textile trade during the 18th century. In Britain, over 50 years, a slew of mechanized inventions revolutionized the manufacture of cotton and wool. The flying shuttle and knitting machines were invented. Hargreaves devised the spinning jenny, Arkwright the water twist frame and Cartwright the weaving loom. And in 1785, when James Watt's steam engine was installed in a cotton mill, the era of mass production began.

Meanwhile, cotton became an industry upon which the American colonies were built. This can be credited to Eli Whitney – a young Yale graduate who travelled and settled in Savannah where he soon invented the saw gin. This hand-operated gadget, which came into operation in 1793, made it possible to separate cotton fibre from the seed.

Previously, the harvesting and manufacture involved in producing cotton had been an arduous task. Slaves picked cotton fleece by hand, a job which had to be done when it was dry, so the best conditions were under the hot sun. Cotton could be churga-ginned, a slow, laborious process that cleaned the seeds from cotton fibre. These fibres were spun into thread by a hand crank. Before the cotton gin was invented, approximately 400 bales of cotton were exported from the colonies to Europe each year. After its introduction, that number escalated to 30,000. By the 19th century, 180,000 bales of cotton were being exported annually.

The cotton industry, however, was morally wrong. Slavery was the only means by which it could thrive. In 1787, a vote in the South had favoured the abolition of slave importation, but in the years that followed Eli Whitney's invention, slavery increased by one-third in the South. By 1810 there were over one million slaves working there. England played an integral part in the slave trade. Ships left Liverpool and landed in Africa where goods were

left: Before the Revolution men's clothes were flamboyant, like this mid-18th century, green velvet coat featuring embroidery with silver thread. After the Revolution, styles became more sober.

exchanged for Africans who were then exported to the Southern colonies. They worked under inhumane conditions, picking raw cotton by hand which was then returned to England for manufacture.

India was another source of cotton. Indiennes and other types of fine Indian cotton material – lawn, batistes, muslins and gauze – were worn by the fashionable from 1780. Marie Antoinette's *chemise à la reine* was made entirely of Indian cotton and featured complex gatherings.

Not only did the production of textiles thrive in the late 18th century, so did the techniques for dyeing and printing cloth. One of the best known printed fabrics of the time was Toile de Jouy – unbleached cotton that was printed with wood blocks or copper plates. It was produced at a textile factory outside of Paris in Jouy en Josas which had been founded and was run by two German brothers, Christophe Philippe and Frederic Oberkampf. The technique for producing Toile de Jouy was originally inspired by Francis Nixon, an Irish artisan who, in 1752, pioneered the use of engraved copper plates to print large-scale illustrations on textiles. Five years later, Nixon had teamed up with an English merchant who had recognized the commercial potential of his technique. The Oberkampfs raised the standard of Toile de Jouy, working with strong-toned, colour-fast dyes and copper plates that made possible the printing of small details. Motifs depicted on Toile de Jouy fabric included – and still include – landscapes, floral patterns, architecture, scenes inspired by passages found in books, plays and mythology as well as leisure activities like ballooning. Marie Antoinette was a Toile de Jouy fan. She had curtains made from it and

covered walls, chairs and beds with the romantic, decorative fabric. When Louis XVI granted the factory a Manufacture Royale citation in 1783, the vogue for Toile de Jouy spread through court circles and the bourgeoisie. It continues to this day.

The craze for chinoiserie necessitated the importation of satin, painted silks (known as pekins and bazins) as well as embroideries from the East. Chinoiserie also inspired European textile manufacturers to add new shades, such as golden yellow and 'Chinese green' to the Rococo spectrum of light pink, dove grey and mist blue. The decorative elements necessary to adorn Rococo dress – lace, ribbons, floral appliqués – were made in Italy. Ikat – a printing technique that originated in central Asia in which yarns are tie-dyed before being woven – appeared on dresses made of silk taffeta.

Make-up and grooming

Washing was not a common practice in the 18th century. Instead people wore make-up to conceal dirty skin. White face paint made of lead continued to be used as a foundation and the cheeks were dabbed with red rouge. People also believed that body odour could be disguised with perfume. Louis XV insisted that his courtiers wore a different perfume every day and Madame de Pompadour spent 500,000 livres on perfumes for herself. She devoted an excessive amount of time to her appearance. Though her bedtime was 3am, it was necessary for her to attend Mass by 8am at which she would appear lavishly turned out. One of the marquise's last acts, after receiving the sacrament, was to call for her rouge pots.

The democratic ideals that swept through France towards the end of the century affected every aspect of personal taste, including a preference for pure, clean air and scent as well as a disdain for strong perfumes. Marie Antoinette had already established a fashion for light scents. Violet and rose were among her personal favourites. Meanwhile, a perfume trade was developing in England. In London's Jermyn Street, Juan Floris, a Minorcan, opened Floris in 1730. Floris became the favourite perfumery of royalty and still exists today as the second oldest perfumery, after the apothecary of Santa Maria Novella in Florence.

In 1770, the Cleaver family established a soap and perfume company. It eventually became known as Yardley, after William Yardley, a maker of sword, spurs and buckles, took over the company from his son-in-law William Cleaver, to save the business from bankruptcy. One of their most popular products was a man's pomander made of Norfolk lavender and bear's grease.

Wigs

Both men and women powdered their hair in the 18th century. To produce the powdered effect, women sprayed wheat meal on to their own hair. Men also used wheat meal, except they applied it to huge white wigs which had been known, since the 17th century, as full-bottom wigs. The Ramillies wig (which took its name from Marlborough's victory of 1706), overtook this style. It featured sausage-roll curls at each ear, with the remainder of the hair tied back at the neck with a black ribbon.

left: Rococo hairstyles reached ever increasing heights as false hair-pieces were added. Such creations were a target for cartoonists of the time.

above: Both men and women powdered their hair in the 18th century – or had someone else do it for them, as seen here in *The Toilet of an Attorney's Clerk.*

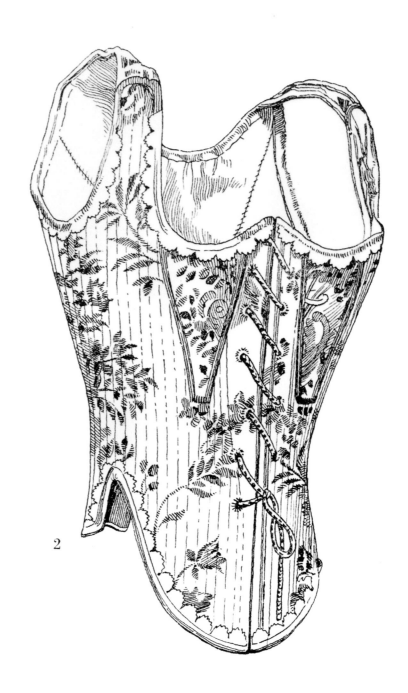

1

2

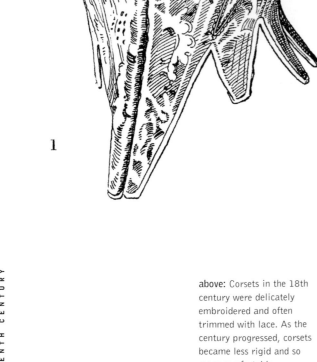

above: Corsets in the 18th century were delicately embroidered and often trimmed with lace. As the century progressed, corsets became less rigid and so more comfortable.

Just as dress-makers were becoming known by name, so too were hairdressers. Hairdressing, in the 18th century, established itself as a legitimate profession. Wigs were made of human hair, goats' hair, horse hair or vegetable fibres. Men and women of all classes wore wigs. Together with her favourite hairdresser Léonard, Madame de Pompadour started a craze for towering artificial hairstyles. They had fanciful names, such as *jardin à l'Anglaise*, mad dog, foaming torrents, and featured decorations which corresponded to the name. The *pouf au sentiment* – a court favourite – featured birds, butterflies, cupids, tree branches and vegetables, all arranged in a towering wig.

Their height inhibited a woman's posture while travelling in her carriage (often they had to kneel on the floor rather than sit). They were also havens for vermin and lice, and women carried scratching sticks to alleviate the discomfort of such pests. Eventually these monstrous constructions fell out of favour.

The taste for all things natural ushered in by the Revolution also did away with powdered hair. Such a time-consuming practice was looked upon with disdain. The democratic forces used the strange ritual as a weapon against the aristocracy, claiming that the use of wheat meal as hair powder had depleted the supply of flour and caused bread shortages. As a result, men wore their own hair and women wore theirs arranged in a variety of loose, natural hairstyles.

The corset

Corsets had been worn by women since the 16th century but by the 18th century they were works of art – or seemed as such to the untrained eye. They may have looked glamorous, but they were the cause of great discomfort. Constructed of restricting hoops of whalebone, corsets were lined with rough, unbleached cotton. Although corsets would later be blamed for a slew of ailments, such as splinters, damaged livers and displaced ribs, they accentuated the female form. Corsets were also considered to be a status symbol: they prevented a woman from over-exertion and so indicated that she was a member of the leisured classes. Corsets were made of satin, embroidered silk and silk brocade. Working women wore a lace-up corselet.

In 1770 a pamphlet entitled *The Degradation of the Human Species Due to Whalebone Corsets* was published. This started a crusade against the corset because the sentiments expressed in the text were backed by progressive thinkers of the day, both men and women – Rousseau being one of the most vociferous. The Revolution did away with bone corsets. From this time on in France women began to wear unboned corsets.

Hats

From approximately 1690 until the Revolution, the tricorne – or three-cornered hat – was worn by professional men. A variety of trimmings could adorn this style of hat: lace, braid or even ostrich feathers. Women, meanwhile, wore cartwheel hats made of straw or felted wool. From 1789 on, men and women adopted a range of military style headgear. Revolutionaries wore the Phrygian cap – the soft, felt hat which was introduced by the Greeks. The tricorne evolved into a bicorne, which was initially worn only by army officers but was eventually incorporated into men's wardrobes.

From the Revolution on, women adopted a number of head coverings. The *Thérèse* – described by Douglas Russell as a 'head bag' – was worn to keep the hair tidy. A variety of bonnets also became popular. The *calash* was made of whalebone hoops which were encased in transparent fabric. This could be raised from or lowered onto the head with the help of a piece of ribbon. The *dormeuse* was a bonnet worn in bed at night and sometimes in the morning at home.

above: Elaborate headgear was typical of the Rococo period.

Membre du Conseil des Anciens.

Membre du Directoire exécutif dans son Grand Costume.

Secrétaire du Directoire exécutif.

Membre du Directoire exécutif dans son Costume ordinaire.

Membre du Conseil des cinq cent.

Ministre.

VUE PERSPECTIVE DE L'INTÉRIEURE DE LA SALLE DES ANCIENS.

Messager d'État.

Membre de haute Cour de Justice.

Membre du Tribunal de Cassation.

Membre du Tribunal Criminel.

COSTUMES

Des Représentans du Peuple Français et Fonctionnaires Public.

Dessiné et Colorié d'après Nature avec la plus grande précision

Les Amateurs pourront demander les Titres en langues étrangères, soit en Allemand, Anglais, Hollandais, Espagnol et Italien.

Se fait et se vend A Paris, chez ANGRAND Fils Peintre, Rue Martin vis-a-vis celle du Vert Bois N.º 337. au premier au fond de la Cour.

Propriété

Huissier du Directoire exécutif et du Corps Législatif.

Président d'administration Municipal.

Membre du Tribunal Civil.

Juge de Paix.

Commissaire du Directoire exécutif près les Tribuneaux.

Membre d'administration Départemental.

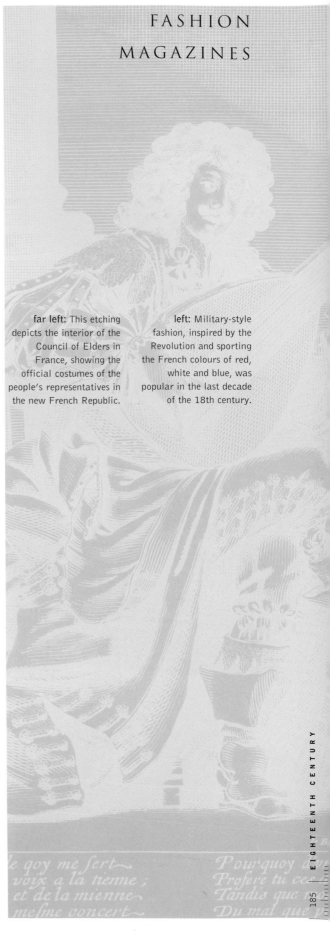

far left: This etching depicts the interior of the Council of Elders in France, showing the official costumes of the people's representatives in the new French Republic.

left: Military-style fashion, inspired by the Revolution and sporting the French colours of red, white and blue, was popular in the last decade of the 18th century.

Fashion magazines

Fashion as a culture was beginning to thrive by the early 18th century. In 1693 the first women's magazine, *The Ladies Mercury*, appeared. A mix of fashion and feature articles — covering subjects like love, marriage and manners — it was published by a London bookseller, John Dunton. Until then, fashion trends had been spread throughout Europe by fashion mannequins.

Costume books, whose pages illuminated the clothing worn during past eras and by ancient civilizations, had been published from 1600, but by the 18th century fashion annuals — almanacs and diaries — were being published. These combined a calendar and information targeted towards women. By 1731 the word 'magazine' had been invented by a British printer, Edward Cave, upon the publication of his *Gentleman's Magazine*. Cave's magazine launched the beginning of a new form of fashion media. From this date on, magazines, copying and modifying his original formula, were produced. In France *Cabinet des Modes* illustrated new fashion with coloured illustrations. 'Fashion' according to the *Cabinet* embraced several subjects: furniture, interior décor, coaches, jewellery and more. Germany's contribution came late in the 18th century: the *Journal des Luxus und der Moden* was first published in 1786. Magazines also featured engravings, or fashion plates, the most memorable of which were designed by Gravelot and Moreau le Jeune.

Originally magazines were aimed at the intelligentsia, but with time they served a wider market. Housewives and servants, intent on learning about current fashion trends, were avid magazine readers. Fashion magazines made a great impact on society. In France, Valerie Steele has observed, magazines made the masses more style conscious, as people saw Parisian fashions and began to copy them. Magazines also began to reflect the concept of lifestyle — that fashion was not just restricted to clothes.

NINETEENTH

THE BIRTH OF THE DANDY

CENTURY

Background

A new spirit of modernity drove the 19th century. The French Revolution had toppled traditions that had governed Europe for centuries. French subjects had become citizens and a new constitution was written. Abolishing the nobility, society was now based on new concepts of toleration and equality before law. Henceforth, France would be governed by an elected, representative National Assembly, a body that could create laws regardless of tradition. Elsewhere, the effects of the Revolution divided politics in the Continent into left (those who supported revolutionary ideas) and right (those who favoured tradition).

Back in France, this new wave of liberty and egalitarianism paved the way for a Corsican, Napoleon Bonaparte (1769–1821), to begin his quest to become emperor. A military genius, Napoleon's rise to the post was swift and steady. Under his guidance, the French army began what historian JM Roberts classified as a career of conquest. Bonaparte's early days as a soldier were unimpressive. During the Revolution, as a lieutenant, he returned to Corsica to organize a revolution but was removed from the army list for appearing at his regiment late. The setback proved temporary. In 1795 Napoleon had helped defeat supporters of the counter revolution in Paris. In 1796, he rose to the position of commander of the French army in Italy, and following a coup in 1799, at the age of 30, he became First Consul.

With his new wife Josephine, who was six years his senior, Napoleon moved from their Paris home in rue de la Victoire to the stately Palais de Luxembourg. His shabby military gear was replaced by an official costume which he had designed himself. Following victories in 1804, Napoleon propelled himself from General to Emperor. And at his coronation, he crowned himself. The French Empire was declared on Bastille Day, 14 July 1804.

In Jacques Louis David, Napoleon found an unofficial minister of propaganda. One of David's chief influences was, as mentioned in the previous chapter, classical Rome and Greece. Using these inspirations, David created Napoleon's interiors at the Palais de Luxembourg and the Tuileries and the ambience for Josephine's home at Malmaison. David's style, which featured such stylistic ideas as imperial eagles – grew to be known as the Directoire. David's furnishings were heavy, reflecting the style found in Roman imperial homes, and his most famous painting, *The Coronation of Napoleon and Josephine*, is most expressive of the style. The huge sweeping canvas, which today hangs in the Louvre, features Napoleon and Josephine inside Notre Dame transformed to look like a Roman temple. He remodelled the inside of the cathedral, laying down the thick green carpet and draping the walls with gold-fringed crimson velvet silk and suspending 24 crystal chandeliers from the ceiling.

Opinion's vary on the coronation gown Josephine wore. Claire de Remusat called it 'a cloud of pink tulle' while Battersby contends that it was made of silver brocade decorated with another symbol of the Empire – dozens of golden bees. No matter what it looked like exactly, Josephine's coronation dress displayed David's major contribution to women's fashion – the Empire line, although some historians argue that the dress was designed by the court painter Isabey and then made up by the tailor, Leroy. Waistless, Josephine's

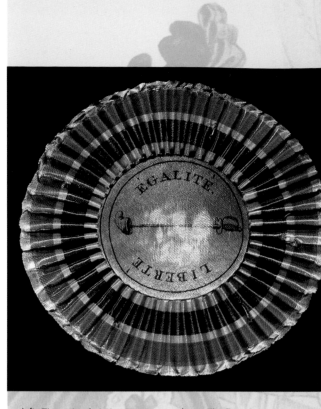

left: The style of clothes which the Emperor and Empress of France chose to wear at their coronation was hugely significant, for it displayed the simple fact that France again was governed by an institution. Jacques Louis David's *The Consecration of the Emperor Napoleon and Coronation of the Empress Josephine* (1806–7) is the most famous painting of their coronation.

above: The French Revolution of 1789 had a profound effect on social, political and sartorial aspects of the 19th century.

magnificent gown featured the flowing lines of Roman costume. Its skirt cascaded from a thin ribbon which travelled in a complete circle beneath her breasts. A pearl tiara, featuring leaves made of diamonds, adorned her head.

Meanwhile, Napoleon's coronation attire was influenced by a combination of sources – the Renaissance, troubadours and François I, as Battersby observes. He wore a doublet made of red velvet, a short cloak lined with satin, silk stockings, a ruff, a velvet cap, a sword and sash. His signature white velvet breeches were met by half boots.

The style of clothes which the emperor and empress of France chose to wear at their coronation was hugely significant, for it displayed the simple fact that France again was governed by an institution. Napoleon's government may not have been monarchy, but the lifestyle of Napoleon and Josephine was every bit as grand and excessive as that of France's former kings and queens. They revived court dress, bringing to an end the sartorial egalitarianism of the Revolution.

But the Napoleonic period – which finally came to an end in 1815 after his defeat at Waterloo – changed not just France but most of Europe. Under Napoleon's direction Paris had been transformed into a modern city: he organized the construction of fine monuments like Chalgrin's spectacular Arc de Triomphe (1805), a copy of a Roman arch, the church at La Madeleine, which followed the feeling of a Greek temple, as well as boulevards and parks. The outdated legal system was replaced with the Code Napoléon – the Napoleonic code of laws which remains much the same in present day France. The territories Napoleon conquered – Italy, Germany and Spain where he installed his brother on the throne – changed too. The ideals of the Revolution, claiming men had rights as individuals, brought to these countries by the French armies would, in time, inspire the inhabitants to turn against their oppressors.

Britain eluded Napoleon. Ruler of the sea, Britain may have lost the New World in the 19th century, but it led the way in the fields of industry, the arts and fashion. Huge factories were built – like Manchester's textile mills – which were manned by cheap labour and driven by steam-powered machinery. The arts flourished: Wordsworth, Byron, Shelley, Keats and Burns published poetry; Sir Walter Scott invented the gothic historical novel and Jane Austen chronicled the daily lifestyle of the English upper class. Painters like Reynolds, Gainsborough, Romney and Lawrence developed English portraiture.

The Romantics – an early 19th-century cultural movement that gained ground in Germany and Britain – expressed the confusion prevalent throughout Europe which followed Napoleon's defeat. Romanticism expressed the insecurity of the unknown. Rejecting the spirit of independent capitalism that was sweeping the western hemisphere, the Romantics championed feelings and emotions. In Britain, the Romantics defended the lower classes whose cheap labour drove the Industrial Revolution. Lord Byron – who lost his life in Greece, where he supported the country's bid for independence against the Turks – was one of its principal players. The exotic Brighton Pavilion, with its lotus-flower chandeliers and lamps of blue Spode porcelain, built by John Nash for George IV in 1822, best expresses the style of Romantic architecture.

left: Fashionable morning dress as worn in London in winter 1837–38. The frock coats were generally dark, the waistcoats colourful, and the outfits completed with top hats and walking sticks.

above: *The Wanderer over the Sea of Clouds*, 1818. The Romantic period firmly established black as the predominant colour for dress clothes.

BACKGROUND

above: Exhibitions were showplaces for the century's great achievements. Inventions from science and industry from around the world were displayed. Seen here is the interior of the International Exhibition in London, 1851.

Despite the harsh conditions that the Industrial Revolution thrust on to the world, science and technology thrived during the 19th century. In 1879 Thomas Edison invented the light bulb. Communication became possible with the invention of the telegraph (1835), and then the telephone (1876). Transportation improved. Streets were paved, the horseless carriage was introduced (1885) and railways were built throughout Europe and the United States. On the sea, the Great Western steamship crossed the Atlantic, travelling from England to New York in 15 days. The phonograph was invented in 1877 and the box camera, which soon followed, allowed people for the first time to capture reality. In the 20th century, as the art and technology of photography evolved, its impact on fashion would prove enormous.

Advances were made in the field of medicine so that people of all classes could better their general health. In England before 1850, five new hospitals were built, and the poor could visit dispensaries to obtain medicine. Charles Darwin (1809–82), an English naturalist, put forth the theory of evolution – the survival of the fittest – which he published as *On the Origin of Species by Means of Natural Selection* in 1859.

Politically, power shifted across Europe in the second half of the 19th century. The Congress of Vienna re-established monarchies across the Continent. But in France, Louis Napoleon (Napoleon III, nephew of Napoleon I) seized power from Louis Philippe, who had set up a new Republic after the Revolution of 1848. His ambition and desire for France to be a world power forced him into a fatal dispute with Prussia which culminated in the occupation of France in 1871. By the end of the century France had become a parliamentary democracy. With the Belle Époque – a period which stretched until World War I – France was the centre of art and culture. Elsewhere, Italy had become united under the leadership of Victor Emmanuel of Sardinia. Germany became an empire in 1871, under Wilhelm of Prussia and his Chancellor, Bismarck, who advanced the country's educational system and industry to new heights. The army and navy were also strengthened under Bismarck and a new feeling of national pride swept through the country. Along with Russia and England, Germany was one of the world's great powers.

In 1837 Queen Victoria (1819–1901) ascended the British throne, where she reigned for 63 years. In 1840 she married Prince Albert of Saxe-Coburg – the force behind the Great Exhibition of 1851. This was the world's first international exhibition, a showplace for the century's great achievements where inventions of science and industry from around the globe could be displayed. Opposition to Prince Albert's plan was widespread. Doctors believed that an attack of the plague would result if too many foreigners visited London at one time. *The Times* also ran a story which claimed that aliens were renting houses near the exhibition site and that these would be used as brothels. Their protest, however, was in vain. Prince Albert's ambition to combine engineering, practicality and beauty was eventually achieved.

Albert commissioned Joseph Paxton, the estate manager to the Duke of Devonshire, to construct in Hyde Park the Crystal Palace, a structure that incorporated 300,000 panes of glass. When the exhibition ended after six months, the palace was dismantled and then

left: As textiles and patterns became more sophisticated, women experienced a greater degree of freedom in their choice of clothing. Madame Moitessier, pictured here, is holding a fan, a favourite accessory of the time.

reconstructed in Sydenham, south London, where it stood until 1936, when it was levelled by a fire. A huge success, the Great Exhibition attracted 13,000 exhibitors from around the globe, allowing over 100,000 products to be observed by the general public. The products included English silk made at Spitalfields, in east London, and many other types of fabric, as well as articles of clothing such as bonnets, boots and bootees, stays, gloves, mittens, muffs, comforters, boas, capes, tippets and shawls.

The profits Albert raised – which amounted to £186,000 – were used to advance science and the arts. Thirty acres of land were purchased in Kensington upon which were built the Victoria and Albert Museum, the Imperial College of Science and Technology and the Royal Albert Hall. Paris soon followed Britain's lead, holding a series of international exhibitions in 1855, 1867, 1878, 1889 and 1900, displaying new wonders of technology alongside decorative objects and fashion designs.

THE CLOTHING
INDUSTRY

above: Before department stores opened people had to travel to specialized shops, each of which carried specific items. Department stores – such as Bon Marché, the first to open in Paris – stocked sartorial and household items under one roof, offering ultimate convenience.

The clothing industry

Advanced technology pushed the fashion industry, or 'needle trade' as it was then known, into new realms of mass production and sophistication. In 1846 the sewing machine was invented and patented by Isaac Singer. His eponymous model was the first to be sold and widely distributed. Although the sewing machine has been called the 'democratizer of fashion', it did little to liberate women. Sewing machines could be purchased and paid for on an instalment plan but the low pay that seamstress work offered women meant that they became slaves to their machines.

But the sewing machine was just the start of new things to come. A standard pattern to make clothes followed its invention. And its use became widespread as smart entrepreneurs such as Samuel Beeton, publisher of the *Englishwomen's Domestic Magazine*, established a pattern service offering women paper dress patterns by mail order.

above: *At the Milliners*,
1822. During the French
Empire, bonnets were low
and oblong and decorated
with ruches, ribbons and
artificial flowers.

Next came a machine that could sew buttons and another that could make buttonholes. The introduction of steam power in 1865 was followed by a machine which adapted the concept to pressing garments. Knitting stools were replaced with knitting machines that were able to introduce high-tech fibres like elastic into the knitwear process. Silk stockings and gloves could now be made with knitting machines, although production of such garments was still complicated as their pieces had to be cut out and sewn together.

The sewing machine and other innovations improved and hastened the production of ready-to-wear clothes, which had been available in certain shops in Paris since 1830. By this time shopping had become a pastime in Paris. The well-off visited arcades and small shops like Belle Jardinière (opened 1824), and the bazaars which had sprung up by the time of the Second Empire (1852–71). These bazaars, like the Galeries du Commerce et de l'Industrie and the Palais Bonne Nouvelle, were filled with stalls and galleries selling ready-

THE CLOTHING INDUSTRY

above: Worth – known as the father of *haute couture* – became dressmaker to Empress Eugénie of France. He was the most famous, the most innovative and the most expensive couturier.

to-wear clothing and other essentials for personal use as well as the home. They were the predecessors of the department store.

A source of much excitement when the first few opened in Paris, department stores gathered ready-made clothing and accessories for men, women and children – what was previously only available in the small shops and stalls – and placed it, for the first time, under one roof. Clothes and accessories that had been once kept in locked glass cases were now out in the open, in full view for the customer to look at or purchase. Browsing was positively encouraged, in order to tempt customers to buy items on impulse.

As men climbed the managerial ranks at department stores, women made popular 'sales ladies' who, with their polite manner, could serve rich clients. Department stores did away with the practice of bargaining, the traditional pricing method of the marketplace and the bazaar, and prices became fixed. Because department store buyers purchased goods in large quantities, they could offer their customers sales, specials and other previously unknown conveniences. Customers could return merchandise and, for the first time, they could buy an entire outfit under one roof. Before department stores opened, people had had to travel from specialized shop to specialized shop – each of which carried one or a few items such as fabric, umbrellas or stockings – to outfit themselves.

In 1852 a husband-and-wife team – Monsieur and Madame Boucicauts – opened one of Paris's first department stores, Bon Marché. Others followed – Magasins du Louvre were among the first to open and then later, on Boulevard Haussmann, came Magasins des Printemps. Department stores were also known in other countries: in 1838 Emerson Muschamp Bainbridge and William Dunn had opened a shop in Newcastle upon Tyne and 11 years later divided the store into 32 departments. In America the department store Wanamakers opened in Philadelphia in 1861.

But truly chic French women shopped in more exclusive environs for their clothes. On the wide tree-lined rue de la Paix, up from the prestigious Place Vendôme, were the maisons of two fashion trailblazers. At number 7 was Charles Frederick Worth (1825–95), and in 1875 Jacques Doucet (1853–1929) opened at number 21.

Charles Frederick Worth

Worth's contribution to fashion history is legendary. He is considered the founder of the fine, hand-made-to-measure clothes which came to be known as *haute couture*, or in English 'the couture' (from the French word for sewing or needlework). The designer, or couturier, as Georgina O'Hara Callan has noted, makes patterns or models of a fine linen or muslin known as toile – bearing the stamp of the designer's name. Clothes are then made to measure – fitted to a client's frame – based on the toile models.

Worth introduced other innovations. He was the first designer to produce an entire seasonal collection of clothing, instead of random, one-off pieces. He also created several designs that shaped women's fashion throughout both the late 19th and 20th centuries. In the 1860s Worth introduced the tunic dress, a knee-length dress which was worn with a long skirt. Some say it was Worth who launched the crinoline, but what is certain is that

he introduced a shorter crinoline – the crinolinette – so that women would be more comfortable while participating in active pursuits such as walking. Empress Eugénie, Princess de Metternich and other members of the inner court circle wore the crinolinette while ice skating on the lake in the Bois de Boulogne.

To the horror of his fashion-conscious clients, Worth eventually decreed the crinoline obsolete in 1864 by introducing a skirt that featured a train and a horsehair pouf (a small saddle) which became known as the bustle. Worth picked up where Rose Bertin had left off, by elevating the profession of fashion designer from a highly skilled trade to an art, so the name of the designer became more important than that of the women wearing the dress.

Worth's life story is cinematic in its intensity. In the spring of 1838, at the age of 13, he was sent by his mother, from his home in Bourne, Lincolnshire, to London to become an apprentice at Swan & Edgar. In 1845, he joined Lewis and Allenby, silk mercers who supplied fine materials to Queen Victoria. At Swan & Edgar, as he unpacked French-made hats and dresses, Worth, it is believed, developed an appreciation for Paris fashion. Alone, in his time off, he visited the National Gallery, studying the clothes which appeared on the canvases of the Old Masters.

WORTH

above: Crinolines were a trademark of the 19th century. Their popularity was due to the freedom they afforded women — large amounts of petticoats were no longer necessary to achieve width.

To further his career Worth moved to Paris in 1846. He found work at Gagelin-Opigez – a prestigious silk mercer that specialized in dresses and shawls, and also sold other dressmaking materials. At Gagelin-Opigez, Worth also met his future wife, a fellow employee, Marie Augustine Vernet (1825–98), and began his career as a fashion designer. In 1855, Gagelin-Opigez entered the Exposition Universelle, Paris's first world exhibition, submitting dresses and court trains. It was Worth's big break. A court train he designed of white gold embroidered silk (bearing an unusually high price tag of US$3,000), won a first class medal. Boosted by his success and perhaps restricted by his work environment, Worth left the company, joining forces with a Swede, Otto Gustaf Bobergh (1821–81). Together they opened the House of Worth at 7 rue de la Paix. Trading commenced in the autumn of 1857. Worth was the creative genius; Bobergh, though a talented sketch artist, was believed to be the business brains.

Their timing was perfect. France at the time Worth and Bobergh set up shop was ruled by Louis Napoleon Bonaparte, Napoleon III, who, just like his uncle, Napoleon, had set about transforming Paris into a grand imperial city. He commissioned Charles Garnier to build the sumptuously ornate Paris Opera House, an architectural monument to the spirit of the age – materialism. Meanwhile, the sartorial symbol of the Second Empire was the crinoline – a cage frame made originally of compressed horsehair hoops and then later of as many as 24 steel hoops. It freed women from wearing numerous underskirts and they fell in love with it. Women of all classes wore crinolines – including factory workers and servants – in all sorts of circumstances, even hiking. The crinoline introduced the fashion for wearing ankle boots. Napoleon III's Spanish wife, Empress Eugénie (1826–1920), the leader of French fashion in her time, was an early devotee of the crinoline and women across Europe followed her influence.

Mrs Worth, Marie Augustine, was the first to recognize how valuable Empress Eugénie and the women in her circle could be to her husband's expanding business. But Marie Augustine approached the matter in an indirect way. She paid a visit to Pauline, Princess von Metternich, the wife of Austrian ambassador to France, and showed her Worth's sketch books. Pauline ordered two of Worth's creations: an ensemble for day and a floral evening dress made of draped tulle. The pair cost 600 Francs. When Eugénie spied Pauline in Worth's dress at the Tuileries, she demanded to know the name of its designer and soon she became Worth's most important client.

It was for Eugénie that Worth created grandes toilettes, state and evening wear, court dresses, day wear and costumes worn for masquerade balls. Worth also made a straight dress for Empress Eugénie which had, beneath the back of the skirt, a horse-hair bustle. The empress was the only client who Worth serviced away from his shop. Clients from all over the world made their way to Maison Worth. Empress Elizabeth of Austria was another prominent Worth client.

In 1871 Worth talked about the spending habits of his international clientèle to the English magazine *Blackwoods*, revealing that Frenchwomen were habitually thrifty,

Englishwomen did not, generally speaking, spend lavishly, while Germans seemed hardly interested in his clothes. His most valuable customers at this time were Russians and Americans, some of whom were spending as much as £4,000 a year in his salons.

His business was thriving. In 1870 Worth had struck out again on his own, severing his relationship with his partner, Bobergh, who went back to Sweden. His business became a family operation, which his two sons, Gaston (1853–1924), and Jean-Philippe (1856–1926), soon joined – the former handled business operations while the latter pursued design.

The ambience at Maison Worth has been compared to that of an embassy. The mood was utterly discreet. Gilt lettering on the door displayed its name. There was no advertising to promote sales. Instead word of mouth drew in clients. Once through the door, a client travelled through a series of ante showrooms. The first displayed fine black and white silks and featured overstuffed sofas and chairs and a curio cabinet inside of which were Worth's antique possessions. A second room, the rainbow room, displayed a range of multi-coloured Lyon silk and Italian brocade and a third room featured British woollens. In a mirrored salon, Worth's designs were modelled by wooden mannequins. These mirrors were strategically placed so that a client could soon recognize, upon entering, how their own clothes seemed somewhat faded next to Worth's new designs. The salon de lumière – the final room – was perhaps Worth's most ingenious idea. Draped in dark silk, daylight was kept out of the room with the help of thick velvet curtains. It was illuminated by gas light to re-create the ambience of a grand ball or reception, so that a client could accurately test the effect of a Worth creation before she later appeared at a function in her frock.

Worth's business survived the transition France made yet again from an empire to a republic after the Franco Prussian War (1870–71). Worth was forced to shut his house during the Siege of Paris but managed to re-open and re-establish his business due to substantial orders placed by foreign clients. Though his business went into decline somewhat in the years before his death in 1895, his sons carried on Worth's mini empire and expanded it in the 20th century. By 1897 clients could order Worth's designs over the telephone, by mail order or by visiting one of his shops in London, Dinard, Biarritz or Cannes. Gaston hired Paul Poiret (1879–1944), a young French designer who had worked with Jacques Doucet. For two years Poiret worked to push the design philosophy at Worth from pure elegance to a more practical elegance. Though his efforts served to irritate Jean-Philippe, he was moving the company in the right direction: by the turn of the century the fashion world had changed as many of the courts of Europe disappeared or shrank.

In 1924 the House of Worth formed Les Parfums Worth and produced its first fragrance, *Dans La Nuit*. Ten more were to follow. The fragrance business outlasted the Worth fashion house, which was acquired in 1954 by the house of Paquin who then closed it in 1956.

Though the business closed, Worth's sons had made their own lasting contribution to fashion. In 1910, Gaston Worth became the first president of the Chambre Syndicale de la Haute Couture, an organization set up to maintain the standards of couture design and

above: Worth designed clothes for women of high society who flocked to his Paris house from Europe and America. Here the Empress of Austria is shown in one of his creations – an evening dress made of draped tulle.

above: Portrait of the Duchess de Morny, one of the many high society women who patronized Maison Worth.

protect couture designers from piracy, which is still in existence today. Jean-Philippe Worth also served as a president. In 1923, during his tenure, he advocated that all couture industry workers should receive paid holidays and he was instrumental in the opening of an Ecole Supérieure de la Couture, a fashion trade school, in 1930.

Other designers became well-known names in Paris at the time of Worth. Empress Eugénie visited Madame Laferrier for day clothes, Felice for cloaks and mantles, and Madames Virot and Lebel for hats. In 1854, when Napoleon III and Empress Eugénie visited Queen Victoria and Prince Albert, the Queen introduced her tailor, Henry Creed, to the Empress. She was so impressed with his work – the Creeds were known for creating finely tailored woollen and tweed suits – that she convinced him to open a shop in Paris.

In 1889 at the Exposition Universelle, Herminie Cadolle exhibited the breast girdle – a contraption that supported the breasts with the help of shoulder suspenders. Cadolle eventually added elastic sections to the breast girdle and called it the 'Bien-être' – or well-being. It was a forerunner of a brassière despite it being fastened in the back to a corset. Cadolle eventually set up shop in 1910 in Paris, where the family lingerie business is still run today on rue Cambon.

Doucet

After inheriting his family's lingerie shop on rue de la Paix, Jacques Doucet opened his own couture house there in 1875. His most popular designs were his tea gowns, tailored suits and fur-lined coats. Fur was important to Doucet. He was the first designer to treat it as a fabric. His otter coats – which were modelled after the style worn by Prussian officers – became popular with his rich clients in the late 19th century.

Doucet derived inspiration for his ballgowns and evening dresses from 17th- and 18th-century paintings. He was considered an art connoisseur, and possessed an impressive collection, including paintings by Watteau and Chardin, among others. The Maison Doucet, with its pink muslin curtains and Rococo salons, was a setting which fell in line with the atmosphere that great writers of the time like Marcel Proust conjured in *Remembrance of Things Past* as well as that which Alexander Dumas's *Le Demi Monde* illuminated. Maison Doucet was a place where society ladies mingled with kept women – the grand cocottes and the demimondaine. Princesses, actresses and mistresses wore Doucet's designs of pale pastel silk organza. In fact, the houses of Doucet, Worth and those belonging to other grand Paris couture designers broke down barriers in society. So long as they could afford the costly creations, women of all types were welcome to shop. Doucet's favourite client was the French actress Rejane, with whom he collaborated on her stage costumes.

American merchants travelled to Paris to buy his models, as well as Worth's, which they exported and copied to sell in the United States. In 1895, Consuelo Vanderbilt married the Duke of Marlborough in a Doucet model, a wedding dress of ivory white satin and Belgian lace which was belted at the waist (a Doucet signature). However, Doucet himself did not design the actual dress. Mrs Donovan, a dress maker popular with New York society ladies, copied a Doucet creation.

Two of the 20th century's most important designers were employed by Doucet before they became known names – Paul Poiret in 1896 and Madeleine Vionnet (1876–1975) in 1907. It was from Doucet that Poiret learned about the business of fashion. When he established his own house in 1903, he emulated Doucet's guise – adopting a groomed beard and perfectly polished shoes. Poiret also learned about business administration from Doucet, finding out how to run and manage a couture house. Madeleine Vionnet's first collection for Doucet, in which barefoot models free of corsets paraded in light thin dresses, was considered ahead of its time.

Women

For the upper echelons of society, the 19th-century fashionable world was a glorious place. For women who worked behind the scenes it was an entirely different matter. After domestic work, the textile industry was the highest employer of women and the working conditions in the factories and textiles mills were harsh. Women were expected to work 12 and 14 hour days, six and sometimes seven days a week. Charles Dickens, political philosophers Karl Marx and Friedrich Engels and the reformer and journalist Henry Mayhew became outspoken opponents of the injustice and exploitation upon which the 19th century textile trade thrived. Upon investigating the factory system Mayhew concluded that it was to blame for the destruction of family life – the wages it offered women were so low that to survive many were forced into prostitution. Work in the needle trade – or the 'sweat shops' as garment factories became known – offered women and children, who worked the same hours as adults, little in return. Wages were low and the conditions unsafe, unheated, unventilated and ill-lit.

The 19th century did offer women more opportunities however. Education, especially in America, was becoming more accessible. Public universities accepted female students and women's colleges such as Smith and Wellesley were founded in the 1870s. Women played sports. Bicycle-riding, swimming and fencing became acceptable active pursuits for women. Some women wore breeches in order to participate: Amelia Jenks Bloomer (1818–94), an American feminist and journalist (she edited a paper called *The Lily*), advocated the wearing of pantaloons as a comfortable alternative to the restrictive corset. Bloomer's costume of a tunic dress worn over loose trousers became a hated symbol of feminism, but she did have her supporters, Britain's *Queen* magazine among them.

There were remarkable role models. In 1854, Florence Nightingale (1820–1910), led nurses during the Crimean War, establishing a medical organization in the British Army. She became a heroine in England when she returned in 1856. Through her career, as adviser to the first district nursing service, set up in Liverpool, she stressed the need for hygiene and appointed women health commissioners. The Nightingale School of Nursing at St Thomas's Hospital, London was set up with public money in gratitude to her work.

The writer George Sand (Amandine Aurore Lucie Dupin, 1804–76), chronicled love, politics and the female experience in 19th-century France. Her life defied convention. Sand advocated sexual equality and lived by her convictions, changing her name, divorcing her

above: After domestic work, the textile industry employed the greatest number of women. But working conditions in the factories and textile mills were harsh. Here women are at work at the Coventry Machinists' Company cycle works in Warwickshire.

WOMEN

above: Though the progress was slow, the path to women's liberation had begun. Here *Le Chalet du Cycle au bois de Boulogne* (c 1868 by Jean Beraud) shows women wearing bloomers – comfortable pantaloons named after the American feminist Amelia Jenks Bloomer.

right: Portrait of Josephine Bonaparte by Baron Antoine Jean Gros (1808). The empress was passionate about clothes. She is wearing a chemise dress with a high waist and slightly puffed sleeves, typical of the period, accompanied by a shawl with embroidered edges.

husband, Baron Dudevant, after nine years of marriage (he later applied for the Legion of Honour, claiming that the courage it took to be married to her deserved public recognition), and then embarked on a series of legendary love affairs (with Frédéric Chopin, among others) and a prolific writing career. A woman of independent means, Sand became the sole heir of her wealthy grandmother's will.

Sand used fashion to make her point about sexual equality. She smoked cigars and adopted a man's wardrobe, striding through the streets of Paris in trousers, a greatcoat and hobnailed boots. Point taken, it seems. Critics of her day considered her as a great writer and her male contemporaries, Balzac and Flaubert, regarded her as an equal.

George Sand was an exception. The majority of women were still concerned with domestic affairs. As men's fashion became more sober women became all the more extravagant. An unspoken rule was established – women were there to display a man's earning power. The 19th century produced a new role for women. They became status symbols to their husbands, or trophy wives, a concept which remains in place today.

Josephine Bonaparte

The first of the kind was Josephine Bonaparte. A divorcee, Josephine met Napoleon through Barras, a high-ranking member of the post-revolutionary Directoire, with whom she had shared a liaison. Napoleon persuaded Josephine to marry him, which she did, and because he was penniless they split the cost of the wedding. Once installed at the Luxembourg Palace and then at the Tuileries, Napoleon, as First Consul, expected his wife to dress in a lavish fashion.

Josephine became the leader of French fashion in clothes made for her by the French tailor Leroy. Like Worth, Leroy became the last word in French fashion after Josephine appeared at a Sunday night ball held at Malmaison wearing one of his creations. The dress – known as the rose petal gown – was a lavish affair. To construct it Leroy had hand sewn hundreds of fresh pale pink rose petals on to a long white satin sheath.

Court dress – on the excessive scale known to pre-revolutionary Versailles – had returned to French fashion. The circle was complete when in 1800 Josephine purchased Marie Antoinette's pearls for 250,000 Francs. She had raised the money in a sideline business – secretly trafficking in army contracts. On the day that she was crowned empress, it was claimed that she outshone her entire entourage. Although she frequently appeared in pink, Napoleon preferred his empress to wear white.

Josephine was fastidious about grooming. She had a personal pedicurist, manicurist and masseuse, and Hebault was her favourite hairstylist. Duplan devised lavish head-pieces from feathers and jewels to match Josephine's ball gowns. Four maids, a personal servant and a wardrobe mistress attended to her daily. Make-up was also important to Josephine. She cared for her skin using face masks, emollients and astringent cleansers. To enhance her features she used face powder, rouge and skin whiteners.

Leroy was also at her service. Though his origins were humble (he was the son of an employee at the Opéra), Leroy had established a reputation for himself before he set to

work for Napoleon and Josephine: he had worked for Marie Antoinette as a hair stylist. Although he was loyal to the monarchy – he continued to appear in pink satin and powdered hair through the Revolution – Leroy reinvented himself to be the model post-revolutionary designer. During the Republic he designed a tricolour dress which incorporated the slogan 'Liberty, Equality, Fraternity' on its border. On its belt were embroidered the words 'Liberty or Death'. By the time Napoleon's empire fell, Leroy was famous across Europe for his work. An international clientèle – made up of aristocratic Austrians, English, Germans, Polish and Italians – kept him occupied. As secret adviser to Napoleon, and as the empress's favourite tailor, Leroy was in a position to influence fashion. His models were published in the *Journal des Modes* for all of Europe to see and copy. His love of French fabrics – crêpe, satin, taffeta and velvet produced by factories in Marseilles and Lyon – revived the French textile industry. He designed dresses in an empire line, featuring deep décolleté and puffed sleeves.

Fashion historians credit Josephine for setting several fashion trends too. She re-popularized white, which became the colour of choice for ballgowns. Fur trim was revived during her reign: pelts of astrakhan, marten and sable were among her favourites. Shawls – made of goat fleece from Kashmir and Russian Kirghiz goats – became as popular as the shatoosh and the pashmina in the late 1990s. Clothes were Josephine's passion, amounting almost to an obsession, as can be seen in an inventory from 1809: it listed that she owned 676 dresses, 49 court costumes to be worn at state functions, 252 hats or head-pieces, 60 cashmere shawls, 785 pairs of slippers, 413 pairs of stockings and 498 embroidered and lace-trimmed chemises.

The return to splendour which Napoleon and Josephine instigated also revived the fluctuating French textile industry. A cotton industry was established at Rouen and lace from Valenciennes was back in demand. Trim for ballgowns, hats and bonnets – once manufactured in Italy – could now be made in France.

If Josephine had a rival it was the French salon hostess Madame Juliette de Recamier (1777–1849), an outspoken enemy of Napoleon, whose portrait by David hangs today in the Louvre. In it she wears her signature style – a dress of soft, clinging fabric cut in the empire line. The style also became known in France as the Recamier line. Graceful and elegant, she was exiled from Paris by Napoleon and settled in Geneva, but returned to Paris after the Battle of Waterloo.

Napoleon's second wife, Marie Louise of Austria, Duchess of Parma, was uninterested in fashion, but was intrigued by the art of perfumery. The violet became the floral symbol of the Bonapartes and in 1817 when she separated from Napoleon she set up a perfume industry at Parma which still thrives today.

Queen Victoria

When Queen Victoria ascended the throne women in England dressed simply. Skirts and sleeves were long. Frocks fitted closely and featured long waists. Evening wear was restrained and gowns had short puffed sleeves and heart-shaped necklines. Well-off women

left: The dress worn here has a wide, trimmed crinoline skirt, long sleeves and bodice (c 1855).

above: Nineteenth-century textiles, such as this red paisley printed on cotton, were sumptuous but produced under harsh conditions. Factories, where the labour was often performed by women, were considered sweatshops.

Jules Brevé

Leroy, imp. r. des Marais, 66.

Ad. Goubaud & fils Ed.rs Paris.

J Bonnard

1077

wore two pairs of stockings – a silk pair over a cashmere pair. In her youth, Queen Victoria was considered one of Europe's style leaders. But she came to view fashion as purely having a functional purpose. Fittings bored her. So she would attend one and have the same dress model made for her in array of fabrics. Her seclusion after the death of her husband lasted for 40 years, and succeeded in lessening the British court's influence on fashion.

Men's clothing

Three men influenced the course of men's fashion during the 19th century: George, 'Beau' Brummell, the Comte d'Orsay and Queen Victoria's husband, Prince Albert. Professionally, Beau Brummell's life was unimpressive. Personally, he led a life of privilege but his huge fame did him few favours. Educated at Eton and then at Oxford, Brummell moved on to London where he was socially in demand. Initially he was a protégé of the Prince of Wales, but his notorious arrogance inevitably proved to be his downfall. Brummell became a social outcast. Debt sent him to France where he led an impecunious existence in Calais from 1816. He proceeded to Caen, where he was appointed Consul by his friend the Duke of Wellington. In 1835, his debtors finally caught up with him and he was imprisoned. Mentally unstable, he was eventually committed to Caen asylum where he died, alone, on 30 March 1840. Although he has never been confirmed homosexual, he was indifferent to women.

Sartorially, George Brummell's life was exceedingly influential: he was the original dandy. Dandyism was a movement which sought to refine gentlemen's dress. Often it is assumed that dandies were effeminate, but in fact they dressed in an understated fashion. They succeeded in jettisoning all that was excessive in a man's wardrobe – lace ruffles, lace ties, white silk stockings, buckled shoes and the three-cornered hat – replacing it with superbly fitting, sober clothes. The plain white linen shirt, the neckcloth, riding boots, the top hat, in short the attire of an English country gentleman – such elements were wardrobe staples to a dandy. By 1830 dandyism had introduced pantaloons and trousers into the male wardrobe. Padding and stays, however, remained. Ornamentation was frowned upon. A dandy's accessories included brass buttons on a cloth coat and a gold watch suspended from a chain. Clothes were cut of soberly coloured cloth: blue or green for day and blue or black for evening.

Beau Brummell's influence also stretched to grooming. Powdered wigs and scent became a thing of the past. Brummell was clean-shaven, wore his hair closely cropped, his shirts bleached and starched to perfection. He prided himself on being so clean as to make perfume unnecessary, Miles Lambert has noted. Brummell's own words sum up the essence of dandyism: 'I cannot be elegant since you have noticed me.' But his affected simplicity took time: it has been estimated that he devoted six hours every morning preparing himself for the day ahead.

Beau Brummell first encountered George IV, the Prince of Wales, at a thatched cottage in London's Green Park. Brummel's aunt, Mrs Searle, kept cows there at a little farm which was run, it seems, for the amusement of the prince who paid irregular visits. The

left: By 1879, the crinoline had been replaced by the bustle – a cushion of horsehair sewn into the back of the skirt. These examples are lavishly adorned with flowers and ribbons and elegantly draped.

above: Sartorially, the life of George 'Beau' Brummell (1778–1849) – whose portrait is shown here – was exceedingly influential. He was the original dandy.

above: The 19th century produced several famous dandies including the writer, dramatist and politician Edward Bulwer Lytton (1803–73).

right: Portrait of Robert de Montesquiou (1897) showing late 19th century male dress which became increasingly plainer and more practical.

provocative Brummell engaged the prince, who soon appointed him to a position in the King's Army – a job that he tired of eventually. But Brummell had passed the test and he was a welcome guest in the highest circles of society.

The Prince looked to Brummell for sartorial advice, and Brummell obliged, persuading him to give up sartorial excesses such as ruffles and diamond buttons. Eventually their relationship became antagonistic and it is believed that the final blow came in the all too appropriate place – Bond Street. Brummell, strolling with a friend, encountered the prince who proceeded to snub his former sartorial advisor. Brummell's reaction was harsh and swift. 'Who's your fat friend?' he asked his companion while the corpulent prince was still in earshot. Soon after, Brummell, chased by debtors, with no friends to rely on, had departed for France.

It was an apt conclusion for his relationship with the prince. Fashion historians believe that Brummell's mission, and the true purpose of dandyism, was to democratize men's fashion, replacing the aristocrats with gentlemen.

The 19th century produced several other famous dandies, both real and fictional: the writer Edward Bulwer Lytton, the Comte d'Orsay (a leading social figure in London and Paris who, among other claims to fame, wrote a fashion column in London's *Daily News* in the 1830s), Benjamin Disraeli, Max Beerbohm and Count Boniface de Castellane. The latter, 'Boni', as he was known by his friends, lived in an enormous pink house in the grand Paris address of Avenue Bois and with his cousin, the Prince de Sagan, threw a lavish party near the century's end which epitomized the excesses of la Belle Époque. Some 15km (9 miles) of carpet were laid across the grass at the Tir aux Pigeons in the Bois de Boulogne, the grounds were lit up by 80,000 Venetian lamps and 3,000 guests were waited on by 60 footmen.

Numerous dandies appeared in William Thackery's *Vanity Fair*. He wrote of Lord Tapeworm, who favoured scented cambric handkerchiefs and high-heeled lacquered boots, Jos Sedley – a rather stout puffy man in buckskins and hessian boots – and Lieutenant General Sir George Tufto KCO, who appeared padded and in stays, strutting down Pall Mall with a rickety swagger. Later, during la Belle Époque, Oscar Wilde created dandies such as *An Ideal Husband's* Lord Goring, Lord Illingworth in *A Woman of No Importance* and Lord Henry Wotton in *The Picture of Dorian Gray*. Marcel Proust's Swann is said to have been inspired by, among others, the French dandy Charles Haas, who also appeared in James Tissot's *Le Cercle de la rue Royale* (1868, see illustration on page 212), a group portrait which explicitly captures the measured style of the late 19th-century French approach to dandyism.

By the mid-19th century, London dandies and other elegant men headed to Savile Row, where the bespoke tailor Henry Poole was one of the first to set up a shop catering to their discerning needs. Henry Poole was the son of James Poole, a linen draper, who became a tailor after the Battle of Waterloo. Henry became an apprentice at his father's firm and then inherited the family company in 1846. Savile Row was originally a street made up of surgeon's offices, but Poole and the other tailors who joined him transformed it into the

above: Prince Albert, the Prince of Wales, became a model of masculine dressing.

centre of influence of men's fashion. The Prince of Wales and Napoleon III were among the many aristocrats who were dressed by Poole & Co.

By the 1860s a number of refined men's clothing styles were named after Prince Albert, such as the Albert Top Frock and the Albert Driving Cape; and into the 20th century, Americans still called a man's frock coat an 'albert'. Near the century's close the Prince of Wales had become the model of masculine dressing. By day or night, whether shooting or yachting, on a State visit or a private party, he had a knack for always dressing in an appropriate fashion. At the time, *The London Tailor* expounded upon the importance of this matter: 'It is an error for gentlemen to go to public dinners or to assemblies where ladies are present, in dinner jackets.' A tail coat had become standard evening attire of the well-to-do.

Although the English gentleman still preferred to visit his tailor, American men began to buy their clothes off-the-peg. The clothing store Brooks Brothers opened in New York in 1818, selling high-quality, ready-made suits for men. Shops like Brooks Brothers emphasized the importance of fit – the most important aspect of men's fashion the 19th-century introduced. They also brought a higher price point to the ready-to-wear market, which, Colin McDowell has claimed, marked the beginning of the idea that if the price of a garment was high, its quality was probably good – a concept which persists, often unwarranted, in today's fashion world. Inevitably this contributed to the improvement of quality ready-to-wear clothes.

Designer jewellery

The 19th century introduced the concept of designer jewellery. Fine, precious jewellery progressed from being a craft carried out by artisans to a commercial trade. The best firms were family run and their names – just like Worth and Doucet – became synonymous with their work. In Paris Etienne Nitot led the way, opening Chaumet & Cie on the rue St Honoré. Early in his career, luck fell upon Nitot: First Consul Napoleon Bonaparte had been in a minor accident outside his shop and Nitot had rushed outside to help him. His goodwill was substantially rewarded, as Napoleon commissioned him to design his coronation crown and sword as well as other important pieces such as a tiara given to the pope. In 1810 when Napoleon married Marie Louise, Nitot designed her bridal jewellery. When Chaumet was appointed to the role of official jeweller to Louis Philippe in 1830, the firm acquired an international reputation, but competition soon arrived. By 1837 Charles Lewis Tiffany founded what has become America's leading jewellery firm, Tiffany & Co. Initially, Tiffany sold inexpensive decorative jewellery but branched out selling more expensive jewellery, watches, diamonds and sterling silver. From the mid-19th century in Paris, French royalty, the Prince of Wales and other wealthy aristocrats patronized Cartier on rue de la Paix, and by the end of the century Cartier had opened boutiques in London and New York. By that time, Sotirio Bulgari, a Greek goldsmith, had opened an eponymous family-run jewellery boutique (established 1881) on Rome's via Condotti. Van Cleef & Arpels, founded in 1906 by Julien, Louis and Charles Arpels and their brother in law Alfred

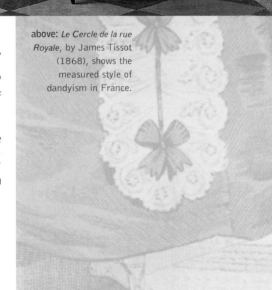

above: *Le Cercle de la rue Royale*, by James Tissot (1868), shows the measured style of dandyism in France.

van Cleef, set up shop on Place Vendôme. The firm found fame later in the 20th century when they created the Farah Diba Crown – a sumptuous head-piece featuring 1,646 gemstones set in gold and platinum – the coronation crown of Farah Diba, the wife of Mohammed Reza Pahlavi, Shah of Iran.

The most famous creations by Russian jeweller Peter Carl Fabergé, jeweller to the Russian court, were Easter eggs. Originally made in 1884 as gifts to the tsar and tsarina, they remain highly prized today. But Fabergé failed to propel his business far into the 20th century. His factory closed after the Russian Revolution in 1918.

12:twelve

TWENTIETH

THE AGE OF DIVERSITY

CENTURY

Background

The 20th century is the story of an increasingly urbanized world. In 1950, 30 per cent of the global population lived in cities; the United Nations predicts that by 2005 this figure will increase to 50 per cent.

It was a century of tragedy and disaster. From the outbreak of World War I in 1914, nearly every decade produced a major conflict, crisis or war. Wars were fought between countrymen (in the Spanish Civil War, Yugoslavia and Kosovo), against neighbours (World Wars I and II), and between alien nations (Korea, Vietnam and the Gulf War). Paradoxically, despite the appalling casualties, the human tragedy and the devastation, society and social conditions improved at an unprecedented pace. Two factors are largely responsible for this – technological innovation and the progression of thought.

Technology was the buzz word of the century. Innovation followed innovation: the aeroplane, cinema, television, the passenger jet, video, the computer, facsimile machines and the internet – all of these have increased the speed of transportation and communication, providing a global awareness. Today there is a continual worldwide interchange of cultural customs. By the end of the century, English had become the universal language of science, commerce, diplomacy and popular culture. The global village, which the Canadian theorist Marshall McLuhan predicted in the sixties, had become a reality.

far left: By the sixties, women's social freedom was reflected in what they wore – Twiggy is shown here in an aggressive stance, wearing a Paco Rabanne mini dress and a coat made of leather which resembles chain-mail armour.

left: Emmeline Pankhurst was the forerunner in the fight for sexual equality for women. She was arrested on 1 May 1914 for staging a demonstration outside Buckingham Palace.

Liberalization

A near equality of the sexes was one of the 20th century's main achievements. In Britain, women's liberation was led by Emmeline Pankhurst, who, in the late 19th century, became the leader of the Women's Social and Political Union (WSPU). Pankhurst led the fight for full women's suffrage, which she witnessed just before her death in 1928. Through the century, dynamic women picked up where Pankhurst left off. Virginia Woolf, in *A Room of One's Own* (1929), discussed the obstacles which thwarted women's achievement. In 1949, Simone de Beauvoir, the French philosopher and writer, published *The Second Sex*, highlighting the oppression of women through several devices: history, myth, political theory and psychology.

In the United States of America, Margaret Sanger opened her first birth-control clinic in 1916 and this was followed in 1921 by that of the British campaigner, Marie Stopes (1880–1958). These clinics served to educate women about safe sex despite opposition from the medical establishment. Stopes' wisdom predated the Pill, which, in the sixties, delivered female independence in tablet form. In 1972 the writer Gloria Steinem published *Ms*, a magazine that made a commitment to report intelligently on equal rights for women. Some 60 years after Nancy Astor became the first female Member of Parliament, women were also taking a more active role in mainstream political life: Margaret Thatcher became

far left: Yves Saint Laurent, shot by Irving Penn. Due to their rebellious nature, his earlier collections, like Robin Hood seen here, shook up the prim Paris fashion establishment.

left: When designer Calvin Klein made Kate Moss his spokesmodel in the early nineties she became the decade's defining fashion force.

Britain's first woman prime minister in 1979, and one of the century's most dynamic politicians.

The Civil Rights movement promoted racial equality, first in America and then around the world. Perestroika liberated the Soviet Union from communism, converting it to a capitalist society with an insatiable demand for western goods and services such as Coca Cola, Levis, McDonalds, *Vogue*, Gianni Versace, and MTV. That demand for western products continued to spread eastward. China's partial liberation from Maoist repression ensured the ever increasing speed of the western consumer culture.

Fashion designers

Designers are no longer artists, as they were during Worth's time; the internationally recognized 'names' assume the combined roles of designer, serious business professional, and glamorous celebrity. Chanel, Dior, Yves Saint Laurent, Ralph Lauren, Calvin Klein,

above: Paul Poiret – whose Sorbet dress is seen here – pioneered the first fashion performance when he went on tour with his models and sewing kit.

right: Madame Vionnet's special way with fabric included the bias cut, which allowed her dresses to fall into flattering folds.

Versace, Miuccia Prada – the best 20th-century designer houses – produce everything from clothes, handbags, scent and make-up to pillows, duvet covers, condom wallets, cappuccino, ashtrays, cigarettes, coffee-table books, dog leads, day beds and skis. Today, anything that can be stamped with a designer's name or initials is produced for mass consumption.

Fashion today is a global, billion-dollar business. The designer as personality has an image which is as manipulated and manufactured as a modern politician's. The fashion industry is run by a team of spin doctors – public relations teams, creative directors in advertising agencies, photographers and savvy fashion stylists, hairstylists and make-up artists. These people work together to perfect the look that is projected to the press at the couture and ready-to-wear shows, as well as to a wider public in magazines, on television and in films. This approach works. Film-makers like Robert Altman, Martin Scorsese and Wim Wenders have captured designers' lives and their work; rock stars wear their clothes on stage; Jean-Paul Gaultier is a television personality; Miuccia Prada has an art gallery and Gucci's Tom Ford has a Hollywood agent who sends him film scripts, just in case he decides to quit fashion and pursue an acting or directing career.

The 20th century has produced too many designers to name them all. Fashion journalism has, through the century, often distorted the work of designers – creating brief fads for their work purely out of sycophancy or because it worked at that moment. Chronicling 20th-century fashion history is somewhat different: it must single out those designers who have made a lasting contribution. Omar Calabrese, in *Versace Signatures*, provided some guidance. Discussing the work of the late Gianni Versace, Calabrese claimed that the mark of a true designer – or what he called a 'great stylist' – is the ability to maintain a distinct personality even in the ever-changing world of fashion. The designers mentioned in this chapter have done exactly that.

Early 20th-century fashion

Jacques Doucet's former in-house designers, Paul Poiret (1879–1944) and Madeleine Vionnet (1876–1975), both eventually established their own ateliers and each of them can share the credit for liberating the female form from restricting, uncomfortable corsets. Poiret believed that the corset made a woman look like she was hauling a trailer and his early dress designs, after he established his own house in 1904, were simple and cut straight. The corset would have altered the silhouette, so Poiret's alternative was the brassière. He focused a lot of his attention on the skirt, shortening it to ankle length. In 1911 he designed the hobble skirt, which freed the hips, but constricted the ankles instead and aroused both positive and negative public reactions, as did his culottes. He also launched a somewhat masculine walking skirt, which he called the *trotteur*.

Poiret was the first French designer to travel throughout Europe and to America in order to promote French fashion. He had a real flair for publicity and made his personal appearances special. As well as using nine models to display his work, Poiret, to the delight of the audience, performed. Standing on a platform with a pair of scissors, a box of pins and a roll of material, he would make a dress in mere minutes.

above: Lady Lucile Duff Gordon was the first to put on a fashion show.

right: 'Coco' Chanel – seen here in one of her designs – was her own best advertisement.

Poiret also understood the power of scent: in 1910 he launched *Roisine* – a perfume named after his daughter. In doing so he became the first French couturier to create perfumes that reflected his image and summed up the mood of his clothes. Leading designers today follow his example.

Madeleine Vionnet confided to the writer Bruce Chatwin that she loved women too much. Vionnet – who opened her salon de couture in 1912, only to shut it two years later because of the war before reopening it in 1919 – was obsessed with the female form. Her dresses, as Valerie Steele claimed, were utterly female. She understood the power of material completely because, unlike most designers, she did not sketch her designs but constructed them in miniature, without using preparatory sketches. Her dresses were made on a scaled-down wooden figure, which shrank the female body to approximately 60cm (2ft) in height, draping and pinning the fabric to form her fluid designs. This miniature form was then translated into life-size proportions and fitted on to a client. The techniques of lingerie – pin-tucking, faggoting and rolled hems – were also employed by Vionnet. And her ground-breaking cuts produced new shapes including the cowl and halter necklines as well as the bias cut – defined by Georgina O'Hara Callan as a cut across the grain of a material which makes the fabric fall in a smooth vertical way thus allowing it to be worked into clinging folds. Guillaume Garnier claimed that the bias cut had already been used in 19th-century dress-making, but Vionnet certainly expanded the possibilities of this discreet, flattering technique.

Less well known than Vionnet and Poiret was Lucile, Lady Duff Gordon (1863–1935). Although she was based in London – where she opened Maison Lucile in Hanover Square – Lucile claimed that she introduced the French word 'chic' into the British vocabulary. Although her sewing skills were minimal, Lucile, who was of Scots-Canadian origin, was the first female English designer to gain an international reputation. As another enemy of the corset and heavy underclothes, Lucile insisted that women should wear glamorous undergarments. As she recalled in her memoirs, *Discretions and Indiscretions*, she liberated London women from flannel underclothes, woollen stockings and voluminous petticoats by introducing them to chiffons and draperies reminiscent of Ancient Greek costume.

But Lucile is remembered more for her innovations surrounding fashion than for her actual designs (her most popular creations were her tea dresses – made from gauze, taffeta, poplin and silk and worn by both Sarah Bernhardt and royalty). She pioneered the first fashion parade – where extremely tall models walked among high profile clients, like Princess Alice, Ellen Terry and Lily Langtry among others, to display her work.

Coco Chanel – the modern fashion house

Gabrielle 'Coco' Chanel (1883–1971) was her own best model. While Vionnet strove to create the perfect shape, Chanel worked with, and improved upon, what she had. Her philosophy was of the 'Total Look', and many still dress by it today. The basic concept is that individual items of clothing are not as important as what they are accessorized with and how they are worn.

Bé" and

Christian Dior
La ligne corolle
Jaquette cintrée en shantung,
jupe longue finement plissée.

Chanel was a complex personality. Her greatest asset, Amy de la Haye has claimed, was that she was shrewd. Chanel picked up random sartorial ideas and styled them to suit herself. Initially, it was her charisma which made her personal style known. But as her business grew, her celebrity made her look world-famous. She was the first designer to work skilfully with wool jersey, buying a stock from the firm of Jean Rodier in 1916, and pioneering a new look of pliant, comfortable, casual, chic clothes, in a material that was originally intended to make sport clothes for men. Designers including Yves Saint Laurent, Christian Lacroix, Adolfo, Franco Moschino and Yohji Yamamoto have all credited the Chanel look as inspiration.

Chanel's legacy floundered in the ten or so years after she died in 1971 – a year after she created a new scent, No 19. Alain Wertheimer, whose family had owned the business since 1924 when his grandfather, Pierre Wertheimer, had helped to establish Parfums Chanel, set about modernizing Chanel, transforming it from a couture house to a globally recognized brand. In 1979 Chanel boutiques were opened around the world in the US, Canada and Europe and in Paris a flagship shop was established on the site of the legendary original house of Chanel on rue Cambon. During the seventies Catherine Deneuve and Cheryl Tiegs successfully promoted Chanel fragrance, but a series of designers failed to make a Chanel couture and ready-to-wear look work. It took the arrival of the German designer Karl Lagerfeld in the early 1980s to breathe new life into the house of Chanel.

Suzy Menkes has rightly claimed that the idea of deconstructing a couture house to modernize it came from Karl Lagerfeld at Chanel in the 1980s. Lagerfeld produced his first Chanel couture collection in 1983, and still has total creative control of the house today.

Holly Brubach noted in the *New Yorker* that under Lagerfeld, the image of Chanel herself as a fashion icon has been replaced by images of other women wearing Chanel. Playing model muse to Lagerfeld a position models including Ines de la Fressanges, Linda Evangelista, Claudia Schiffer, Stella Tennant, Karen Elson and Devon Aoki have enjoyed – means instant visibility. Lagerfeld promotes a model's image, his own and Chanel's all at the same time. Models and celebrities – such as Shalom Harlow, Carole Bouquet and Vanessa Paradis – pose for his perfume advertisements.

Despite some critics' suggestions that Lagerfeld's creations are self-glorifying and contrary to what Chanel herself stood for, he has managed to maintain Chanel as utterly fashionable – merging the Total Chanel Look with the spirit of the times. In the eighties it was about the excessive use of the Chanel signature but through the nineties Chanel fused fashion with increasing functionality.

The New Look

Chanel was utterly sceptical of the talent of Christian Dior (1905–57), wondering, in exasperation, whether he was mad or making fun of women. How, she wondered, could they function in 'that thing?' 'That thing' was the 'New Look' – fashion editor Carmel Snow's name for a silhouette introduced by Dior in 1947 (Dior originally called it the Carolle line). Colin McDowell is suspicious about the newness of Dior's look, claiming that its calf-length

CHANEL

left: Christian Dior's Carolle line was christened the 'New Look' by Carmel Snow, Editor of *Harper's Bazaar*.

above: Stella Tennant was one of several nineties models who became the face of designer Karl Lagerfeld's Chanel.

skirt with padded hips, nipped-in waist and fitted jacket with soft shoulders had been seen before in Hardy Amies' collection of January 1946. But Dior was one of the first to pick up on an idea launched elsewhere and produce it with more polish and appeal – a trend which continues today among French designers. Chanel may have expressed disdain but Dior's curvaceous silhouette had an instant appeal for women in the west, who had been so starved of glamour during and after World War II. Dior's New Look copies were sold in America for $24.95.

Dior introduced several fashion innovations, like the high-waisted princess line, cartwheel and coolie hats, and brought men's suiting features to women's clothes in 1954. He also popularized the wearing of ropes of pearls. He ran a sound business and his backer, Marcel Boussac bankrolled the company generously. Dior was the first designer to license his name – initially launching a line of Christian Dior stockings. In 1948 he opened Christian Dior, New York, to produce his ready-to-wear in the United States where his name was already well known, thanks to generous fashion editorials in both *Vogue* and *Harper's Bazaar*.

Unlike Dior's New Look, the influence of Cristóbal Balenciaga – who had set up a couture house in 1937 at 10 Avenue George V – was gradual, and is still guiding designers today. According to Colin McDowell, the concept of unstructured yet tailored clothes, exploited so successfully by names such as Giorgio Armani, Calvin Klein, and Ralph Lauren, was originated by Balenciaga in the early fifties. The style of evening wear produced by designers like John Galliano and Romeo Gigli was completely in line with Balenciaga's thinking and the sharp discipline of Gianfranco Ferre's cutting is not far off the standard that Balenciaga always insisted upon. Balenciaga was the mentor of Hubert de Givenchy and two of his former employees – Andre Courrèges and Emanuel Ungaro.

In 1957 Dior died suddenly of a heart attack, but Boussac wasted no time in finding a successor to his thriving fashion empire. Yves Saint Laurent, a 21-year-old apprentice in Dior's atelier, was elevated to the position of designer-in-chief. Saint Laurent became (and still remains) the youngest couture designer ever to head a French house. His first show was a smash. The young, shy designer became an instant star as well as the lover of Pierre Berge, his future business partner, who was then an outspoken political raconteur and a full-time agent of the painter Bernard Buffet. But two years after Saint Laurent's stellar Dior début, he was fired by Boussac who – like Dior's prim clientèle – was less than impressed with the 1960 presentation of Dior couture: the Beat collection of slinky black cashmere turtlenecks and mink-lined crocodile jackets.

The House of Christian Dior experienced stability from the sixties through until the nineties. Marc Bohan, the first director of the company's British operations, produced a series of successful collections which attracted younger customers. In 1989, after 29 years with the company, he moved to London to join Norman Hartnell. His successor, Gianfranco Ferre, was ousted after less than a decade and a high-profile search was launched by Bernard Arnault, the president of Moet Hennessy Louis Vuitton (LVMH), the French luxury goods conglomerate that now owns Dior.

left: Cristóbal Balenciaga – who designed the dress seen here – was mentor to Hubert de Givenchy, Andre Courrèges and Emanuel Ungaro.

above: John Galliano created a new modern glamour for Christian Dior. A dress from his spring/summer 1998 collection is seen here.

THE NEW LOOK

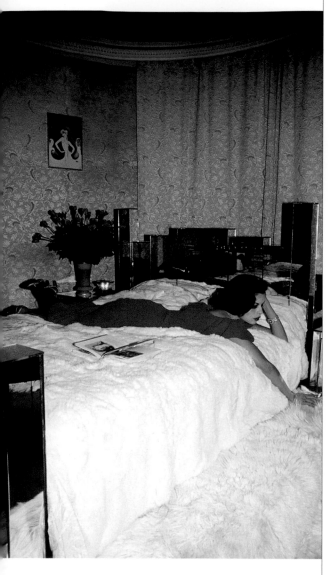

Designers including Vivienne Westwood and Gaultier were rumoured as contenders for the key position at Dior. But in a surprise move, Arnault appointed John Galliano. The boy wonder of British fashion studied at St Martin's School of Art in the early eighties. Joan Burstein, owner of the exclusive London boutique Browns, bought his graduation collection, Les Incroyables. Though Galliano struggled to produce his own independent collections through the eighties and early nineties, he was helped by *American Vogue* – particularly by its editor Anna Wintour – to find financial backing and by introducing him to high-profile women who placed orders for what became his signature look – bias cut dresses.

Galliano's arrival at Dior, it was hoped, would inject new life into couture – which since the 1960s has suffered from dwindling sales and a beleaguered reputation as a dying craft. His appointment followed an 11-month stint at the house of Givenchy – founded by Hubert de Givenchy in 1952, who remained designer-in-chief until 1996. Upon Galliano's departure, Alexander McQueen became designer-in-chief of the fashion house.

Galliano confessed, upon his appointment to Dior, that the New Look was closer to his own aesthetic than the conservative linear designs of Givenchy. In terms of publicity, Arnault scored a coup with Galliano at Dior's helm in the late nineties. His flare for costume produced beautiful collections which merged the silhouette of Dior with innumerable cultural references, tribal themes, modern accessories and theatrical catwalk shows. His first couture show in 1998 at the Opéra Garnier was a triumph. But from that point, the production level of his shows seemed to overshadow the workmanship of his clothes. Several outspoken critics wondered if Galliano's clothes for Dior were merely high priced costumes. A headline that accompanied a story by Suzy Menkes, fashion editor of the *International Herald Tribune*, spoke about 'Dior Delirium'. Menkes was unsure what was going on in his show. Galliano had been inspired by the science fiction film, *The Matrix*, but Menkes claimed that his collection amounted to Gothic make-up, discarded battle dress and dead birds and animals. Galliano has pushed costume to the extreme, and his customers and critics seem to want clothes that capture the romantic beauty of his past collections with a more modern – not futuristic – silhouette.

Today, following Arnault's example, more and more new designers are being appointed to revitalize French fashion houses. British designer Stella McCartney works at Chloé. And there are the Americans – Michael Kors at Celine, Marc Jacobs is the creative director at Louis Vuitton and Narcisso Rodriguez designs for the Spanish leather goods house, Loewe.

Modern dressing

The turn of the millennium seemed somehow an appropriate time for the fate of the 20th century's most famous fashion house, after Chanel, to be decided. Saint Laurent, Menkes reported when his ready-to-wear successor, Alber Elbaz débuted his first collection in March 1999, is a designer who established the template of modern dressing. His revolutionary genderless daytime pantsuits and evening tuxedos reflected a modern society in which feminists had earned a place for women in a man's world.

far left: From the late sixties, Yves Saint Laurent made the pant suit (or trouser suit) an acceptable ensemble in a woman's wardrobe.

left: Saint Laurent's timeless classics, like this sheer chiffon blouse, continued to win acclaim from critics into the late nineties.

With his business partner Pierre Berge at his side, Saint Laurent, like Chanel, became the originator of a number of fashion firsts. He introduced a 'little girl' look, the A-line silhouette, and see-through blouses. His styles of skirts ranged from sophisticated longer versions to drastically shorter styles. He featured metallic and transparent fabrics in his sixties collections. In the seventies he pioneered the peasant look. Pierre Berge said that Coco Chanel had given women freedom, adding that Yves gave them power, reducing the sartorial differences between men and women. Before Yves Saint Laurent created his legendary tuxedo trouser suit 'Le Smoking' in January 1966, trousers on women were associated with butch lesbian writers, according to Alice Rawsthorn in *Yves Saint Laurent*,

above: After designing hats for Jackie Kennedy, Halston became the quintessential American fashion designer of the seventies.

A Biography. But after Le Smoking's launch, trousers on women were the height of French chic, very acceptable and influential. As Grace Mirabella says, in *In and Out of Vogue*, Yves Saint Laurent's trouser suit marked the beginning of a new concept of what constituted sophisticated daytime dressing, which had a profound influence on the later work of such designers as Calvin Klein, Ralph Lauren and Giorgio Armani.

Name a major moment, or a continuing theme in 20th-century fashion and it was Saint Laurent who defined it: the 1965 collection of Mondrian shift dresses which were the first dresses to marry Pop Art with high fashion, the safari look, hippie de luxe, forties hemlines, the versatility of a wardrobe of basic black and his use of colour. Then there were all of the looks he dreamed up in the decadent seventies: animal prints, backless, topless, sheer, the

Ballet Russes collection (which, like nearly all of Saint Laurent's collections, was endlessly copied, prompting the sale of countless peasant skirts worldwide) and biker chic.

Saint Laurent's empire includes accessories, household linens, fragrances, men's clothing and make-up. Up until his retirement he was content to reinvent his old classics, but contemporary designers – namely Eric Bergere – are still as influenced by Saint Laurent's work as they are by that of Chanel. "Every collection I see, has in some way, a reference to Saint Laurent's work," stylist Carine Roitfeld said. "It's like he has written the grammar of fashion." Gucci's designer, Tom Ford, received the ultimate prize when, in the year 2000, he was appointed as designer-in-chief of the house of Saint Laurent.

The rise of American designers

Although Paris remains, rightly, the world's eternal capital of fashion, during the late 1930s, fashion ceased to be dominated by French designers and became an international business. The New York department store Lord and Taylor started to promote American designers as early as 1933, commissioning Elizabeth Hawes and Muriel King to design ready-to-wear collections. In 1938 *Vogue* published its first annual American issue.

The turning point arrived with World War II when French fashion houses shut down. Afterwards, money was scarce and American magazine editors simply didn't have the means to travel to the haute couture shows, so they championed the work of American designers. At the forefront were Claire McCardell – who invented the concept of easy, elegant, separate-led American sportswear – Norman Norell, Mainbocher and Charles James. Although designers did work in Los Angeles – where James Galanos and Rudi Gernreich set up ateliers in the fifties – and Chicago, New York became America's fashion capital. It was a city where fashion magazines were published and most clothes were made.

In its early stages the American fashion scene was far from glamorous. Bill Blass changed things. In 1946, when he returned from the war, he entered the fashion world, joining the dress house of Maurice Retner as a designer. Blass was part of a cool post-war café society, moving between New York night clubs such as El Morocco, Blue Ange, Monte Carlo and the 1-2-3. A friend introduced him to Diana Vreeland, the legendary editor of *American Vogue*. He met society girls who were models and fashion editors. Once they started wearing his clothes, so did lots of other New York women and soon the demand for Blass' work spread.

Like Chanel, Blass became his own best model. In 1965 he appeared in an ad with a model. Both were dressed in houndstooth check suits. The caption was tongue in cheek: 'Who needs Paris when you can steal from yourself?' His move paved the way for other American male designers who produced fashion – notably Ralph Lauren and Calvin Klein – to do the same two decades later.

The London scene

Two designers shaped London in the sixties – Mary Quant and Ossie Clark. Quant, with her husband, Alexander Plunkett Green, opened a Chelsea boutique called Bazaar in the fifties,

above: Bill Blass created elegant clothes for American society women through his 50 year career as a designer.

above: Mary Quant was London's best known designer in the early sixties. Here Jean Shrimpton wears one of her sixties dresses.

stocking adventurous clothes by other designer labels. When she became dissatisfied with the merchandise she had, she struck out on her own – designing a look that expressed the Swinging London vibe – mini skirts, hipster belts, skinny rib sweaters and coloured tights. The hair stylist Vidal Sassoon cut her hair into a bob, and, in 1966, Quant launched her own make-up line. Although her22 work is no longer as popular as it once was, she still has a cult following and runs her boutiques and produces a make-up line.

Shortly after Ossie Clark's death, Kathryn Flett Flanagan noted that he was as swinging as it was possible to be and stay upright. Mick Jagger wore Clark's clothes twice while performing with the Rolling Stones: at the Stones' free concert in Hyde Park, London in 1969 and again while on tour in the mid-seventies. Bianca Jagger was Clark's best customer, commissioning him to design her dresses up until 1996, the year he was murdered, bankrupt and penniless, by his lover. Clark's wife, Celia Birtwell, a textile designer – with whom he split in 1974 – produced most of the fabric for his clothes. Clark also commissioned the then unknown, but now globally sought-after, shoe designer Manolo Blahnik to design shoes to go with one of his collections in 1972. His most successful years were spent designing for Quorum, one of Chelsea's most fashionable boutiques, in the late sixties. His genius was as a cutter. Hot pants, maxi coats, gypsy dresses, leather and snakeskin clothes were Clark's signature style, and one of his most celebrated creations was an ankle-length, wraparound dress, which fitted at the back in such a way to leave a triangle of bare skin.

Seventies New York

What Clark was to swinging London, Halston was to New York's disco era – a designer at the nexus between young, hip society and the art world. Halston had a tribe. As Andy Warhol noted in his diaries, they would talk to each other before they went out to choose a colour theme that they would all wear.

Originally a milliner, who made pillbox hats for Jacqueline Kennedy, Halston radically shifted his design philosophy in the seventies – making minimalist knitwear – wide-leg jersey trousers, cashmere dresses, halterneck dresses and, most notably, a suede shirtwaister dress that inspired countless imitations. Halston produced an eponymous perfume, commissioning his friend Elsa Peretti, who had modelled for him and made his accessories, to design the bottle. She produced a teardrop shape – and moved on to design jewellery for the American company Tiffany & Co.

In the early seventies, Diane von Furstenberg, a beautiful, New York-based Belgian who married Prince Egon von Furstenberg, started her career in fashion as a model. Bored of modelling, she turned to fashion design. Her first pieces were simple, T-shirts, shirt dresses and a little wrap-top with a skirt to go with it. Her bright idea was to combine the wrap top and skirt to make a dress. Von Furstenberg's 'wrap dress' was an instant hit – during the seventies she sold five million of them. In 1976 she appeared on the cover of the American magazine *Newsweek*. She became a role model – a modern, powerful female

designer – to whom other women, both inside and outside of the fashion industry, would look for inspiration.

Although the craze for the wrap dress cooled, in the mid-nineties von Furstenberg, still a recognizable household name in America, revitalized her business – appointing her daughter-in-law, Alexandra von Furstenberg (née Miller), as creative director – and relaunched her fashion label, which remains a best seller in boutiques worldwide.

Eighties fashion

The designs produced by Giorgio Armani, Gianni Versace, Missoni, Franco Moschino, Gianfranco Ferre and Valentino all helped to build Milan into Italy's fashion capital. When Armani introduced a slightly lower-priced line called Emporio in 1981, he pioneered what has become known as the diffusion line – an example that countless designers around the world have copied. Vivienne Westwood and Katharine Hamnett established themselves as the best designers working in London, while in New York

above: The supermodel was a phenomenon invented by the late Gianni Versace.

designers Ralph Lauren, Calvin Klein, Oscar de la Renta and Donna Karan were in the midst of successful careers. Lauren has become a billionaire by regurgitating aristocratic English and preppy American styles. Klein capitalized on sex appeal – selling sensuous ready-to-wear which emphasizes cut, provocative designer denim, heady, heavily marketed scent and inventive cotton underwear. Donna Karan became the quintessential female designer, marketing herself as an earth mother whose big idea was 'the body' – a body suit that, as she demonstrated by wearing one herself, could work with day and evening wear. Karan's fashion logic is to liberate women from constricting clothes by giving them pieces which are comfortable, wearable and chic.

In Paris, Japanese designers Rei Kawakubo, Yohji Yamamoto and Issey Miyake fascinated the critics and buyers with their art-inspired designs. A host of young Belgian designers, including Anne Demeulemeester and Martin Margiela, began to make inroads on the Paris fashion scene too. The late eighties introduced the work of Austrian designer Helmut Lang and the German designer Jil Sander.

Megabrands

In the nineties, competition increased to such an extent that fashion in the last decade of the 20th century was no longer about globally recognizable labels, but about megabrands.

Proof of this is the $1 million budget that Alexander McQueen was given in 1999 by American Express to stage a fashion show – this budget could bankroll the cost of producing an independent feature film (most designers spend about 100,000 dollars on an hour-long presentation). At the beginning of the 20th century, fashion shows were lavish private tea parties where ladies observed clothes worn by about a dozen models. In the mid-century, most designers had show spaces in their ateliers; and in the nineties France's minister of culture, Jacques Lang, incorporated into the Louvre, Paris's premier art museum, a special space – Le Carousel – for designers to hold catwalk presentations. Elsewhere, designers had updated their premises lavishly. Versace's atelier on Milan's Via Jesù, boasts a Plexiglass catwalk where at least 100 television sets flash his creations as the models stalk in front of the guests seated on his signature velvet pillows. The *New Yorker* described Giorgio Armani's private catwalk, built beneath his palazzo in the centre of Milan, as having an atmosphere similar to a Noh amphitheatre.

The job of fashion designer no longer stops at clothes and accessories but is about curating a lifestyle. Designers now own restaurants (Armani, Joseph, Donna Karan, Alberta Ferretti, Ralph Lauren) and make furniture – what the fashion press calls 'homewear' – a move Ralph Lauren instigated in the late eighties and which has been copied by Bill Blass, Nicole Farhi, Tom Ford at Gucci, Versace, Kenzo, Calvin Klein, Consuelo Castiglione of Marni, Tommy Hilfiger and Joseph. Alexander McQueen paid American Express back for financing his show by designing for them a credit card which features his own glinting eye in the centre.

Further proof that fashion is more about brand image than actual clothes design is that the names of the businessmen that run fashion are as known as those of the designers who create clothes. Take Bernard Arnault, president of LVMH, who has built his company into the largest luxury-products company in the world. *Women's Wear Daily* has dubbed Arnault the Pope of fashion.

With $15 million of his own money, Arnault – together with Antoine Bernheim, a managing partner of the French bank Lazard Frère and Co – raised the $80 million necessary to purchase Boussac, the then bankrupt company that owned Christian Dior. In 1987 Arnault was invited to invest in LVMH by the company's chairman, Henri Recamier. Investing through a joint venture with Guinness, Arnault soon ousted Recamier and started to sweep a slew of fashion companies into the LVMH fold: Christian Lacroix, Givenchy, Kenzo, Celine, the leather goods company Loewe, the jeweller Berluti, the perfume and make-up company Guerlain, the DFS group (the world's biggest duty free chain) and Sephora, a chain of perfume and make-up superstores.

Arnault became known as the man who revitalized couture. Though he is both loved and loathed by fashion critics and colleagues, he is unrepentant about his approach, saying that he is only interested in the youngest, the brightest and the very talented. In 1996, after he moved Galliano to Dior and appointed Alexander McQueen to replace him, he then hired Marc Jacobs, a young American designer, to the post of creative director of Louis Vuitton,

above: Giorgio Armani's pared down suits became an unlikely status symbol in the eighties.

above: More theatricality by Alexander McQueen. Here, model Shalom Harlow is paint splattered during his spring/summer 1999 show.

the maker of luxury leather goods. Michael Kors, another American designer of deluxe sportswear, was appointed to Celine, and Narciso Rodriguez, a designer who had worked with Calvin Klein but shot to stardom after he designed the wedding dress of the late Carolyn Bessette Kennedy, was installed at Loewe. Although the work of these Arnault-appointed designers is distinct, they share a common approach to casual luxury.

Prada and Gucci are LVMH's only other rivals. In 1978 Miuccia Prada set about transforming her family's leather goods business (which opened in Milan in 1913) into a fashion empire with her husband Patrizio Bertelli. By the nineties both had built Prada into a US$800 million business. The business was built on functional fashion. Prada designs a mix of nylon handbags and ultra hip clothes.

As Prada established her own thriving Milan based ready-to-wear business, Bertelli

left: Gucci's designer, Tom Ford, initiated a tasteful brand of sex appeal in nineties fashion.

concentrated on building the business into a megabrand. In 1999 he acquired Jil Sander, a move that *Women's Wear Daily* claimed marked the birth of Italy's first privately owned luxury goods group (a year later Sander left the company due to creative differences). He also negotiated joint ventures with Helmut Lang (acquired early in 1999), Italian eyewear maker De Riga and an 8.5 per cent stake in the British footwear company Church & Co.

Gucci's designer, Tom Ford – who journalist Katharine Betts referred to as the man who transformed the Italian company Gucci from a duty-free-logo-laden, and virtually bankrupt, fashion house to a US$4.3 billion public company – resisted, with Gucci's CEO Domenico De Sole (another businessman whose name is becoming as well-known as Ford's), a hostile take-over from Arnault. Ford is the archetypal modern designer. He is a businessman, designer and glamorous public personality. Together with De Sole, he forged

above: Tom Ford gives seventies sensuality a rebirth with this slim halterneck dress with leather rose detail for Gucci, October 1999.

right: Claire McCardell was sensitive to the needs of the modern woman in the post-war era, designing glamorous, yet functional clothes.

a business deal in 1999 which made Gucci part of Pinault, Printemps Redoute, a new luxury goods group that owns French department stores and the Yves Saint Laurent fashion and fragrance empire (the French billionaire François Pinault controls it). Ford can talk knowingly about Wall Street, stride confidently down the catwalk and hang out with Hollywood's main players like Tom Hanks, Rita Wilson and Lisa Eisner – all of whom wear his sexy yet wearable shoes, clothes, watches, accessories and scent.

Functionality

Women started wearing trousers long before Yves Saint Laurent presented Le Smoking in the 1960s. During World War II, trousers became a part of the woman's wardrobe. Some women, short of money to buy clothes, simply started wearing clothes belonging to their husbands who were away fighting the war. After the war, designers picked up on the need to dress the new, increasingly mobile modern women. Claire McCardell was one of the first to sense the changing style times. McCardell's début collection for a New York label, Townley Frocks, featured the first of what would become several classic designs such as the Monastic. Unconstructed, this tent dress was waistless and dartless. McCardell also produced shorts and trousers. She designed for the lifestyle and attitudes of free-moving American women and her name became a byword for functional, casual clothes that were both easy to wear and glamorous.

Critics claim that McCardell drew up the blueprint for American sportswear, but she was not the first designer to make it. French couture houses had been making sportswear since the Paris Olympics of 1924, as Valerie Guillaume observed in her book about Andre Courrèges and Wimbledon champion Suzanne Lenglen's tennis clothes were designed by Jean Patou. McCardell did, however, introduce denim into working women's wardrobes and, along with fabrics such as jersey, ticking and cotton calico, it became a mainstay in her portfolio of designs.

Denim clothing was the brainchild of Levi Strauss, a Bavarian who immigrated to the US in the mid-19th century. At 20, Strauss began to sell canvas tents and wagon covers to prospectors who flocked to California during the Gold Rush. Denim was originally called *serge de Nîmes*, a durable cotton fabric made and worn in the South of France. Strauss consulted a San Franciscan tailor on how to best make trousers and began to import the French fabric which he dyed indigo blue. The initial market for his trousers was among Californian miners, but things soon changed, and before long he was able to open a shop in San Francisco.

Every decade of the 20th century since Levi Strauss introduced denim can be associated with the material, but for different reasons. In the fifties, jeans were the trousers of choice for a group of people – teenagers who were obsessed by rock 'n' roll. In the sixties, loose bell-bottom jeans signified the free love attitude of hippies in England and America, while tight black or white Levis, black poloneck sweaters and wraparound sunglasses were the uniform of Andy Warhol's Velvet Underground. The look expressed the band's and their followers' sense of artistic cool. Designer jeans – launched shortly after Levi Strauss won

above: Designer denim – such as pictured here by Gloria Vanderbilt, created in the late seventies – continues to hold appeal to consumers in the year 2000.

the Coty Fashion Critics Award for world fashion influence in 1971 – worn so tight that, as a French jeans store owner claimed, they would make your eyes bulge out when you first put them on, summed up the decadent, sex-mad seventies. Calvin Klein and Gloria Vanderbilt made designer jeans famous, as did the Italian fashion retail entrepreneur Elio Fiorucci, whose 'Safety' jeans, came in every colour of the rainbow, including gold lamé.

Meanwhile, ripped jeans became a symbol of aggression favoured by London punks. Marshall McLuhan declared that jeans represented a rip-off and a rage against the establishment. When everything went big in the eighties – hair, shoulder pads, egos and salaries – jeans became baggy. Distressed denim was symbolic of the recession in the early nineties and through that decade, as social and sexual barriers became blurred, jeans were the outfit of choice for a relaxed Generation X, captured in Steven Meisel's advertisement campaign for Calvin Klein's unisex scent CKOne. New York designers X-Girl and Daryl K reinvented denim trousers, feminizing them so that they flattered the female form, rather than constricting it. In the late nineties Helmut Lang re-introduced the concept of designer jeans, although they had never really disappeared. In the age of the mega designer, the price tags were mega as well. In 1999 Gucci's spring/summer collection included a pair of ripped, feathered and beaded denims bearing the stratospheric price tag of £1,910. The following season, for autumn/winter, several other leading designers launched high-priced denims including Stella McCartney for Chloé (£350), Louis Vuitton (£465), Michael Kors (£375), Hussein Chalayan (£180) and Valentino (£850).

It seemed odd that when denim's popularity was at such an all-time high, sales figures had plummeted. In 1999 denim sales figures dropped by 11 per cent in Europe, and, as a result, Levi-Strauss was forced to lay off 6,000 workers. In just one year the company lost sales worth £1 billion. The popularity of Levi Strauss was at an all time low. Fashion designer denim obviously presented Levis with competition as did cult labels worn by young people including MUDD, JNCO and Evisu – a jeans line launched in the eighties by a Japanese businessman, Mr Yamane, who bought the looms that had made denim for Levi Strauss. He juggled the letters of a well-known name and called his jeans Evis, but under threat of legal action from Levi's he changed the name to Evisu.

If cult labels presented Levi's with competition, so did the market for combat trousers – made chic by the London label Maharishi – and chinos – khaki trousers made popular globally by the casual fashion retail empires such as Club Monaco (which is owned by Ralph Lauren) and the Gap. Launched in 1969 as a San Francisco shop selling only Levi's jeans by real-estate developer Don Fisher and his wife Doris, the Gap created its own line of clothing in 1975. In 1983 the Fisher family hired Millard Drexler, the former president of fashion label Anne Taylor. Drexler's mission was to make Gap ubiquitous, *Fortune* magazine noted in 1998, and he succeeded. *American Vogue*'s 100th Anniversary Special Issue in 1991 featured the world's most recognizable supermodels wearing Gap jeans and T-shirts. In 1996 Sharon Stone wore a Gap mock turtleneck to the Oscars. Advertising campaigns shot by the world's best fashion photographers, including Annie Leibowitz, Steven Meisel and Mario Testino, also secured the Gap's globally dominant retail position. Between Drexler's arrival in 1983 and the *Fortune* article, Gap had expanded from 566 stores to 2,237, with new ones opening at the rate of one a day.

Activewear

If Claire McCardell launched the idea of casual sportswear, Andre Courrèges can be credited with the introduction of activewear. Leaving Balenciaga in 1961 to start his own fashion house, Courrèges was inspired by gymnastics, dance and music. He accessorized his collections with flat shoes because he believed that women needed to be able to walk and run again after so many years in high heels. Courrèges produced modern body-conscious clothes, an attitude which, Valerie Guillaume claimed, inspired him to create the first mini-skirt in 1965.

American Vogue claimed that the eighties was the 'Age of Exercise'. Triple gold medallist Florence Griffith Joyner, combined superb athleticism with femininity and was a role model

above: The Gap's success was summed up by this American *Vogue* cover (April 1992) in which the world's most popular models wear Gap's simple clothes.

for many women. Geoffrey Beene – who had created the ultimate exercise-inspired take on black tie evening dress in the sixties – a floor-length sequinned football jersey – like many other designers made his silhouette more body-conscious and claimed that his fitted jump-suit was the 'ballgown of the future'.

Norma Kamali, a New York-based designer, merged the comfort-factor of fleece sweatshirts with high fashion tailoring in the 1980s. Shirts with shoulder pads, pull-on skirts, leggings and long, flared skirts made of pink, grey and white fleece sold by the tens of thousands and inspired countless knockoffs. The Algerian-born, Paris-based Azzedine Alaia created what became the little black dress of the eighties from clinging Lycra. His sexy, skin-hugging Lycra dresses, tops and leggings became the wardrobe staple of girls who did aerobics by day and clubbed by night. Tina Turner, a twentysomething Madonna and a long list of supermodels including Naomi Campbell (his early muse), Stephanie Seymour and Linda Evangelista were his best customers.

In the nineties, active took on a new meaning: jet set travel. Miuccia Prada's functional nylon handbags reintroduced functionality into men's and women's wardrobes in the nineties. So successful were her rucksacks and non-creasable nylon trench coats that in 1998 Prada launched Prada Sport – a designer line of sports-inspired shoes and clothing. In the autumn of 1999, Neil Barrett, an English designer who designed Prada's menswear for eight seasons, introduced Samsonite Active Wear, a unisex range of fashion products for the American luggage line. Geared at people on the move, Barrett utilized fabrics such as Cordura, an industrial trademarked nylon used heavily in the Prada range, for jackets. Barrett's clothing merged functional with technical. The Wear Bag, for instance, is a raincoat which folds into a small zip-up pocket. Some jackets featured neck pillows – collars that are inflated by blowing into a concealed tube – while other jackets have in-built digital alarms.

These designers have all cashed in on a late 20th-century sportswear boom which followed after Nike, the active footwear brand, launched in the US in 1971. As it did, a jogging craze started in North America before spreading to England and then around the world. Trainers were first conceived in the 1860s when the British began to wear canvas leisure shoes. They were popularized initially by Converse, which created the canvas All Star in 1919 (it remained the most popular sneaker in America for the first half of the century). Nike has become a niche brand, merging technical design with of-the-moment cuts and colours. Nike capitalized on the exercise craze of the late seventies and eighties, prompting designers like Chanel, Ralph Lauren (who commissioned Reebok to make Polo Sport athletic shoes) and Rifat Ozbek to introduce trainers into their collections. Nike was referred to by *American Vogue* as the closest thing to couture in the world of sport, producing an enormous range of sports-related fashion with both sophisticated clothing and highly designed shoes.

High tech Nikes went slightly out of favour when the rock-fuelled youth movement, Grunge, introduced the rage for decidedly low tech Puma, Adidas and Converse among teens and twentysomethings. Nike, however, regained its position, opening a chain of

left: Azzedine Alaia's clinging designs allowed women in the 1980s to display their gym-toned physiques.

above: Andre Courrèges' simple designs liberated women from long hemlines and cumbersome clothes.

above: Missoni, the Milan-based, family run fashion label, produces distinct, colourful knitwear.

superstores called Nike Town. The *Times* called it a colossus when Nike Town opened in London in 1999. The largest store owned by the sports conglomerate, it occupies 70,000 square feet and stocks 47,000 pairs of shoes as well as 135,000 pieces of sports-inspired clothing. Nike Town's formula has worked for the brand. In 1999, Nike reported a worldwide turnover of US$8.8 billion.

Fashion, art and popular culture

Prior to the 20th century painters such as Ingres and Courbet, Monet, Manet, Degas, Whistler and Toulouse-Lautrec were fascinated by the fashions their subjects wore and painted them in great detail. But the 20th century reversed the cycle. Designers who were both artists and dress-makers – or simply fascinated by art – produced fashions that merged the two disciplines. Paul Poiret was the first designer to work closely with artists, commissioning Raoul Dufy and André Derain to design fabrics for his couture collections. In 1911 Poiret founded the Ecole Martine, his own art school, named after one of his daughters. There both artist and amateur were given the chance to paint, and Poiret used their work to create fabric designs. It was sold along with pottery and lacquer furniture in his shop on the rue du Faubourg Saint-Honoré.

The artist Sonia Delaunay also worked in the fashion industry – first designing textiles and then moving on to work as a couturier. The Soeurs Callot – with whom Vionnet trained – were inspired by Orientalism and Cubism. But as Richard Martin noted, referring to a lime green silk embroidered day dress, which is a part of the Metropolitan Museum of Art's costume collection, their influence, unlike Poiret's, was often conceptual rather than literal.

Mario Fortuny and Elsa Schiaparelli were other notable designers who put art ahead of fashion. A talented painter, Fortuny's first major contribution to fashion was the Delphos dress, which he did not merely create. Fortuny claimed he 'invented' it, patenting the finely pleated silk shift that hung from the shoulders to the ground. The inspiration for this dress was ancient Greece, but he also took ideas from Renaissance art for his trained, panelled velvet dresses.

Coco Chanel regarded Schiaparelli as a rival yet their creations were at opposite ends of the sartorial spectrum. While Chanel created clothes which were functionally luxurious, Schiaparelli's creations were fantastical. Though she was inspired by Cubism and African art, Schiaparelli's primary artistic influence was Surrealism – her thirties hat shoe being the most obvious of her surrealist accessories. She collaborated with artists such as Salvador Dali, Jean Cocteau and the fashion illustrator Christian Bérard, and was friendly with Andre Breton. Later, in the eighties and nineties, Franco Moschino would revisit Schiaparelli's sartorial Surrealism. Schiaparelli made buttons which were created in the shape of acrobats, a clear plastic necklace printed with insects, commissioned fabric printed with newsprint from which she made scarves, and music-box handbags. Later Moschino made similar sartorial puns producing a jacket with windmill buttons, a dinner jacket with a knife and fork appliqué and a belt emblazoned with the words 'Waist of Money'.

left: Rock'n'roll stars –
like the Rolling Stones,
seen here with Patti Boyd
– became fashion icons in
the late sixties.

The sixties started a cycle which continues today – art and fashion merged so seamlessly that they were one and the same. Meanwhile the definition of art broadened to include popular culture – a movement which was inextricably linked to fashion. Everything went pop. With his soup can paintings, Andy Warhol pioneered Pop Art. Elvis, the Beatles and the Rolling Stones were at the forefront of music and film and television translated the cultural shifts to the world.

Yves Saint Laurent understood the new artistic mood. In 1965 he produced a line of dresses inspired by the Cubist painter Piet Mondrian. The Mondrian shift became, and remains, a source of countless copies. Saint Laurent also dressed the actress Catherine Deneuve for her role in Louis Buñuel's *Belle du Jour*. His feminine costumes for Deneuve continue to inspire designers – traces of the refined style turned up in Miuccia Prada's

FASHION, ART AND POPULAR CULTURE

above: Giorgio Armani became a household name after Richard Gere, pictured here, wore his clothes in *American Gigolo*.

Spring/Summer 2000 ready-to-wear show. Saint Laurent also befriended Warhol, whose muse, Edie Sedgewick, was the century's most memorable 'It Girl' (even is Clara Bow was the first to be crowned with the title). Edie had the necessary It Girl requirement – personal style. Her signature look – a pair of black tights, a striped T-shirt and a pair of ballet flats – remain youthful classics.

Hubert de Givenchy dressed Audrey Hepburn for her film roles including *Breakfast at Tiffany's* and *Sabrina*, forging a personal relationship and a valuable professional partnership. Givenchy created a chic simple style for Hepburn. For five consecutive years she was placed on the International Best Dressed List, and their relationship paved the way for successful collaborations between designer and celebrities which continues today: Debbie Harry of Blondie's early punk/pop image was created by Warhol, protégé the New York designer Stephen Sprouse; Sharon Stone has strong links with Valentino; Cher's outrageous persona was masterminded by Bob Mackie.

The Sex Pistols were Malcolm McLaren and Vivienne Westwood's vehicle which propelled them to sartorial notoriety and spearheaded punk – a youth culture movement, which like the fifties Beat Generation, sixties and seventies Hippies and nineties Grunge, used fashion and pop music to demonstrate youthful dissatisfaction with the state of society. The Sex Pistols were a nexus point where art, fashion and music all came together. Punk spawned a slew of subversive musical spin-off cults complete with their own dress codes – the New Romantics, Goths and in the nineties, Grunge. Punk provided inspiration for fashion designers – the late Gianni Versace produced a punk-inspired collection in 1995. And punk was Vivienne Westwood's launch into mainstream fashion.

Japanese designers have always stressed the importance of art in their work. Regarding the work of Rei Kawakubo, the designer of Comme des Garçons, Yohji Yamamoto and Issey Miyake, Peter Wollen claimed that there was no clear-cut distinction between arts and crafts, between the clothes and the environments they are created, shown and sold in.

Celebrities

Paul Schrader's suit scene in his 1980 film *American Gigolo* – during which Richard Gere surveys his closet full of Giorgio Armani suits – started a love affair between Hollywood and Armani. From the late eighties, Armani suits became de rigueur for American male and female film executives and film stars. Meanwhile, Elton John became Gianni Versace's best menswear client and Elizabeth Hurley became a spokesmodel for the sexy-starlet Versace look. The Versace family were perhaps the 20th century's most prominent designers to exploit the power of famous personalities to sell their clothes. Gianni Versace realized how potent a statement supermodels could make in his clothes and supplied them with pieces from the collections for parties and special occasions. Donatella dressed rock stars like Courtney Love, John Bon Jovi and Madonna. But Madonna, shrewdly, did not restrict her look to the responsibility of one designer. Her image makeovers have been helped by numerous designers: Jean-Paul Gaultier, Dolce e Gabbana, Olivier Theyskins, Chloé's Stella McCartney, Gucci's Tom Ford and Miuccia Prada as well as the Versaces.

Designers such as Versace, Valentino, Tommy Hilfiger and Armani employ public relations executives to ensure that celebrities are seen at events, such as the Oscars, in their creations. And prominent political wives and members of European Royal families too have forged links with designers to heighten their image – Jacqueline Kennedy employed Oleg Cassini when she was America's first lady in the early sixties; Nancy Reagan was James Galano's best-known client in the eighties and Hilary Clinton wore Oscar de la Renta for state functions, important public appearances and photographs, such as when she appeared on the cover of *American Vogue* in December 1998. Princess

above: Hussein Chalayan merges artistic technique with dress design.

above: Carolyn Bessette Kennedy became a minimalist role model when she chose to wear Yohji Yamamoto's clothes after her marriage to John Kennedy Junior.

right: Alexander McQueen's futuristic look appealed to critics who were, by the century's close, pondering fashion's future direction.

Caroline of Monaco wears clothes designed for Chanel by her friend Karl Lagerfeld. Princess Diana initially relied on Catherine Walker who produced appropriate clothes for her public appearances and court functions, but after her divorce, Diana became less restrained, opting to wear Valentino and Versace as well as becoming famous for favouring accessories such as Ray Ban sunglasses, JP Tods loafers and a Christian Dior handbag which became known as the Princess Diana handbag.

Caroline Bessette Kennedy – a former public relations executive for Calvin Klein – epitomized the designer's stark chic style but when she married John Kennedy Junior she shrewdly shied away from wearing Klein, forging her own image in a simple white sheath designed by Klein's former assistant Narciso Rodriguez. Bessette Kennedy then began to wear Yohji Yamamoto clothes and shoes designed by Manolo Blahnik almost exclusively.

Photography and the Internet

In the early 20th century magazines were a creative outlet for photographers and illustrators. Cecil Beaton, Baron Adolphe de Meyer, George Hoyyningen-Huene, Erwin Blumenfeld, Horst P. Horst and Man Ray worked for the early issues of American, British and French *Vogue*. At *Harpers Bazaar*, Alexey Brodovitch nurtured the talent of fashion photographers Richard Avedon, Blumenfeld and Lisette Model, among others, as well as commissioning art photographers Henri Cartier-Bresson, Brassai and Bill Brandt to shoot reportage. At *American Vogue*, photographers Irving Penn, Helmut Newton and Norman Parkinson flourished under the guidance of editorial director Alexander Lieberman.

By the century's end fashion magazines had become increasingly driven by commercial considerations. Because advertisers dictate the terms in which their clothes are shot – insisting that their clothes be photographed as complete ensembles rather than mixing pieces by other rival designers – much of the creativity involved in fashion editorial shoots has diminished. Advertisements today are often more creative than fashion editorials. And though they still attract leading photographers, most of these seek out other outlets for creative stimulation and satisfaction. Less mainstream fashion publications – like *Visionaire, ID, Dutch, It, Tank and Joe's Magazine* – are the source of a new breed of fashion art work. These publications give collaborators complete creative control over the work they produce but the participants forfeit money (often working for free) for the sake of creative freedom.

The Internet is another new potential outlet for artistic fashion expression. Although most fashion websites on the Internet are uninteresting shopping portals, by the year 2000 the British graphic designer Peter Saville and fashion photographer Nick Knight had launched www.show.uk.com ('show'), a fashion-focused website devoted to revealing creative work conceived by some of the most dynamic fashion industry professionals as well as that created by cutting edge artists. "The Internet has the potential to open up the industry," Nick Knight explained. "I like the idea that you can be on a beach in Sweden, in a tower block in London or on a freeway in Tokyo and it will all be there. All you need is a computer."

Aldred, Cyril. Akhenaten and Nefertiti, Thames & Hudson, 1973

Amphlett, Hilda. Hats, a History of Fashion in Headwear, Richard Sadler, 1974

Anderson Black, J. & Garland, Madge. A History of Fashion, Orbis Publishing, 1980

Batterberry, M. Fashion: the Mirror of History, Columbus Books

Bindman, David (ed). The Thames and Hudson Encyclopaedia of British Art, Thames & Hudson, 1988

Bomberg, Craig. The Wicked Ways of Malcolm McLaren, Omnibus Press

Boucher, François. 20,000 Years of Fashion: The History of Costume and Personal Adornment, Harry N Abrams, 1987

Boucher, Francois. A History of Costume in the West, Thames & Hudson, 1996

Bowman, Sara. A Fashion for Extravagance, Art Deco Fabrics and Fashions, Bell & Hyman

Braithwaite, B. Women's Magazines, Peter Owen, 1994

Breward, Christopher. The Culture of Fashion: A New History of Fashionable Dress (Studies in Design and Material Culture), Manchester University Press, 1995

Brody Johansen, R. Body and Clothes, An Illustrated History of Costume, Faber & Faber, 1968

Browning, Robert. The Byzantine Empire, Weidenfeld & Nicolson, 1992

Cassin-Scott, Jack. The Illustrated Encyclopedia of Costume and Fashion: From 1066 to the Present, Sterling, 1994

Chenoune, Farid. A History of Men's Fashion, Flammarion, 1993

Colle, Doriene. Collars, Stocks, Cravats, White Lion Publishers, 1972

Collins, Winston. All About Shoes, Footwear Through the Ages, Bata Limited, 1994

Contini, Mila. Fashion From Ancient Egypt to the Present Day, Paul Hamlyn, 1965

Corson, Richard. Fashions in Make Up, Peter Owen, 1972

Cosgrave, Bronwyn. 'It's Show Time', British Vogue, September 1999, p.148

Dictionary of Biography, Brockhampton Press, 1995

Douglas, Russel. Costume History and Style, Prentice Hall, 1982

Eco, Umberto. Art and Beauty in the Middle Ages, Yale University Press, 1986

Ewing, Elizabeth. Everyday Dress 1650–1900, Batsford, 1990

Finkelstein, Nat. Andy Warhol: The Factory Years 1964–1967, Canongate, 1999

Fontanel, Beatrice. Support and Seduction: A History of Corsets and Bras, Harry N Abrams, 1997

Foster, Vanda. Bags and Purses, from the Costume Accessories Series, Batsford, 1982

Ginsburg, Madeleine (ed). The Illustrated History of Textiles, Studio Editions

Gregorietti, Guido. Jewellery Through the Ages, Hamlyn, 1970

Griffin, Victoria. The Mistress, Bloomsbury, 1999

Groom, Nigel. The Perfume Handbook, Chapman & Hall, 1992

Hart, Avril and North, Susan. Historical Fashion in Detail, the 17th and 18th Centuries, V&A Publications, 1998

Hart, Avril. Ties, V&A Publications, 1998

Hartnell, Norman. Royal Courts of Fashion, Cassell

Hennessy, Edmund. American Vogue, 1987, p.323

Hollander, Anne. Seeing Through Clothes, University of California Press, 1993

Hughes-Hallett, Lucy. 'The Women Who Dared', The Sunday Times Books Review, 23 August 1999, p.6

Hume, Marion. 'Portrait of a Former Punk', American Vogue, September 1994, p.194

Irvine, Susan. Perfume, The Creation and Allure of Classic Fragrances, Aurum, 1995

Jacobson, Dawn. Chinoiserie, Phaidon, 1993

Kennett, Frances. History of Perfume, Batsford, 1985

Kitto H. D. F. The Greeks, Peter Smith, 1988

Kohler, Carl. A History of Costume, Dover Publications, 1983

Kraatz, Annie. Lace History and Fashion, Thames & Hudson, 1989

Lambert, Miles. 'The Dandy in Thackeray's Vanity Fair and Pendennis, An Early Victorian View of the Regency Dandy', The Journal of the Costume Society, no. 22, p.60

Lambert, Sylvie. The Ring, Design Past and Present, RotoVision, 1998

Laver, James. A Concise History of Fashion, Thames & Hudson, 1969

Laver, James. Dandies, Weidenfeld & Nicolson

Lehnert, Gertrud. Fashion A Concise History, Laurence King, 1999

Levron, Jacques. Pompadour, translated by Claire Eliane Engel, George Allen and Unwin Ltd, 1963

Maniche, Lise. An Ancient Egyptian Herbal, British Museum Press, 1989

Maniche, Lise. Sacred Luxuries, Fragrance, Aromatherapy and Cosmetics in Ancient Egypt, Opus Publishing, 1999

Maine, Henry. Village Communities, 3rd edn, 1876

Marcus, Greil. Lipstick Traces: A Secret History of the 20th Century, Penguin Books, 1999

Martin, Richard. The Ceaseless Century, 300 Years of Eighteenth Century Costume, The Metropolitan Museum of Art, 1998

Martin, Richard. Cubism and Fashion, The Metropolitan Museum of Art, 1999

McDowell, Colin. The Etruscans

McDowell, Colin. The Man of Fashion, Peacock Males and Perfect Gentlemen, Thames & Hudson, 1997

McDowell, Colin. Shoes Fashion and Fantasy, Thames & Hudson, 1989

Mirabella, Grace and Warner, Judith. In and Out of Vogue: A Memoir

Mulvagh, Jane. Vivienne Westwood, An Unfashionable Life, Harper Collins, 1998

Mulvagh, Jane. Vogue History of 20th Century Fashion

Newman, Harold. An Illustrated Dictionary of Jewelry, Thames & Hudson, 1987

O'Hara Callan, Georgina. The Thames & Hudson Dictionary of Fashion and Fashion Designers, Thames & Hudson, 1998

Oldenbourg, Zoe. Catherine the Great A Biography of the Empress of all the Russians, Gallimard, 1965

Pick, Robert. Empress Maria Theresa The Earlier Years 1717–1757, Weidenfeld & Nicolson, 1966

Putnam, James. Pyramid, Dorling Kindersley, 2000

Roberts, J. M. Shorter Illustrated History of the World, Helicon, 1993

Roberts, J. M. Twentieth Century, A History of the World 1901 to Present, Allen Lane, 1999

Robbins, Gay. Women in Ancient Egypt, Harvard University Press, 1992

Sage, Elizabeth. A Study of Costume, Scribner

Scaribbrick, Diana. Jewellery, the Costume Accessories Series, Batsford, 1984

Siloti, Alberto. Egypt: Splendours of an Ancient Civilisation, Thames & Hudson, 1994

Simon, Marie. Fashion in Art, Zwemmer, 1995

Skira, A. The Great Centuries of Painting, Watteau to Tiepolo, Skira

Somerset Fry, Plantagenet. Kings and Queens of England and Scotland, Dorling Kindersley, 1997

Squire, Geoffrey. Dress, Art and Society, 1560–1970, Studio Vista, 1974

Steele, Valerie. Paris Fashion, A Cultural History, Oxford University Press, 1988

Street, Julie. 'The Ancient Egypt in our Fantasies', The European, 28 January– 3 February, 1994, p.8

Turner Wilcox, R. The Dictionary of Costume, Batsford, 1992

Uglow, Jennifer. Women's Biography, Macmillan, 1982

Webber, Paul. Shoes, A Pictorial Commentary on the History of the Shoe, Verlay, 1982

Wilkie, Angus. 'Toile de Jouy', Elle Decor, April 1999, p.88

Wollen, Peter. Addressing the Century: 100 Years of Art and Fashion, Hawford Gallery, 1999

Zemon Davis, Natalie and Kerr Conway, Jill. 'The Rest of the Story', New York Times Magazine, May 16, 1999, p.84

THIS BOOK IS DEDICATED TO MY MOTHER, FATHER.
THANKS TO MY RESEARCHER AND GREAT FRIEND
ISABELLE MARIE CREAC'H.

Picture Acknowledgements

AKG, London front cover centre left and centre right/Musée du Louvre, Paris front cover below centre right

Bridgeman Art Library/British Museum London front cover below centre/British Library, London front cover top left/Chateau de Versailles, France front cover bottom left/Private Collection front cover bottom centre

ET Archive front cover top centre, front cover below centre left

Hulton Getty Picture Collection front cover bottom right

Mary Evans Picture Library front cover top right, front cover centre

Advertising Archives 242

AKG, London 27, 54, 56, 63, 76, 87, 90, 92, 93, 98, 100, 144, 167, 192/Bibliothèque Nationale, Paris 184/Bussy-Rabutin, Chateau 155/Deutsches Historisches Museum, Berlin 189/Galleria degli Uffizi, Florence 114, 131, 134/Galleria dell'Accademia, Venice 116, 130/Gemaeldegalerie, Dresden 123/Herakleion, Archaeologisches Museum 33/Heraklion, Archaeologisches Museum 36/Kunsthistorisches Museum 47/Kunsthistorisches Museum, Vienna 12, 168/Louvre, Paris 18, 50/Musée Conde, Chantilly 139/Musée du Bardo, Tunis 79/Musée du Louvre, Paris, 120, 140/Musée National du Chateau, Compiegne 200/Museo del Prado, Madrid 126/Museo Nazionale di Villa Giulia 62/Museo Nazionale Romano delle Terme/Erich Lessing 72/National Gallery, London 110/National Museum of Archaeology, Naples 78/Paris, Private Collection 174/St Petersburg, State Hermitage 58/Staatsgalerie, Stuttgart 135/Trier, Rheinisches Landesmuseum 75/Victoria and Albert Museum, London 142/Woburn Abbey, Bedfordshire 121.

Bridgeman Art Library, London/New York 10/Agnew & Sons, London 129/Alte Pinakothek, Munich 173/Ashmolean Museum, Oxford 14, 22, 49, 133/Bibliothèque de l'Arsenal, Paris, France 96/British Library, London 13, 15, 94, 101, 102, 103, 104, 109, 111/Bundesmobiliensammlung, Vienna 199/Chateau de Versailles, France, 145/Collection of the Earl of Pembroke, Wilton House, Wilts, UK 150/Fitzwilliam Museum, University of Cambridge, UK 141, 158/Galleria degli Uffizi, Florence, Italy 124/Guildhall Library, Corporation of London 190/Johnny van Haeften Gallery, London 154/Kress Collection, Washington D.C, USA 122/Kunsthalle, Hamburg 191/Longleat House, Wiltshire 118/Loseley Park, Guildford 136/Musée du Louvre, Paris 16, 17, 29, 132, 188/Musée Carnavalet, Paris 146, 166/Musée d'Art et d'Histoire, Palais Massena, Nica, France 205/Musée d'Orsay, Paris 209/Museo Correr, Venice 138/National Gallery, London 161, 193/O'Shea Gallery, London 206/Palazzo Medici-Riccardi, Florence, Italy 117/Pergamon Museum, Berlin 41/Philip Mould, Historical Portraits Ltd, London 137/Private Collection 67, 157, 169, 181, 195, 207/Private Collection/Copyright Sevenarts Ltd 2000. All Rights Reserved, DACS 4/Rafael Valls Gallery, London 183/San Vitale, Ravenna, Italy 85/Schloss Charlottenburg, Berlin 172/The Design Library, New York 178, 203/Victoria & Albert Museum London 97, 164, 179, 212, Copyright ADAGP, Paris and DACS, London 2000 220/Walker Art Gallery, Liverpool, Merseyside 128/Wallace Collection, London 9, 125.

Christopher Moore Ltd 214, 227, 238, 249, 251

The Conde Nast Publications, Inc/Patrick Demarchelier 243

The Conde Nast Publications Ltd 232/Eric Boman 228/De Meyer 221/Nathanial Goldberg 240/Hoyningen-Huene 222/Peter Lindbergh 244/Tom Munro 229/Nick Night 39/Softroom 215

Corbis UK Ltd 233/AFP 231/Richard Bowditch 219/Mitchell Gerber 250/Hulton Deutsch Collection 230/David Lees 237/Vittoriano Rastelli 236/Vanni Archive 24

E.T. Archive 32, 48, 57, 59, 60, 61, 64, 77, 80, 82, 84, 86, 119, 175, 180, 194/Archaeological Museum, Naples 73/Bibliothèque de l'Arsenal, Paris 105/Bibliothèque Nationale 99/British Museum 149, 162/Castella di Manta Asti 107/Musée de Cluny, Paris 88/Musée de l'Ile de France 204/Musée de Versailles 152/Musée du Louvre, Paris 153, 171.

Fashion Institute of Technology 241

Glasgow Museum: Burrell Collection 197

Hulton Getty Picture Collection 216, 217, 223

Image Bank/Archive Photos/Tim Boxer 235

Jean-Loup Charmet 148, 182, 196, 211/Copyright ADAGP, Paris and DACS, London 2000 224

Collection Kharbine-Tapabor 177

Mary Evans Picture Library 7, 19, 30, 34, 35, 37, 38, 40, 42, 44, 45, 46, 51, 53, 66, 68, 69, 71, 74, 106, 108, 112, 113, 147, 151, 156, 159, 160, 165, 170, 185, 186, 201, 202, 208, 210

Missoni 246

Museum of London 176

National Gallery, London 127

NETWORK/Rapho 8

Nick Knight/Virtual Catwalk for showstudio.com 6

Philippe Garner 198, 226, 245

Rex Features 225

The Ronald Grant Archive 248

Victoria & Albert Museum/John French Archive 218, 234, 247

Werner Forman Archive 20, 43, 70, 83, 89/Antiquarium Gallery, New York 52/E. Strouhal 28/Egyptian Museum, Cairo 23, 25, 26/Thessaloniki Archaeological Museum 91/University College London, Petrie Museum 21